A NOT SO FICTIONAL FALL

A MARRIAGE OF CONVENIENCE ROMCOM

SAVANNAH SCOTT

Connect with Savannah Scott

You can connect with Savannah at her website
https://SavannahScott.website/

You can also follow Savannah on Amazon.

For free books and first notice of new releases, sign up for
Savannah's Romcom Readers email at https://www.
subscribepage.com/savannahscottromcom

~

For Jon
Marrying a romance author
isn't always the stuff of fiction.
You've given us a love story worth fighting for.
Thank you for the belly laughs, the shared dreams, and for being
my soft place to land.

~

For the bookish community—
Especially those bookstagrammers who sing the praises of well-
told stories,
cheer for authors in ways that put
rabid sports fans to shame,
and fill their TBRs and bookcases
with our words turned into worlds.

🤍

You are the ones I write for: my friends, my "fans,"
my favorite people.

~

Falling in love can be surprising,
unexpected, even scary.
It's like standing in line for a roller coaster
and then stepping on.
Once you've buckled in, there's no turning back from
the thrill and rush of it all.

~

1

TASHA

Being a fan doesn't mean being there from the start.
It means being there till the end.
~ Alex Gaskarth

"**I** got my ticket!" I nearly squeal to my sister Heather. I'm trying to tamp down my excitement and failing miserably.

She's wrapping up closing up shop at Cataloochee Mountain Coffee, otherwise known as Catty Coffee by most of the locals. I'm standing around feeling useless while Heather checks machines, writes lists, and inventories the coffee supplies—managing this place like she owns it.

"Are you sure I can't do anything?" I ask again.

"You're going to California!" She ignores my offer and adds a strained note of enthusiasm for my sake.

Nate, my adorable nephew, pops his head of curly brown

hair in from the back of the store where he's been hanging out.

He walks over to Heather, stands on tiptoes and tugs at her shirt. When she bends, he whispers something in her ear.

"Yes," she says in that tone of voice that sends me back to my own childhood. "You can play with the iPad for exactly thirty minutes."

"Don't I get a hello or a hug?" I lean my forearms on the counter and wag my eyebrows at Nate.

"Oh, Hi, Aunt Tasha. What's shakin'?"

"What's shakin'? Are you serious with that?"

Nate stares at me like I'm old. I'm not. He, on the other hand, is. Way too old for his seven years of life. He's seven going on seventeen most days.

"It means, *How are you*?" Nate explains to me, dragging out those last three words.

"I know what it means, you booger—at least what it meant in the 1970s … nevermind. Come over here and give me a hug."

Nate ambushes me, running full speed and leaping into my arms. I wobble when he hits me.

He wiggles out of my embrace as quickly as he landed there and looks over his shoulder in Heather's direction. "This hugging time doesn't count toward my thirty minutes."

"I know. I know." Heather's voice lacks her usual energy.

"Are you coming home with us? We're getting pizza!" Nate asks me.

"I could eat some pizza. Sure. Let me see what your mom thinks. I have to drive back to Asheville tonight, so I can't stay late."

"M'kay."

Nate rushes off without another word. The door between the main area of the shop and the back kitchen and office swings on its hinges in his wake.

"If life gave out report cards, I'd barely be getting a passing grade," Heather says, walking up front to double check the lock and flip the old fashioned sign in the window from Open to Closed.

"You're doing great. Single moms are rock stars. And you get extra bonus points for being a one-man, parenting band while running your own business."

"It's not my business yet." Heather pushes a chair more fully under a table while she makes her way back to the counter.

"You know it will be."

She's quiet. And I don't blame her for feeling uncertain. I have enough belief in her for the both of us.

"Anyway," Heather says, "Let's get out of here and you can tell me all about your plans for this trip."

Heather hits the last light switch and the room goes mostly dark except for the late afternoon sun streaming in through the front windows. We stop in the office to gather Nate. His eyes remain glued to the game he's playing, even when he stands and follows us out the back door.

"That's a skill," I whisper to my sister.

"Zombie walking while playing a game and tuning out everything around you?" she asks with an amused look on her face.

"Yeah. I'd break a leg for sure."

"You would!" She laughs. "Want to drive us home? I walked in this morning and Mom dropped Nate off after school."

"I don't want to walk," Nate says from behind his screen, never looking up.

"I'll drive," I say. "I'm parked around the corner, I snagged a space in front of the General Store."

We walk down the alley behind Cataloochee and turn up Maple, toward the street that's home to many of the quaint shops that have been the backdrop to our childhoods. A few newer stores have taken over some of the old spaces, but enough of the originals remain to make me feel nostalgic.

As we drive toward Heather's, I take in the awnings and brick facades of the thrift store, Apple-A-Day Gifts, Domenico's Jewelers, DeLucca's, and Book Smart, feeling the familiar pang of homesickness that often strikes me when I come back to Harvest Hollow. We drive out of downtown into a more residential section of town. A lot of these homes are still owned by elderly couples who settled here when they were newly married. They raised their children in this neighborhood and are now spending their retirement in the same house that holds all their family memories. I wonder what that kind of stability would feel like.

I resume my conversation about my trip, barely able to contain my excitement, but also acutely aware that Heather's life definitely does not include jaunting off to exclusive island resorts.

"Can you believe it's a seven and a half hour flight from Asheville to LA, including a layover in Chicago?"

Heather's laugh sounds tired, but amused.

"Why? Who plans these routes?" I ask rhetorically. "And is that man related to the guy who decides which items go in each aisle at the grocery store?"

"I love how you assume it's a man," Heather muses.

"Yeah, well. I just think women would arrange more

direct flights, and also create a more sensible order in the Publix. Why is bread near the liquor aisle? But peanut butter is all the way by the cereal? And the cream cheese isn't near the other cheeses. Like it's this whole other special cheese, so it gets to be by the butter and yogurt. I need someone to mansplain this to me."

"You won't get any argument from me there. You know how I feel about the male population."

I pause and look over at Heather, changing my tune before I solidify her single status for life with my faux griping.

"I didn't mean to bash all men. And don't you go throwing away the entire male race based on one jerk who didn't know a good thing when he had it."

"Ix-nay on the ivorce-day alk-tay," my sister warns me in Pig Latin.

I lower my voice. "Sorry. I forgot he was in the back seat. He's so absorbed in that game."

"I'm still listening," Nate chimes in, surprising the heck out of me. "And I speak Pig Latin, Mom."

"Sorry, Nater Potater. I didn't mean to bash anyone."

"Yeah, you did," he says. "It's okay. My dad should have done a better job staying with Mom and me."

Sheesh. I don't even know what to say to that.

"Let's work on forgiveness and living forward. Okay, Buddy?" Heather says softly.

Nate and I both say, "Yes."

Heather looks at me and laughs. I guess I need to release the grudge I have against my sister's ex if she's willing to. Maybe I will. Maybe I won't. He did a number on her—and Nate—though that kid is remarkably resilient.

"Anyway, after my flight to LA, I'll take a two-hour bus to

this beach town, Ventura, and then a boat over to Marbella Island. It's basically a full day of travel each way."

"And then ...? I'm living vicariously through you, so spare me no details here."

"I have a room at the Alicante Resort and Spa. Four days on an island. The Meet-the-Author event starts Thursday. I'm going to finally meet Winona, Daisy, Brianna, and Cass, my online booksta-besties, in person! And then," I pause for dramatic effect and put on my well-practiced French accent. "The pièce de résistance: I can't believe I'm finally going to meet Amelie De Pierre in the flesh. My all-time favorite author. She's been a total recluse for years. This is the first public appearance she's made, and I'll be there to witness it. I'm packing my five favorite books of hers to have her sign them. That's not excessive, is it? I'd pack more despite extra baggage fees, but I don't want to fangirl so hard I send off stalker vibes. You know?"

"Back the train up. You're going to an island off the west coast, nearly 2500 miles away from North Carolina, and you are meeting two total strangers there?"

"Four, actually. And they're not total strangers. We talk every day online. They have bookish accounts on Instagram."

"You don't know if these are actual people, Tash. What if some creep is using these accounts to pretend like he's this avid book lover just so he can lure unsuspecting young women to islands and ..."

"I saw a thing like that on Lifetime," Nate chimes in from the back seat.

"What? When?" My sister is horrified.

"Grampa and I watched it."

"I'm going to kill our father," Heather murmurs to me. "They can put his murder on Lifetime."

I'm smiling big at my sister's reaction, and also her over-the-top fear about my bookish friends. "What would this creepy fake book guy do? Read to us? Come on, Heather. I watch these girls' reels. We message daily. We collaborate. They share my recordings and help promote my author services. They're real people. I know it's unconventional how we met, but I really know them."

Heather sighs.

"Don't be a wet blanket," I plead. "Trust me, there's no stranger danger. The four of them have actually become good friends of mine. If it makes you feel any better, I'll send proof-of-life photos every step of the trip."

"It does make me feel better. And you're probably right. As long as you're really meeting book-loving friends and your fave author, I'm excited for you. And, when did you start speaking French?"

"I don't. I just figure, meeting Amelie, it might come in handy to have some phrases under my belt. You know, like, *Bonjour, Comment allez-vous*, things like that."

"And *pièce de résistance*?"

"Exactly. I can complement one of her books that way. Only, I'll have to decide if it's *Lovestruck in Lyon*, *Married in Marseille*, or *Ravished in Rouen*."

"Decisions, decisions," Heather teases me.

While I'm the romantic in the family, she's the pragmatic. Her idea of a good book is a hiking manual with a thick, backwoods first-aid section.

"Will you come back to Harvest Hollow to see us before you go?" The pleading note in her voice isn't even disguised.

"Probably not ... maybe. I don't know. I want to."

"Nate misses you."

"I'm right here. He's really missing me. He's probably going to need therapy from missing me so much."

Heather's laugh is soft. "You know what I mean. We only see you every few weeks. I miss having you in town. If you moved back here, we'd see each other nearly every day." She pauses, smiling over at me with an imploring look. "I'd give you free coffee."

"Way to pull the guilt trip and the incentive program. Using my seven-year-old nephew against me—and coffee. I think you are surpassing Mom in your skills of persuasion."

"Persuasion. Yeah. Let's go with that."

We both laugh.

"Seriously," I say. "If I can fit in a visit, I will."

I feel it too—the ache of the distance between us. Heather isn't only my older sister. She's my best friend. Technically, we're less than an hour away from one another, separated by rolling hills and blue-green mountains, but our lives are so full we rarely even see one another more than twice a month these days.

"You can always come to Asheville." I say it, but I know better.

Nate's old enough to travel easily—not like he was a few years ago when he'd end up crying for at least the second half hour of the drive. But now, Heather can't freely leave on weekends, or any day, for completely other reasons. Her work demands odd hours and devotion—especially if she hopes to take over Cataloochee Coffee in the coming years.

Besides, she doesn't want to accidentally bump into Andrew. Asheville's big enough. He moved there after their divorce was final. I rarely see him. But knowing my sister's luck, she'd land smack dab in the middle of his trajectory. It happened once a few months ago and Andrew was with *her*. I'll make the trip home to see Heather regularly if it means never putting her—and Nate—through that kind of excruciatingly awkward encounter again.

Heather orders pizza while we're making the drive to her house. It arrives about ten minutes after we do. It's a little early for dinner time, but Heather's had a long work day, and Nate can always eat. I don't know where that kid puts it all. Heather makes Nate put the iPad up and we all hang out, laughing and devouring the pizza right out of the box on paper plates in their living room. When we finish, I make the drive back to my current home in Asheville.

It's not even seven when I walk through the front door of the little house I rent month-to-month in a small residential neighborhood. Still, I change into pajamas and pick up my latest Amelie De Pierre book: *Nuzzling in Nante*. Granted, it's the weirdest of her titles to date, but I'm sure it's a challenge trying to find alliterative titles that contain a city in France and a romantic term with the same first letter. At least it's not *Nookie in Nante*. I guess it could have been *Nuptials*. *Nuptials in Nante*. But she just released *Married in Marseille* this spring. *Needy? Necking? Nurtured?* ... Yeah. Nuzzling it is.

I focus on the book, and am immediately transported to northwest France, two hundred miles south of Paris. I'm the heroine, Genevieve, and Luc, my book boyfriend, is completely smitten with me, or at least he will be shortly ...

LUC'S HAND finds the small of my back. It's an innocent touch, like all his touches—the times when his fingers graze mine as he passes me a cup of my favorite coffee, or the moments when he has swiped a piece of windblown hair and tucked it gently behind my ear. He's free with his physical affection, hugging me in greeting, or brushing my cheeks with barely a kiss when we say goodbye. I never know if he feels the same surge of electricity dancing across his skin as I do, or whether he's thinking the kinds of thoughts I am—about how his lips would feel if he brushed them against my mouth instead of the side of my face—if he let them linger and pulled me in for something deeper and more meaningful.

I'm restless around him, but also more calm than I've ever felt anywhere else on earth. I fantasized I'd find a French boyfriend when I came to university from America. I couldn't have dreamt of a man like Luc. He's cultured, serious, and intelligent. But at times, he's playful. And even though he hasn't told me he has any romantic feelings for me, he acts in a way I can only describe as possessive whenever we're in a crowd, like he's keeping me to himself.

Luc extends his other hand to stabilize me as he helps me board the evening cruise on the Loire River. He easily steps onto the deck behind me, barely looking away from my eyes to acknowledge the river guide who will lead our tour and the chef who will serve the passengers hors d'oeuvres and chilled wine. I've never felt so wholly cherished. Luc's green eyes rove across my features as if I'm priceless. His gaze heats me from within, staving off the breeze coming in from across the water.

"Come over here," he says in a voice intended only for me. "I wish to show you the view before we take off."

Luc leads me to a spot separated from the other people already gathered on the benches at the center table. I wonder if this will be the moment he confirms what I've suspected. Am I imagining the way he always studies me—the way his eyes seem to secretly seek mine from across any space we share? Will he finally kiss me?

· · ·

MY DOORBELL RINGS. I'm tempted to ignore it. This story is just getting good. There hasn't been any nuzzling in Nantes, not even a nip or a nudge. It's been a torturously slow burn between Luc and me—er, Genevieve. And I'm ready. Genevieve's ready. Is Luc ready? I'll have to find out later. I set my book down, quickly tearing the receipt off last night's empty pizza box on my coffee table to mark my place. Pizza here, pizza with Heather ... at least I'm consistent.

What makes Amelie De Pierre write book boyfriends that are so wholly captivating? How does every word she writes grip me and sweep me up into her stories? It's like she knows exactly what to say so I'll forget everything around me. Her characters feel real, as if I could hop on a plane to France, and there they'd be—Luc and Genevieve—waiting to meet me. Of course, Amelie De Pierre is talented. She wouldn't have every single book she's written translated from French into multiple languages, including English, if she weren't. It would be a dream to work with her one day, even indirectly. I can barely believe I'll be meeting her in less than a month.

A young man wearing a brown button down shirt and matching shorts is standing on my welcome mat when I answer the door. He's holding a rather large package in one arm.

"Tasha Pierson?"

I nod. "That's me."

He extends an electronic clipboard in my direction. I move the stylus across the screen in a signature and accept the box from him.

Shoving the door closed behind me with my foot, I set the package on my counter and check the return address. Ahhh. The stickers for our subscription boxes. I grab my phone off the charging station and shoot Lindsay a text. She's one of the authors I serve as a personal assistant. We've put together a quarterly romance collection with swag and books for readers—and, when I say we, I mean me. It was a brainstormed idea I had to help generate a little side income and some reader loyalty for all the authors who contract with me. I take a cut of the proceeds for being the one to assemble and ship everything.

All these various projects—editing, running social media, coordinating book launches, and the subscription box, help supplement my income as a voice artist narrating books. I'm still neck-deep in student loans even though I graduated over seven years ago. The last thing I want to be forced to do is to take a full-time job just to keep up financially. I'd lose recording gigs and never get ahead in a field I feel born to work in.

Heather tells me I should pursue a career in stage acting too. She dreams that would lead to big things, like a TV role or even movies. Even if that weren't a pipe dream, acting's not my passion. Books. Books are my passion.

As much as I stand out with my curly auburn hair and light complexion, I don't have any desire to be on stage. I prefer to be the voice behind the characters, bringing them to life, amplifying the vision of the author who fashioned them into existence.

If only one day I could have the honor of lending my talent to the romance heroines of Amelie De Pierre.

2

THE AUTHOR, AMELIE DE PIERRE

Secrets: Can't live with them,
can't live without them.
~ Gail Baltz

I sit in my living room on a Zoom call, my eyes drifting over the top of my laptop, out past the solid wood walls and sliding doors into the dense green woods just beyond the deck.

I'd rather be hiking. How many times have I seen that saying on bumper stickers since coming to North Carolina? Today, I understand the sentiment.

Stuart drones on about the Meet-the-Author event on an island off the coast of California. I make a half-baked attempt at focusing, reminding myself what Mamie always said, "Après la pluie, le beau temps." It means, after the rain, good weather—basically our way of saying not to lose hope.

"... and you'll have accommodations in the Honeymoon

Suite, I guess. It's the nicest room they have. Besides, I figured it was fitting for a romance author. Honeymoon. Romance. It's perfect, no?"

Stuart likes to add in French words or sayings, poorly pronounced, and ineptly placed whenever we speak, as if I'll think of him as somehow more continental and less of a pain in my derriere. There's a French word for you, Stuart. Unfortunately, life as an author has perks and pains. Publicists and agents are both, or either, depending on the day.

"Sounds fine," I answer. "Merci."

Stuart also loves when I pander to him by speaking French words that anyone who has read the children's book, *Madeline*, would understand. It makes him feel as if I believe he's as worldly as he attempts to behave.

"It's a big trip for you," Stuart reminds me. "This is the year the world finds out the person behind the pen of Amelie De Pierre is actually Pierre Toussaint."

"Yes. I know."

My family didn't even know about my nom de plume before Stuart cooked up this scheme. Of course they had heard of Amelie De Pierre. In France, everyone has heard of the best-selling novels which some even hold responsible for increasing tourism to France by romance enthusiasts—a phenomenon my country's people simultaneously love and loathe. We are not always fans of Americans, the culture tends to be more brash and less ... I don't know ... just more, and less, than the French way of life. Though, I will say, I have been happy so far in my temporary home on the outskirts of Harvest Hollow here in the Blue Ridge mountains of North Carolina.

I had my relatives all believing I wrote articles for various travel journals and ghost wrote for novelists. I kept it all relatively vague, explaining I couldn't reveal any author I represent due to confidentiality issues. It was a lie that was near enough to the truth, and it kept them from poking around. Did I like selling my family a half-truth? No. Did it spare me humiliation? Absolutely. And, not only that, my secret remained safely concealed between me, my publicist, my agent, and a few select people in my employ—each one signing an NDA before even meeting me through a video chat.

I wrote my first romance story as a response to a dare from one of my classmates at university. It was more of a novella. He followed that dare by taunting me, saying he was quite certain I would hide my story in a shoebox rather than publishing it. That was when I coined the name De Pierre. It literally means *of the rock*, but in my case, *of Pierre*. I hid my identity in plain sight. I always loved the name Amelie, the name of my grand-mère.

On a whim, I got on Amazon one night, after sharing a few glasses of Pinot Noir with my apartment mates, and I published the book under my new pen name. Little did I know, someone influential would trip across my manuscript and find it charming enough to reach out to me. And from there, my path as an author grew, like a garden weed, but one with great benefits and fulfillment I never imagined.

The only hitch? I have to live a double life. Well, I did have to. Until this tour.

I made the call to my family before we even began planning to unveil my true identity. I insisted on it. Family is most precious to me. I adore my family. Telling them I had hidden this facet of my work—the entire reality of me being a world-renowned romance author, and writing under a female pen name—well, that did not go over so well.

I talk to my papa twice a week. Mamie has always had a very strict way with me—strict, but affectionate. She saw my secret as a betrayal of sorts. Why would I not trust my parents? Did I think so poorly of them that I couldn't share my life? But now, a month into the planning of this tour, they have forgiven my faux pas and are basking in their newfound pride over my accomplishments. They are itching to tell everyone they know, but are waiting until the first few stops of the tour are underway because I asked them to honor the plans of my publicist and agent.

"And with California being the first stop in this tour," Stuart continues, "the buzz will start after this initial Meet-the-Author event. People will be giddy with interest. The news will leak and people will question if it could be true. Could the greatest romance novels in the world truly be written by a man?"

By a Frenchman, *oui*. Yes, of course.

But I don't say that to Stuart. He already assumes my French arrogance. I would say confidence is not arrogance if it's factual. I'm not one to say French men are superior. What I will say is we are steeped in a culture devoted to cherishing women, appreciating them, and seducing them. We aren't known for this worldwide for nothing. We have earned our reputation. I'll be the first to admit some Frenchmen are more seductive than romantic, especially in our larger municipalities where the men can be downright brutish in their directness. But nonetheless, we Frenchmen know romance and we know it well enough to write a book—or twenty-two, my current number of published titles. That is, if a Frenchman were able to write well, which, some can, and some, sadly cannot.

I'm still unsure about this plan of Stuart's. My books are

doing fine. I make a very good living doing what I love. People line up in bookstores on pub day whenever a new book of mine is slated to release.

According to Stuart, and my agent, Bob, "fine" is dangerous. We should never settle for *fine*. The slope is slippery, they warn me. One day I'm fine, the next, like the dinosaurs, I'll be obsolete. Only, according to Stuart, I won't be remembered like the ancient reptiles. No one will have child's toy figurines and museums set up in my memory. So a revealing, possibly shocking, tour has been planned, and by the end of this week I'll be letting my secret identity out to the public, whether I'm ready or not.

Stuart reviews the plans for the first half of the year-long tour. First Marbella Island, then, I'll return to North Carolina for a month to write and do some local appearances. Then we'll have tours in New York and Boston. Back to North Carolina, and so on ... He reviews each spot on the itinerary in great detail along with the breaks I'll have for writing between tour locations, as if I'm not reading the same attachment to the email he is.

Finally, he bids me "Adieu," and hangs up to leave me questioning all my life choices—well, most of them. Writing novels will never be something I question. It's in my blood. I owe that university friend of mine, Nicolas, a debt. Crafting stories comes as naturally as breathing. I can't imagine doing anything else. And I never would have started were it not for his dare.

I take my coffee and laptop out on the porch to write for a bit. The air is crisp and brisk this morning, a hint of the coming fall season. Soon my woods will be the color of flames, matching the fire burning in the stone hearth in my living room.

The phone rings. When I see the caller ID, I quickly do the mental math to figure the time in France. Midafternoon.

"Allô, Rene. Ça va ?"

"Allo," my oldest friend in the world answers me, the mirth in his voice already preceding whatever taunt he's about to throw my way.

We speak in French, and it instantly reminds me of home —the stone wall surrounding the old papal residency, the buildings covered in ivy, the theater festival held every July. I miss walking old streets, traveling further into Provence on weekends for a hike or a lunch at a family-owned establishment. I miss the culture. I miss my family. I miss Rene and my other friends.

"How is our hometown Romeo today?"

My parents and older sisters may have moved on from my secrecy. Rene has not. He's a good sport in all things, fun-loving, witty, too charming for his own good, so he has made light of it. Underneath the joking, I know he's still upset at me for not telling him about my pen name.

"I'm actually finally sitting to write. Stuart had me on a call for an hour going over things I could have discerned in ten minutes of solitude."

"You poor dear."

"Aren't you supposed to be at work?"

"I'm a Frenchman through and through. I feel the ancient call of my ancestors to rest after my mid-day meal."

"You're so full of it."

"And you are one to talk, man of mystery."

"I am sorry, Rene."

I say it every time we speak. Eventually, he may accept my apology and move on. I hope he will.

"What is the current project?" Rene neatly avoids the topic of my indiscretion and repentance.

"After the insistence from my publisher that we give my last novel such a ridiculous title, I have the working title of *Adored in Aix-en-Provence.*"

Of course, my French Titles aren't so cutesy. It doesn't matter to the French that all the words don't start with the same letters the way the American publisher insists they do. It's almost more refined when they don't align. None of that mattered as much to me when I was writing behind the curtain of a pen name. Now every choice feels more exposed, more open to direct judgment and critique.

"My leading male is an art gallery owner, a man who is only slightly obsessed with the works of Cezanne."

"Only slightly obsessed. As if everyone there isn't slightly obsessed—rightly so. They have the history of his life and works to their name." Rene pauses. "And is this leading man based on a certain agent immobilier who has a way with women?"

"No. I do not base my characters on you."

"Who else could you base them on? And what would Camille say of this—her ex-boyfriend, the romance novelist?"

"She would say I must base them on you as I am so poor at romance," I admit.

"Of course she would. And she would be right. But the numbers don't lie. You are finding inspiration somewhere. People eat up these books of yours. I'm happy for you. And me—since I'm certainly the inspiration."

"Congratulations. You inspire me."

"I knew it!" He chuckles. "Now. If I could only inspire you

in real life. Maybe in America you will find a woman, someone who loves not only the books, but the author too?"

"No. I'm here for business. It's not a trip for love."

"Spoken like the truly romantic man you are." Rene laughs again. This time more fully.

I smile. He's not wrong. The irony of me being a romance novelist isn't lost on me. I didn't choose it, this profession chose me. And, I'm so glad it did. Romance is easy in books —where the female lead character is looking for love, instantly smitten with the male love interest, and he knows all the things to say and do when she overwhelms him. Of course, my characters experience challenges and conflict, but they will always make it through by chapter thirty or so. In real life, there are no such guarantees.

"So, tell me more," Rene asks. "Who is the woman worthy of my love—in this story?"

"His love. My art gallery owner. He is the one falling in love, not you, Casanova."

"Details. We both know who he really is. So, who is my woman?"

"The leading lady, the woman who will win Jean Paul's heart, is a shy young woman whose family runs tours for visitors to the region. The extended family grows lavender in the fields outside town."

"Yes. Lavender fields. You must have those. And a fish-monger. And a town market."

"All included already."

"Good. Good. Is she beautiful, this future love of my life?"

"Yes. Of course she is. Beautiful, feminine, and reserved. But not so reserved once you get to know her."

"That's what I'm talking about. Where can I meet her?"

"In my books. And this—what you are feeling—is why they sell."

"Maybe—no promises—I'll read one. Especially since all the men are based on me."

"They aren't."

"Of course they aren't. They are based on all your life experience collected somewhere and distilled into the pages of your stories. I know. Your wealth of romantic success has to translate onto so many pages." Rene laughs good-naturedly, softening the impact of his statement only a little.

I hear Mamie's voice, the words she said after the shock of my revealed secret wore off: *How do you write romance, my son, when you have rejected love yourself?* I laughed off her words at the time, assuring her my sales and international popularity were proof enough that I could write on the subject with proficiency. She argued with me, quoting a famous saying, "Il n'y a qu'un bonheur dans la vie, c'est d'aimer et d'être aimé."

There is only one happiness in life, to love and be loved.

I assured her I'm happy. And I'm loved. *What greater love is there than a mother for her son?* That statement put a stop to her need to foist her opinions about my personal life on me. She sighed and said, "You are right, of course." Still, my writing feels slightly flat since that conversation. Her accusations continue to fertilize the seed of self-doubt she planted. *How can I truly write romance if I have rejected it in my own life and heart?*

3

TASHA

You give me the kind of feelings
people write novels about.
~ Unknown

"Watch your step," a young woman in a white polo shirt and pressed khaki shorts says to me as I plant my foot on the long wooden dock stretching from the charter boat to shore.

Her name tag says *Summer.*

I quickly move aside so the other passengers can disembark and scoot past me. It seems like many of them have been here before. There's a comfortable familiarity in the way they walk off the boat toward the crew member standing near the pile of luggage a short distance down the dock.

The island air smells of ocean and sunshine. I close my eyes to let the warmth seep into my skin. Everything's already slower and less urgent. A soft breeze blows my hair back from my face. I already know it's a mess of curls and waves, and I can't bring myself to care. When I open my eyes, Summer is staring at me with not exactly a smile on her face. It's not unfriendly. Maybe it's curious? Possibly impatience cloaked in hospitality.

"Well, let's get you checked in," Summer says to me and a few other stragglers who are also staying at the Alicante Resort and Spa.

"If you want a tour of this side of the island, I'll be with a few other resort hosts at the front of the main building for the next half-hour. We're available to take you on golf carts through the resort buildings and surrounding island community to give you a feel for what we offer and how to get around during your stay." Summer talks to us from over her shoulder as she continues to lead the seven of us down the pier, toward the sand.

I follow Summer along the dock which is made up of about forty feet of evenly cut and sanded wooden planks set off by low pylons. In the distance, the island stretches out to the north and south of us. Sailboats bob in the harbor at their moorings to our right. Evenly spaced lounge chairs with red umbrellas dot the southern section of the sand near the shoreline to our left. The clean white stucco of the resort buildings with their tile roofs stand out behind a row of quaint streetside shops in various bright colors. The stores face a walk path along the edge of the beach. The whole scene looks like a vacation postcard.

When we hit the sand, a gorgeous young man with tousled light brown hair and a sun-kissed tan approaches Summer. He's obviously physically fit, the way his white

Alicante Resort & Spa T-shirt clings to his muscles. He's wearing a pair of navy board shorts and flip-flops.

He addresses the group of guests in a charismatic and carefree voice. "Welcome to Descanso, the resort town on Marbella Island. I'm Ben, one of the watersports instructors, lifeguards, and evening cruise directors. Let me know if you need anything water-related during your stay. You can find me over there at our watersports rental shack."

Ben points toward the northern section of the beach.

Then he turns to Summer, winks at her in a way that nearly makes my knees weak, and says, "And *you* let me know if you need anything water or land-related. Anything at all."

Ben smiles a winsome smile at Summer, and then turns that same smile toward the group. His face could put him in a commercial, or even the movies. He's not really my type, but then again, he sort of seems like he ought to be everyone's type. With a wave, he does this smooth exit, taking two jogging steps backward and then turning to slowly run toward the area of the beach where he had pointed. A small, painted white wooden hut sits close to the water with a turquoise wooden sign overhead that says *Rentals-Lessons-Tours*.

Summer shakes her head as she watches him go. She seems completely unamused and definitely not charmed by Ben.

I hear her mutter, "Not everything dangerous on the island is submerged in water."

The romance fanatic in me is already shipping them. My sister would chide me. According to her, I can't even go out to a restaurant without playing silent matchmaker. She's not totally wrong. But she's not here, and I am—here for all things romance this weekend. Well, not my romance, of course. Literary romance, safely tucked between two covers. Book covers, not bed covers ... you know what I mean.

We cross the street, which is more like a glorified side-walk since there are no cars allowed on the island aside from small delivery trucks. Golf carts are parked in various spots near bike racks filled with two-wheelers and electric scooters. A pedal-surrey shop catches my eye. We walk down a wide cobblestone area between two of the shops, colorful canopies hang overhead for shade, and bistro tables line the walls. Then we emerge, past the rear of the shops in an oasis. A large cement entry patio is filled with elegant lounging spots and various clover shaped pools. Behind all that are the sprawling stone steps leading to the main building of the resort.

"Here we are," Summer announces. "Alicante."

She waves her hand in a game show hostess flourish toward the main building and then around at the surrounding beauty of the resort entrance.

"I'll be right over there, near the golf carts. Straight through those doors you'll find the lobby and front desk. Our guest services hosts are aware of your arrival. You'll find your luggage with a porter next to the front desk, along with your itineraries for the weekend if you are here for the Meet-the-Authors event. When you get your room keys, let the porter know and he'll arrange for someone to accompany you to your room with your bags."

I never want to leave.

Living alone, I carry all my own bags and cook my own meals—unless Domino's cooks for me, which they often do. Is it a crime to know all the employees' names at my neighborhood pizza place? If so, arrest me now.

Still, I definitely could get used to island living—at a resort, of course. I'd miss Braydon, Missy, and Carter at the local Domino's—and the garlic bread knots. I'd miss those a whole lot. But I'd get over it. Having someone so attentive to the small courtesies—porters to carry my bags, cute hostesses to drive me around touring the island, a concierge to plan my itinerary? Yes. I'd adapt to this deliciously indulgent lifestyle in a hot minute. But to be truthful, I'd miss fall if I lived in the eternal summer on this island. Fall is my favorite season. Especially fall in the Blue Ridge Mountains.

We walk through the double-high glass doors into a casual and simultaneously elegant lobby with its white and light blue beach theme. My eyes stop on a man. Forget that guy Ben. This. This is a man. He's wearing a suit with a tie gracing the collar of his crisp, white, dress shirt. He's impeccable, and standing casually as if being dressed for a business meeting around a small crowd of people in beachwear doesn't faze him in the least. His brown hair is cropped short around the sides and neck, and tastefully slicked back on top. His skin is lightly olive, his eyes framed by these black, Clark Kent style glasses which perch on his beautifully defined nose. He's perfection.

I can't stop staring. Which is a problem, obviously. I force my eyes away, and then the little rebellious orbs drift back in his direction until I'm taking him in as if I'm on an exclusive, behind the rope tour of the Mona Lisa. More like Michelangelo's David. Because, though this man isn't as built as Ben, the charmer out at the waterfront, he's got muscles and a lean, toned physique. He looks like a professor you'd crush on all four years of college.

Gah. I look away again. And look back.

Until I hear, "Miss?" and again, "Miss?" And I realize the

front desk clerk is calling me. When my eyes snap away from this vision of perfect manhood standing across the lobby to answer the resort employee, he's got a soft, knowing smirk on his face. Yeah, buddy. I was totally checking out the hot professor. Sue me. I'm on vacation.

I approach the desk and check in, every so often allowing my gaze to drift to my right, where the hot professor is now holding up a wall, looking just the right blend of impatient and at ease. How does one pull off both those looks at once, and will I see him in a swimsuit this weekend? These are important things I need to know.

Is it strange that I no longer feel as much of the burning obsession to meet Amelie De Pierre? Instead, I'm wondering when I'll see this man again. Why? It's not like I'll meet him, or talk to him. But this is why fantasies are so fun. We can dream. Like considering the hot professor with those glasses I'd like to take off and set to the side so I could really kiss his perfect lips. Not that I would. I wouldn't. I haven't kissed any lips in ... well, it's been a long enough time to make me wonder if I still know how.

But back to the fantasy. I imagine the hot professor would stroll over here, introduce himself, and then we'd have this instant connection ...

Oh! Record scratch.

That's not a fantasy. He is walking over here. And he's looking at me—with my crazy windblown hair and an outfit that's just endured over ten hours of travel after waking early to make it to the airport. Not my best look—by a longshot.

I feel the heat creep up my cheeks. And then he speaks. Oh, sweet baguette with a chunk of gourmet cheese, this man is French.

Keep talking. Keep talking. Keeeeeep talking. Oh, the things I would do to hear this man speak forever.

"Pardon me, sir," hot French professor says to the clerk working next to mine.

"Yes. How can I help you?"

"My bags were supposed to meet me here. The young valet said he was bringing them from the front to me. If it's no trouble, could you help me locate my luggage?"

His Rs roll in the back of his throat with this sexy softness that makes me want to curl up on a hammock and listen to him speak all day, and he says *luggage* like lahgeejshuh.

When he thanks the clerk, he says, "Sank you so much for seez."

I'm done. Put a fork in me. I'm done.

Am I staring again? Well, I'm not alone. Two of the women behind the desk are also ogling this man. I'm assuming they see gorgeous men from other countries all the time. This man still attracts their attention. What he has goes beyond looks. It's something deep within, compelling all of us to pause whatever we're doing and take note. And, he seems relatively oblivious to his own magnetism.

He turns with a quiet air of confidence, and his eyes meet mine. He gives me a polite smile, lips closed in a soft line, eyes trained on mine. He nods lightly and walks back to his spot along the lobby wall as if our imperceptible interaction hadn't just rolled through me like a category five hurricane setting my nerve endings ablaze with tingles.

What is happening to me? Yes. I'm here for a weekend focused on romance authors and romantic novels, but this is not my usual reaction to men. I live in North Carolina. Men around our area tend to be outdoor enthusiasts. They stay in shape hiking, rafting, and cycling. No man has ever made me feel so alive, or been so alluring to me before.

Note to self: save for a trip to France.

Also note to self: stop in airport bathroom to freshen up after flights in the future.

My thoughts are interrupted by excited squeals and laughter across the lobby—calling my name.

"Tashaaaa! Tasha, you're heeeere!"

I take my key and itinerary from the clerk with a polite smile, and turn to see my four booksta-besties flying across the lobby as if we're in a roadside McDonald's, not a posh, five-star, island resort. I step away from the counter and drop my belongings at my feet so I can pull each of them into a hug.

They're all chattering at once.

"I can't believe you're here—we're all here—together, in person!"

"Did you check in?"

"Have you seen your room yet?"

"Of course she hasn't seen her room. She obviously just got here. You're next to us. We're all together."

"Here. Let's get your bags."

I'm swept along in their exuberant welcome. When I glance at the wall where my perfect guy had been standing, he's gone like the dream he must have been.

4

PIERRE

We grow fearless by walking into our fears.
~ Robin Sharma

"Oui," I say absently into the phone as my oldest sister grills me about the resort.

Is it beautiful? Of course it is. Resorts like this are designed to take a human being out of their life and make them feel elevated, removed, pampered. We don't call them paradise for no reason. I suppose it's the same effect my books have on readers, in a much less visceral way—providing sweet escape and refreshment.

"A slice of paradise," I add. "I'll send you photos later."

But I am not here to indulge myself in island tranquility. This is a work trip. At that thought my stomach knots slightly. After today there will be no turning back. The whole world, or at least the segment that matters to me, will know Amelie De Pierre has been a mask—something I've conveniently hidden behind while writing books I couldn't bring myself to fully own as my creations.

As usual, Colette senses something. I swear she would be capable of reading my very thoughts from across a continent and the Atlantic even if we weren't on the phone.

"Nervous?"

"Un peu." I admit to a fraction of what I'm feeling, throwing her a bone to keep her from going deeper.

"With you, a little is the tip of an iceberg. It's okay to be nervous, baby brother. You're coming out as a man. That's a big deal."

I chuckle at her choice of words, but then a seriousness overshadows the joke.

"I am nervous, Colette. What if people turn away? What if my sales plummet and I can't recover? My publicist, Stuart, thinks this is a brilliant PR move. It will attract attention. He uses the saying, *all publicity is good publicity*. That saying alone makes me anxious. I don't want to disillusion the readers I've worked so hard to engage. They trust me. What will happen when they find out I've been hiding behind a nom de plume?"

"They will still love you and your books. Lots of writers use pen names. You are important, but not that important, I hate to tell you. These readers of yours have lives. Voilà."

"Of course they have lives."

"Meaning, they won't lose sleep over your gender. Besides, they might like it even better that you are this man who can write such romantic stories. Though, I'll never know how. Just keep writing books they call, how do you say it? Ah. Swoony." She says that last word in English.

"Swoony, yeah."

I don't bother to defend the depth of my characters or

the difficulty of writing a whole, cohesive story. I allow her to poke fun. She's my sister. She loves me more than I probably know. She can mock a little. Marguerite, our middle sister, had joked that I should do a gender reveal party like an expectant couple. Set off a blue confetti cannon, or let blue balloons into the air. She couldn't stop laughing at her own joke. I smile now, hearing the sound of her laughter at my expense almost as if she's right here in the hotel with me.

"You'll be fine, mon petit mignon."

Her little cutie pie. At least the world will never hear that nickname. Colette's only slightly over two years older than me, and she still treats me like there's a ten year gap.

We chat a little longer. Colette fills me in on everything going on back in Avignon. Then she says she loves me, wishes me luck, and we hang up.

Less than an hour later, Stuart's knock sounds through my room like a death knell. *Death to Amelie.* If I were writing another genre of books, that might be a potential title.

"Coming!" I say, making my way toward the door.

With a steadying breath, I open the door to Stuart's overeager smile. If this publicist gig doesn't work out, I think he could do well in the used car business.

"Pierre. Pierre. Pierre. This is the day. The jour, no?" He says *jour* with such a strong R sound I nearly wince. French is spoken with restraint and finesse. He is a butcher, and not even one with a sharp knife.

"Oui. The jour."

Stuart walks past me into my suite, looking around and letting out a low whistle. His eyes rove the furniture and walls as he walks further into the space.

"What's this?" He asks from the restroom. "No! Tell me they didn't!"

I'm afraid they definitely did. The central fixture in the restroom, before the large jacuzzi bath and oversized shower, is a toilet made for two. The bowls are set adjacent to each other, but facing one another. If anything ever made me less eager to settle down and get married, that porcelain monstrosity confirmed my bachelor status. Some things should not be shared. Ever.

"At least they have a bidet!" he shouts, pronouncing the T.

"Small wonders and blessings," I murmur to myself, wondering if Stuart would know what to do with a bidet if he found himself the opportunity to use one. Okaaaay. Enough of those disturbing thoughts.

Stuart emerges from the restroom, snapping into business mode as quickly as he sloughed it.

"Everything downstairs is ready. You will have a special area set apart from the other authors this afternoon. The rest of the event you will be included with the others. The resort has a back patio area roped off with a table, the display of your books, and two barstools near a mic. We'll start with me announcing you. And then you will step out. I'll say, 'Ladies and gentleman, the brilliant author behind the romance books of Amelie De Pierre.' That's your cue."

I nod, unable to find a gracious response if I searched with a flashlight and a magnifying glass. Maybe I need a new publicist. Though, Stuart has steered me well over the years, guarded my secret as his own, and always been fair and honest with me. So, he's a bit gauche. I'll deal.

"Thank you, Stuart."

"Don't thank me. I love repping you. Look at me. I'm in paradise and getting paid to be here. We're living the dream, Pierre. Living the dream."

Or ... the nightmare. Only time will tell.

I divert myself with thoughts of the next scene in my current work in progress as the elevator transports Stuart and me down to the first floor. The rear of the building is as beautiful and immaculately landscaped as the front. A small crowd has gathered already, filling rows of chairs aimed at the mic. Most of them are women, though a few are men. No one pays a bit of attention to me and Stuart when we walk onto the patio. Of course, they are awaiting Amelie—a woman.

A hotel employee I met yesterday, shortly after I arrived, approaches me.

"Good afternoon, Mister Toussaint."

"Good afternoon." I glance at his tag and add, "Cameron."

"If you'll follow me, we'll wait over here behind this partition."

I nod to Stuart, who is already moving in the direction of the mic, eager, as they say in the states, to rip the bandaid. We have a saying a little like this, to seize the nettle. Either way, it is going headlong into the possibly painful thing— not my usual approach, as we all can ascertain based on how long I clung to this pen name instead of coming forward as the man I am.

I follow Cameron to a spot behind a trellis covered in a perfectly manicured flowering vine. In France, especially our region of Provence, vines grow wild on old stone buildings and walls. I close my eyes, imagining Avignon while Stuart drones on a short distance away.

Cameron's voice pulls me back to the moment.

"I think he's about to introduce you."

I nod, straightening my tie. I don't know why I wore a

suit, except it gives me an air of legitimacy. I have less formal outfits packed for other events over the coming four days.

"By the way," Cameron says, "my sister literally devours each of your books in less than a day as soon as they hit the stores. I didn't tell her your identity yet, of course, but I've been dying to. I'm going to call her after this event is over. She's going to freak."

"Freak good? Or ...?"

Cameron doesn't have time to answer because Stuart says the words he's been anticipating saying for over a month. "Ladies and gentleman, the brilliant author behind the romance books of Amelie De Pierre."

I look at Cameron, take a breath, and step out toward the mic. There is a moment of silence, during which I hear Cameron say, "A good freaking out. Very good. She's going to love this."

And then there's a collective gasp and a murmur that grows louder as people comprehend that the man approaching the empty stool in front of the mic is the beloved and renowned Amelie De Pierre.

Me. Pierre Toussaint.

Every eye is on me—including those of the reporters I didn't realize would be here. Their lanyards with the word *PRESS*, along with the way they eye my every move, distinguish them from the rest of the crowd.

I take a seat and smile a comfortable, confident smile at the audience which has grown now. From what I can tell, every seat is filled. People are lined up at the back of the patio, and more keep arriving, probably out of curiosity as to why the crowd has started making a low-grade commotion.

"As you can see," Stuart says, looking over at me with a wide, friendly smile. "Amelie is a man. More precisely,

Amelie is the pen name of the very male, French author, Pierre Toussaint."

Remarkably, he pronounces my last name as if he were born and raised in France. What's even more odd is how his accurate pronunciation calms my racing heart.

"Bon après-midi," I say, followed by the translation, "Good afternoon."

The chatter of the crowd stills at the sound of my voice.

I look around, searching for a friendly face, and find expectancy and bewilderment everywhere I look.

"I am sure my announcement and presence is quite a surprise to all of you. And I would like to introduce myself, and to tell you how I came to take on the pen name of Amelie de Pierre. Then I will welcome your questions before I move over there."

I motion to the table with a banner featuring my latest release, *Nuzzling in Nantes*. That tragic title. Ah, well. Stacks of my novels flank the table on both sides.

"I will be available to sign books and meet you after our Q and A, my dear readers."

I tell them of the dare I took in college, how I wrote the novella and published it, because in those days I never passed up an opportunity to show my peers I had hubris, which I mistook for confidence. Then I tell them of the day I got the email from someone in the publishing industry who had found my novella and searched for me through the link on my book sales page. I recount how that one contact led me to my first book contract. I explain how I fashioned the pen name as a joke at first, but once my first book took off, the name was solidified. Amelie De Pierre was my new identity as an author. I confess how it became a sort of security blanket, or a garden gate, protecting me and keeping me comfortable. A light laugh ripples through the audience when I say that.

"I never intended to be a romance author. I was at university studying business when my friend issued the dare that changed the trajectory of my life. My minor was communications. I had no idea the path ahead would lead me to all of you."

I glance at Stuart. He's smiling. The crowd has settled over the past fifteen minutes while I brought them up to speed. Many are smiling. No one looks disappointed or betrayed.

"So, now that you know, I am open to any questions."

I barely have the offer out of my mouth before one of the reporters has her hand in the air. Cameron and another hotel employee are ready with roving microphones.

"Why now?" she asks. "You've been silent all these years. Why come out now?"

"Well," I say, pausing to allow a thought to come. Why didn't we prep for this question? It was bound to come. I look to Stuart for some sort of clue as to what to say. He only nods, as if I can say whatever I want. I'm not telling them the truth. Then again, maybe I will.

"It was the hairbrained idea of my publicist," I say with a soft laugh.

Stuart laughs with me. "True story!"

The audience laughs loudly. We even have to wait for the laughter to die down before the reporter can ask her follow-up question.

"So, you would rather have remained anonymous and shrouded behind a female pen name?"

"In all honesty? Yes, I would. I am not a man who likes the spotlight. I can function in it. But I am a simple man. I like my morning coffee—black and sipped in quiet solitude —a good walk, a long discussion with friends, a meal with my family. I don't need to be seen or known. I have enjoyed my lack of notoriety. I love writing stories. It has been a privilege to create them for you. And it has been comfortable for a man like me to remain unknown while Amelie gained all the fame."

The reporter smiles at me, obviously satisfied with my answer.

A hand is raised in the back of the room. When she is handed a microphone, the young woman who appears to be in her early twenties asks, "Where does your inspiration come from? Are you that romantic in real life? And ..." she giggles lightly. "Are you single?"

I smile warmly at her, realizing these people now imagine me to be as personally as romantic as the men I write. If only Rene were here. He'd set them straight—and have a good laugh while doing it.

"I am not sure where my inspiration originates. Can any of us really say where creativity originates? I imagine my parents' good marriage is partly responsible. I have grown up watching people fall in love as we all have. And I live in France. Well, most of the time. For the time being, I am in America while I'm on tour. We aren't all sitting around kissing one another and drinking cappuccinos at the local patisserie all day as the movies would make it appear, but I have seen my share of romance—done well and poorly. Enough to draw from for my novels."

"Are you single?" the friend of the woman who just had the mic asks, leaning over to grab the mic to ask her question. If I am seeing correctly, her friend blushes.

"I am single," I reluctantly admit. I'm happily single. I don't add that far-too-personal detail.

Women audibly sigh, and a few shout out things like, "I'm single too!" and "You're so handsome!" and "I'll be your inspiration, Pierre!"

I was not prepared for this reaction. I had been so sure people might be upset that I never considered the opposite reaction—infatuation and misplaced adoration.

Stuart eats it all up and laughs at my side.

He whispers to me, "You've got a few days ahead here. Prepare to be hit on daily."

Fantastique. Très fantastique.

5

TASHA

Some people are worth melting for.
~ Olaf, Frozen

Hurry. Hurry. Hurry!
I'm dying a slow and painful death waiting here in the hallway for my friends to come out of their rooms so we can go to the exclusive Meet-the-Author event for Amelie De Pierre. Yes. She'll be here all weekend. And yes, there are panel discussions, opportunities to win a dinner with her, which I'm hoping and praying I do, and so much more. Plus, we're all here through Sunday late afternoon, so I may bump into her oh-so-casually in a very not-fangirl-stalker way, say, in an elevator or poolside. And then I could very smoothly mention the novel I'm reading.

What? You wrote Nuzzling in Nantes? Oh. Wow. I love your books.

I run other possible scripts through my head as to what

I'll say when I meet Amelie, or maybe she prefers Miss De Pierre. It might be Mrs. De Pierre. She's French. I wonder if that man from the lobby yesterday is related to her. Could he be her husband? No. He was traveling alone. So it seemed. I've thought of him entirely too much over the past twenty-four hours, hoping to spot him on the beach, near a pool, in the lobby, or at the quaint shops while browsing with my four friends. I'm nearly convinced I dreamt him up.

Speaking of my four friends, where are they? I glance at the time on my phone—again. It's official. We're late. Shifting my stack of Amelie De Pierre novels to my other arm, I juggle my phone into a position where I text Cass.

Tasha: Where are you? Should I meet you down there?

Cass: We've got a situation.

Tasha: A situation?

Cass: Winona was drying her hair, tipped her head upside down, and a chunk of it got stuck in the dryer. It's like a third of her hair is permanently wound inside this machine. Leave it to my twin to have a wrestling match with a common household appliance and lose. We're trying to remove her hair without her ending up with a bald spot or a buzz cut in the process.

Tasha: Oh my gosh. Do you need help?

Cass: No. We've already got three of us working on

this. You go ahead down. We'll meet you after the hair surgery.

Tasha: Are you sure?

Cass: Yes. Amelie De Pierre is your fave author. Don't miss this chance to see her. She's the main reason you came on this trip.

Tasha: I came to see you four too. And the other authors.

Cass: We know. Now scoot. And get a selfie with Amelie if you can.

I set my stack of books at my feet, plop my phone into my purse, pick up my books, and take off as fast as I can manage without breaking into a sweat toward the elevators around a corner at the end of the hall. When I get there, the doors of all three elevators are wide open and a man with a walkie-talkie and a tool box is squatting on the ground listening to someone on the other end.

He looks up at me. "Sorry, Miss. Elevator trouble. Some kids were in here hitting the buttons the way kids do. Something froze. We'll have 'em up and running in no time. Meanwhile, you can take the stairs."

He points further down this section to a more industrial style doorway where another employee is standing. She waves at me and I take off in her direction. Voices carry up from deeper in the stairwell. It's only a five-story building. Maybe I could scale the exterior?

"Sorry for the inconvenience," the hotel employee says as

I resign myself to my slow descent toward the lobby along with what feels like half the hotel's guests.

"No problem." I scoot past her and make my way down a flight before I come to a standstill.

We're moving. It's just slow, with a lot of stopping, and slightly hot. All this body heat, and I'm cradling my precious novels in one arm, which may never unfold completely after holding them for so long. I shift the books to my other arm and make my way step-by-step to the first floor. Once I'm out of the stairwell, I beeline to the back of the lobby and out onto the large terrace. An employee standing just outside the exit asks me if I'm headed to the Meet-the-Author event.

"I am. And I'm late because of the elevators."

He nods. "Right this way."

He points toward a spot where a crowd is gathered, standing room only, on a patio off to the back of the terrace, set off by planter boxes holding trellises of beautiful, tropical-flowered vines. I thank the resort staff member and walk toward the crowded space, only slightly sweaty from my nerves and the sauna that was the stairwell. I'd like to be more pulled together when I meet Amelie, but beggars can't be choosers, and she's a woman. She'll understand.

The crowd is standing up from their chairs and moving around. A woman turns to me and says, "The author is going to sign books now. He just finished answering questions."

My face scrunches up. "He?"

Someone waves to the woman and she walks up to cut in line about seven people ahead of me.

Am I at the wrong author event? No. I can't be. This event was scheduled separately before the rest of the weekend line-up officially kicks off. Probably because Amelie De Pierre is so famous she needed her own opportunity to greet her fans before the rest of the authors. An opportunity I missed because of a hairdryer and an elevator. Curses on the industrial revolution. Except airplanes. And motorboats.

I can practically feel my hair frizzing. It's not exceptionally hot. The island climate is temperate, even cool enough that I wore a light sweater in the morning and evening. But between my rush to get ready and the long, hot trip down the stairwell, I'm sure I look like I stuck my hand in a light socket and pulled it away just in time to survive the shock.

I try to look over the heads of the crowd, but as thick as it is, and with me measuring in at 5' 4", there's no way. People are chatting. A lot of them saying things like, "Wasn't that a surprise?" and "Who would have guessed?"

I careen my neck so I can peer around people and when I do, I see a man seated at the table. And not just any man. It's him. The French professor.

Why is my first thought, "Darn it"? It's not like we were about to date. Still, it feels like a loss after all the pining I've been doing yesterday and today—a fact that will go with me to my grave. He's probably Amelie's sexy, mysterious husband. No wonder she writes such hot male leading men in her stories. I'm quite sure each one is based on this guy—the Gregory Peck of all France—with a slightly more pronounced nose than the classic film star, but no less alluring or mesmerizing. Actually, that nose is amazing. Who would think I could be attracted to a nose? Noses are weird when you think about it. Little funnels for air right in the middle of our faces. Why couldn't our ears just do double duty? But we have a nose. Which is convenient when wearing glasses, for sure. And we have two nostrils. Even the word nostril is funky. I wonder how they ever came up with it.

I imagine two guys just sitting around naming parts of the body.

"Hey, Joe. What's this?"

"Why, Bill, I'd say that's an elbow."

"Elbow?"

"Yes. It's like a bow that can be bent into the shape of an L."

"Makes sense to me."

And, that does make sense. But, nostril? Not so much.

"Joe, I got a stumper for ya."

"Lay it on me, Bill."

"What are these holes on the middle of my face at the end of my nose? We did say this is a nose, right?"

"You are right. And I'd say those are nose-trills."

"Trills?"

"Yes. That trilling noise you make when you sleep? Maybe one day they'll have some sort of sticky strip to put over the bridge of your nose to stop that incessant whistling from waking me all night long."

I chuckle softly to myself. No one—and I repeat, no one —should ever hear my inner monologues.

The line inches forward, readers chatting with Amelie's husband. Him signing their books. What? Why is he signing her books? I'm about to ask the woman ahead of me when she turns and says, "Can you believe it?"

We're only five people away from Amelie's husband now —the hot French professor.

"Can I believe what?" I ask.

"Oh! Weren't you here earlier?"

"No."

Did Amelie De Pierre cancel? Is her husband signing her books in her place? I'm sorry. He may be hot. I may be more obsessed with him than I've ever been with any stranger, or anyone I know personally for that matter, but no one is signing my books but Amelie herself. I'll be so bummed if she's not here. Maybe it's jet lag. She might be resting, preparing herself for the rest of the weekend. But why would she miss this, the one event that focuses on her alone?

I barely hear the words the woman in front of me says next.

"Wait, what?" I ask.

Did I hear her right?

The line shuffles forward again as yet another reader leaves with her pile of books and a huge, dreamy smile on her face. Yes. He does have that effect, and apparently not only on me. Amelie is so lucky.

"I said, that man, Pierre Toussaint, announced that he's been using Amelie De Pierre as a pen name all these years. He's Amelie De Pierre. The person behind the pen is him."

The next three things that happen all occur as if in slow motion.

My mouth drops open.

I go to slap my hand over my mouth.

The hand that is attached to the stack of Amelie's books.

Amelie—the hot French professor.

The books go flying in five directions. Five books. Five directions. Loudly slapping the concrete and scattering.

I gasp, and my head snaps up to see Amelie—not Amelie, but yes, Amelie, the man, Pierre—staring at me. Our eyes lock. I'm not just saying this in some metaphorical, I'm-the-star-in-my-own-romcom sort of way. Our eyes lock, like a mechanism sliding into place and finding the niche that fits it perfectly. I'm bonkers. I know. Nothing about Amelie—

Pierre—is made to be seamlessly compatible with me, obviously.

Pierre gets this amused grin.

I realize my mouth is still wide open. I hear the voice of Mary Poppins in my head saying, *"We are not a codfish."*

I slap my mouth shut, which is probably just as attractive of a move as dropping it wide open in the first place.

And then ... in slow motion, like a lifeguard running in *Baywatch* (If you haven't seen that old show, look it up) ... Pierre stands and pushes his chair back, his eyes still trained on mine.

He leans over to the woman whose book sits open in front of where he was sitting and says, "If you'll excuse me a moment."

That voice. Butter melting on toast, with sprinkles of chocolate on top, and a cozy fire in the fireplace and my favorite slippers and ... oh, sweet breakfast pastries ... he's walking over. To me.

Pierre smiles this sexy, soft smile. And then he talks. To me. "I am guessing you got the news late?"

"Uh. Yes. Late. The elevators. And the hair dryer. And, well. Winona's hair was tangled—stuck like gum on a boot heel. I hope they get it out. And it was broken. So we had to take the stairs. So, yeah. Late."

Pierre chuckles this amused laugh as he bends down to collect my books. Which, of course, I can't let him do. So I bend down to join him. And now we're both squatting here, faces too near to one another, groping for books, and still carrying on the most embarrassing conversation of my life.

"None of what I just said made sense, huh?"

"Not completely, but English is my second language, so it could be entirely my fault."

"Nope. Not even one percent your fault. I just babbled. Which I never do. I'm just. Excuse me. I'm in shock."

"I understand," he says. "It's shocking. I was supposed to be a woman. Not in life. I'm quite sure I was supposed to be a man in life."

"Oh, me too. Sure you were supposed to be a man, that is. Not me. I wasn't supposed to be a man. But you obviously were. Obviously. I mean, look at you."

Whaaaat? Shut the pie hole, Tasha.

He chuckles again. I might pass out on the spot. Which, come to think of it, would be awesome in its own way. Maybe when I wake, I can avoid Pierre the rest of the weekend.

A hotel employee wearing the name badge, Cameron, comes over to where I am squatting with the world-famous author I have loved for years. Just hanging out down here collecting books and acting like a dork, making a first impression that should go in all Meet-the-Author instruction manuals as an example of what not to ever do when you meet your idol and he turns out to also be the hot French professor.

But, seriously. Tell me you wouldn't have dropped something—as in your jaw and your books.

Right? Right.

Pierre gracefully stands, holding two of my books—his books, that are mine. And he extends me his hand. I'm holding one book. Cameron has the other two. I look up at Pierre with an expression that says, *You want me to hold your hand? Are you out of your mind?*

He chuckles again. "Let me help you up, Cherie."

I somehow manage to put my hand in his and stand without flipping my sundress over my head or some other absurd display. I mean, I could go three for three in the embarrass-myself-beyond-measure category today. Why not? I'm nothing if I'm not memorable right now.

And, yes. Tiny zips of pleasurable tingles race across my skin causing my nerve endings to erupt in the French national anthem. Vive la France!

Pierre hands me the two books he picked up. "I have to ..." He gestures to his book signing table.

"Of course. Of course."

"Your name was?"

"My name? I'm Tasha."

"Tasha. My pleasure. I am sorry to have shocked you. I hope you will stay to have these books signed anyway."

"I wouldn't miss it. Thank you, Pierre. Mister Touissant."

"Pierre. Just call me, Pierre."

6

PIERRE

Fame is a delicate and dangerous creature.
~ Patrick Dempsey

I return to my signing table. Stuart gives me a look as I take my seat. I don't know what made me stand, abandoning my other readers to help pick up the books Tasha dropped. Maybe it's the training of my mother and sisters who taught me always to step in when a woman is struggling. Though, that doesn't seem to quite explain whatever compelled me.

The next three women in line approach me one by one, handing me a book or three to sign, telling me I'm one of their favorite authors, smiling smiles that seem like they might be different from the smile they would have given if Amelie were actually a woman. Being a man writing romance apparently gives women ideas. The wrong ideas.

I look up after handing a book back to a blond woman

and thanking her for her compliment. There she is. Tasha. She's so very American—a little loud, unrestrained, and definitely rough around the edges. She shouldn't intrigue or amuse me, but she does. In a sea of women who all seem to be sending me not-so-subtle messages that they would be interested in me for more than my books, Tasha's slightly unpolished and candid presence is refreshing.

"Hi," she says sheepishly. "So. Um. Could we possibly have a do-over?"

"A do-over?"

"Yeah. You know? Like pretend I didn't drop my jaw and my books and make a complete buffoon of myself back there? I mean, maybe I'm just an average reader like the rest of these women who are obviously maintaining their composure much more effectively and being less blaah-ahhh-aaahh ... like I was?"

She waves at all the women in line and then turns to me, making a crazy face while she waves her hands in the air to demonstrate what she means by blaah-ahhh-aahh.

"Do over? Sure." I smile and extend my hand. "Hi, Tasha. I'm Pierre Toussaint. I'm the author behind the books written under the pen name Amelie De Pierre."

She returns my smile. "Hi. I'm Tasha. Obviously. You said that. Didn't you? I'm a huge fan. Which, I'm sure, doesn't surprise you since I'm carrying five of your books. But also, I'm here. Hence: fan. So. Yeah. Nevermind. This do-over isn't going to work. Apparently, I can't keep my wits together in front of you. So, here."

She sets the stack of books down on the table and shoves the pile at me en masse.

"I think the do-over went well," I tell her with the kind of warm smile I would give my sister, Marguerite. I can't help but think how Marguerite would love a woman like Tasha. She's the more outspoken and unabashed of my two sisters.

The do-over didn't go well, of course. But it would be a shame for Tasha to continue to feel so flustered around me. I'm just me, Pierre. This day has probably been more nerve racking for me than it has for her. She has no idea.

I lean nearer to her, and in a low, conspiratorial voice, I say, "You know, I was nervous today too."

"You were?"

"I was. Imagine, I've had the safety and comfort of this nom de plume. And now, it is ripped away like a bandage. I had no idea what people would think or how they would react."

Tasha's face morphs from the nervousness she has been displaying since she dropped her stack of books to something more like a look my mother gave me after a hard day at school. Her eyebrows lift toward the center of her forehead, and her eyes widen. A softness takes over her demeanor and voice.

"That must have put you in knots."

"It actually did," I say, pulling one book from the stack and signing it. "I couldn't even eat my lunch."

I choose a quote from Balzac to inscribe the title page: *Love is like the wind, we never know where it will come from.* Then I sign beneath the quote, *Amelie De Pierre.*

"Does it feel weird to sign your pen name?" she asks softly.

"It does. But then again, she is me, isn't she?"

"Weirdly, yes."

I laugh. "You missed my story of how she came to be?"

"I did. Sorry. As I said. I was delayed."

"Well, maybe someday I will tell you."

"I would like that. Thank you. And, by the way, I am guessing things went well with you ripping off the bandaid." She looks behind her at the line of readers still wrapping around the designated patio area into the more public section of the terrace. "Everyone seems eager to meet you and not the least bit unhappy with you being a man." She giggles lightly.

"I guess so. That's a relief."

Though I still need to see what life will be like now that I am known by my face. Maybe it won't change much. After all, I'm not in the movies. I'm only a writer, and I'm not J. K. Rowling or Stephen King. I bet most of their fans wouldn't even recognize them in a line-up.

I sign the next four of Tasha's books without another word spoken between us. She takes the stack when I am finished, thanks me, and turns away from the table.

Then she pivots to look at me one last time. "You really are my favorite author. I love your work. It's so cliché, isn't it?"

"A good cliché." I smile at her.

Her mouth turns up slightly in a soft grin.

"Bonjour, Tasha."

In very perfect French, she answers me, "Bonjour, Pierre." Her Rs are soft, sitting at the back of her throat where they belong. Her vowels are short and tight. Does she speak French? If not, she at least has practiced. Intriguing.

Tasha leaves, and I don't really give her another thought. I'm swept up in the stream of women, and a few men, who come one by one to the table, extending books for me to sign, asking for a picture with me, or discussing parts of my books they have loved most. It's simultaneously flattering and draining. Stuart brings me water, smiling brightly like one does to their dog after he has retrieved a stick for the first time.

The line is thinning finally. I've spent nearly two hours sitting in the same chair, with the exception of the brief minutes I stood to help that woman, Tasha, pick up her strewn books. A slight commotion on the other side of the trellis at the edge of the patio pulls my attention away from the book I'm signing, causing me to nearly scribble, *Pierre Toussaint*. I recover and write *Amelie De Pierre* just in time.

"No. You guys. No. It's fine." The female voice sounds familiar, but why?

"You need to do this. He'll understand," another voice answers.

I smile at the next reader approaching my table. "Hello, thank you for waiting all this time to meet me. I'm sorry you've had to stand for so long."

"It's my pleasure. I love your work. It's so fun knowing I was here the day you revealed your secret identity."

Her attention shifts to the back of the line where four young women are pulling another woman into line. I try not to be conspicuous as I glance to see what is going on. Stuart stands from the bar stool he's pulled off to the side behind me. He gives me a look that says he's got this handled. I turn my attention back to the reader in front of me.

"I'm sorry." I smile. "You were saying?"

Before she answers, I hear Stuart's voice asking the young women what is going on. The reader in front of me, obviously as intrigued as I am, abandons our conversation to watch the interaction between Stuart and whoever just arrived late. I catch glimpses of clothing, but cannot make out any faces from my seated position. I can hear Stuart, though.

"Ladies, may I help you?" A pause, but not long enough for them to answer. "This line is for the fans of Amelie De Pierre. The event on this patio is for guests who have reservations to attend the event. It was a paid function. The author will be available throughout the weekend."

I nearly groan at the thought. After a few hours of greeting fans, I'm weary and in great need of some solitude. It seems that might not come until I'm back in my temporary home on the outskirts of Harvest Hollow, North Carolina at this rate.

One of the women answers Stuart. "We did pay for the event, only my sister here caught her hair in a blow dryer and it took us a half hour to extricate her from the contraption, and then we had to figure out how to even out her hair since a bit of it was cut off in the process, so we missed everything."

Hair dryer? Hmmm.

I turn my attention back to the woman at my table. She asks me about my inspiration for my characters. I assure her it's not from my personal life. Then, when she makes it clear she would like to inspire me, I cordially inform her I'm so busy with the tour I have no time for personal romance. We talk about her favorite scene from the latest book, and she goes on about the plot twist I inserted close to the end.

"You should consider writing mysteries too. Maybe under another pen name."

"Maybe someday," I offer, thanking her again for waiting when she collects her books to leave and make room for the next reader to step up.

The commotion at the back of the line has settled. Another few women come forward, and I go through the motions, trying to give them the same energy and attention

I've devoted to each fan. I allow a little extra time with each one of them since they had such a wait, standing on their feet on concrete just to see me. It's overwhelming. I'm aware I'm well-known and well-loved. This event gave me a tangible experience of that in a way nothing else has.

I peer over the shoulder of the next woman stepping up to my table and see Tasha standing there with a look on her face that can only be described as apologetic. She's surrounded by four other women who, by the way they easily interact, all seem to know one another. Maybe she was the one arguing outside the patio a few moments ago.

After signing, taking a selfie, and allowing a hug I hadn't anticipated, the reader leaves, and Tasha and her four friends approach. One of them has an unusual haircut, longer in parts than others.

I acknowledge Tasha by name, causing an eruption of excited giggles from her friends along with their curious glances which roam from me to Tasha and back.

"I'm sorry," she says. "They made me come back because I didn't get a selfie with you."

"Oh. Of course. We did forget that, didn't we?"

She nods. One of her friends takes out a cell phone. Tasha comes around the table to stand next to me and I loop an arm around her shoulder. I haven't embraced other readers, and I realize at once how inappropriately familiar it makes us seem. But removing my arm now would draw more attention to my faux pas, so I keep my arm in place. We smile when prompted and her friend snaps the shot. Next, we drag Stuart over to take a group photo of Tasha and all her friends with me in the middle, each of them holding a different novel of mine. Not one of them asks for an autograph.

"We've taken up enough of your time," Tasha's friend explains. "We just didn't want her to leave without a photo with you. We're all fans, but she's ... well, you're her favorite author by a long shot, so we wanted to make sure she got what she wanted."

"You are very lucky to have such good friends," I say to Tasha.

Suddenly bashful, she smiles at me and says, "I am."

The women leave much more quietly than they came. I sign a few more books, and then Stuart and I wrap up for the day.

Room service. That is what I will have for dinner.

Something small and private, and then a shower and bed.

It's been a whirlwind. And for some reason, one reader's face stands out from all the rest—the woman with auburn hair, a slight lack of composure, and a deep love for my writing. I don't feel anything romantic for her, obviously. She simply caught my attention and turned an otherwise challenging and stressful day into something more.

7

TASHA

Extraordinary things are always hiding
in places people never think to look.
~ Jodi Picoult

The chill in the air contrasts with the warm water swirling around my shoulders and knees. A soft island breeze flows through the palms lining the pool edge.

"This is the life," Cass says from her spot next to me.

Our arms are resting behind us on the coping while we lazily tread water with our legs extended out in front of us. Our other three friends are splashing around and swimming right now.

"I'm pretty sure there aren't any bugs here either," Cass says. "Girl, back in Tennessee, we've got bugs a plenty. I'd probably have already been bit up good by now."

I chuckle softly.

"What a day," I sigh.

"For you, especially."

"I hope you all had a good day too."

"We did. After we saved my sister from the hair dryer. We're going to have to hustle her to a hairdresser as soon as we get home, poor thing." She giggles, and adds, "Bless her heart."

"Tonight was amazing," I sigh.

Cass nods, silently agreeing with me.

We had dinner together at one of the little restaurants facing the beach. Nothing fancy, but a view of the sand and water across the street from the shops. Then, we attended the official opening ceremony for the weekend with each of the authors giving short presentations about their writing lives. We met so many authors in person. After the formal part of the ceremony, we all mingled in the ballroom: authors, readers, bookstagrammers, agents, and publicists. For book lovers, this would be the equivalent of our Comicon or the Cannes film festival.

"You actually met Pierre Toussaint twice!" Cass says.

"I know. It's unbelievable. I don't know if I've even had time to absorb the reality completely. I always imagined Amelie De Pierre as being this middle-aged French woman who was slightly glamorous in a scholarly way. It's going to take some time for me to see Pierre's face when I think of Amelie."

"It won't take me any time at all to see his face. Bam. I see it. Ooooh-eee. Yes. I do. What a face."

"Stop."

"Why? That man is fine as strawberry wine. He is as cute as a new pair of boots. He's ..."

"I got the memo." I laugh. "He's attractive."

"I'm just playin' with ya. Y'all can keep Pierre. I'm just gonna picture him every so often whether you like it or not. Fine. Fine. Fine. Mmm mmm."

Our other friends swim toward us. We transfer into the hot tub and soak for a little bit and then we all agree we ought to head up for the night.

I'm packing up the bag I brought down with me and making sure I don't drip water on my Kindle.

"You guys go ahead. I'll be right in."

"We can wait," Winona answers.

"No need. I'll be right there."

My friends exchange glances and walk off toward the large doors leading into the lobby.

I wrap my towel around me, throw my bag over my shoulder, and take my keycard out so I'm ready to let myself into my room. A shower and bed sounds like heaven right now.

I'm walking through the lobby, and for some reason, my attention is drawn to a small decorative turnout in the wall. A tall potted plant fills the space. Something moves. Then I see him: Pierre, huddled behind the plant. He's trying to melt back into the wall, and failing.

"Pierre?"

"Shhhh."

I look around. "Are you alright?"

Pierre's appearance is slightly disheveled—less polished than usual. I try not to notice the casual clothes he's wearing, a far cry from the suit he had on when I first saw him in the lobby or this afternoon at his book signing. He's wearing shorts and a polo shirt with deck shoes, and he looks like someone who hangs out at a yacht club and knows his way around a boat. His hair is rumpled and his face is flushed.

He actually looks like a man who has been well-kissed. Was he recently well-kissed? Images of Pierre kissing fill my head.

I clear my throat.

Pierre answers me with a near whisper. "Whether I'm alright is debatable. I ate dinner in my room. But then Stuart wanted to meet in the bar. I should have told him to come to my room. I am a naive and foolish man, Tasha."

"What happened?" I ask, matching my volume to his, and stepping closer to the alcove he has tucked himself inside.

"Tasha?" Winona calls from up ahead. My four friends have already made it more than halfway across the lobby.

"I'll be up in a minute. Go ahead."

Her face scrunches up, but she nods.

"A woman approached me in the bar. She was ... how do you say it? Agh. Très coquette."

"Very flirtatious? Forward?"

I've taken to listening to French lessons. They teach the oddest phrases, but also some useful ones. I skipped ahead to the one on love and relationships—obviously. And it's a good thing I did. I wouldn't have known *très coquette* last week. I learned that phrase in the lesson I reviewed on the plane. Instead, I would only know how to say, *May I have some cheese with my baguette?* Or *Hello, Grandmother.* And the ever helpful, *This is a pen.* None of those sayings would have been at all useful to Pierre at this moment.

"Oui. Yes. That is the way. Flirtatious. Forward. She was running her hand up and down my leg while I was sitting at the bar with Stuart. He found this oh so amusing. I wish she would have shifted her attention to Stuart. I'm sure he would have been happy to entertain her this evening." Pierre pauses. "Did you see her? She is a woman with light brown hair, about this long, but some streaks of blond are in her hair also. She is wearing a green sundress and sandals of the same color."

I look around the lobby and see no one like that at first, but then I see a woman matching the description Pierre just gave me, walking around looking like she just lost her puppy.

"I see her. She's in the lobby."

"Quel désastre!"

I want to ask Pierre why and how he ended up on the other end of the lobby, a good distance from the restaurant and bar which are set off down a short hallway in the middle of the main room. But we obviously don't have time for explanations with the groupie in the green dress getting closer every second.

"She's coming this way," I whisper, stepping in the direction of the woman and putting a little more distance between me and Pierre.

I pretend to adjust my towel and start searching for something. I don't know what. All I know is I have to throw her off. Pierre doesn't need this hassle. He's obviously rattled. If I can help him, I will.

The woman stares directly at the potted plant, the only thing keeping her from seeing Pierre are the large green leaves. Not only would her catching him hiding ruin his night, but she could make a deal out of it. If she publicizes the fact that he purposely hid from her in a hotel lobby, the press he'd get would not be good.

On a whim, I casually toss my hotel key onto the floor in a spot between me and the crazed fan.

"Oh gosh!" I say in a slightly too-loud voice. "My key!"

Her gaze shifts from the potted plant to me.

"I dropped my key," I repeat.

I'm clutching my towel with one hand, not that I couldn't drop the towel, but I am only in a swimsuit underneath it.

"Could you ...?" I ask the fangirl in green.

"Oh. Sure."

She bends over and grabs my key. I take it from her when she stands up.

"Thank you so much. I hate when I lose something, don't you?"

"Um. Yeah." She looks around again.

"Did you lose something?"

"Actually, I'm looking for that author, Pierre Toussaint. The one who writes the Amelie De Pierre books. I saw you at his book signing line today."

"Oh, yeah. That was crazy. I was just in shock."

"Right? I mean who knew those books could be written by a man? And a man like that? Wow. He's so virile and breathtaking. And he's got this quiet magnetism. Like a man of mystery. Such a gentleman too, the way he helped you pick up your books. A man who writes like that and is that chivalrous has to know his way around everything a woman needs."

My eyes go momentarily wide, but I school my features, hopefully fast enough for her not to notice my reaction.

"I think I saw him head to the elevators." I pause, looking off in the distance as if I'm trying to verify what I saw. "Yep! There he is!" I point to ensure she looks.

"Where? Where is he? I don't see him."

The frantic tone in her voice only confirms that there are times in life when white lies are acceptable. Pink lies. Yellow lies. Whatever color you want to paint your lie. Throwing this woman off Pierre's scent is worth a fib. I know I'm misleading her and I feel one hundred percent right in doing so.

Poor Pierre. Pierre, who is crouched behind a potted tropical plant on a day when he poured himself out for his fans and walked through the stress of revealing his pen name to the world. I may have been attracted to him at first —okay, I am still very attracted to him. But I'm keeping my cool. Now. I'm cool now. Forget earlier. That was awful.

"Oh! You just missed him!" I exclaim. "He went up in that last elevator. That one that just closed. Maybe you can follow him?"

She looks like she just might. Which is equal parts frightening and disturbing.

I hear Pierre's voice—in my head, not from behind the fiddle leaf fig—*Quel désastre!* I don't have to be a French major to know that means *What a disaster!* No kidding.

The crazed fan looks at me with a wistfully resigned look on her face. "I guess I'll just head to bed, then."

"Probably a good call. We have a long day ahead of us. Three more days, actually. Have a good night."

She turns toward the elevators. I pivot in the opposite direction and fake as if I'm going toward the pools. As soon as she vacates the lobby, I'll give Pierre the go-ahead to make a clean getaway.

I walk slowly, glancing back over my shoulder occasionally until I see her get into an elevator. Once the doors are shut, I walk back over to Pierre.

"Coast is clear. You can come out of hiding."

"Oh. Thank you. Merci beaucoup. I am in your debt, Tasha."

"You aren't. That woman was so out of line. Totally over

the top. Let's call it even after the display I put on at the signing."

"Completely understandable. You were in shock. And, I understand even more, because, after all, I'm chivalrous," he chuckles. "A man of mystery. Virile, even."

"Exactly." I laugh, realizing he heard every word the rabid woman in green said about him.

He smiles a relieved smile. "I'm going to make a break for it before she changes her mind."

"Good call," I say. "Goodnight, Pierre."

"Goodnight, Cher. And thank you again."

Cher. I never loved a word so much as I love the sound of that term of endearment coming out of Pierre's mouth from where he's still hiding behind a potted plant. Obviously, it's a word he'd use with anyone. Can I help that it sends chills skittering across my skin, and a sweet flip and flutter inside my belly? I'm lighter than air, and completely and utterly content—more than content. I could possibly skip the elevators and float up to my room.

I step back, giving Pierre space to leave his hideout. He smiles as he slips past me. Then he walks away, softly grinning back at me once. I may as well pack my bags and go home. This event couldn't get better than tonight's strange, but personal, encounter with Pierre Toussaint.

8

PIERRE

We don't meet people by accident.
They are meant to cross our paths for a reason.
~ Unknown

I'm lying on my hotel bed, not exactly sleeping, but not really awake either. Who could have guessed the qualities women would attribute to me once they found out I was the man behind these novels? Obviously, Stuart. He's nearly gloating at my misfortune. And then gloating that I think it's a misfortune.

Do you realize how many men would give up their salaries, cars, and vacations to trade places with you for a day? All this female attention. It's nearly every man's dream, he had said over breakfast on his balcony. I insisted on room service after the fiasco in the bar two nights ago. Thanks to Tasha, I made a narrow escape from that crazed reader. Tasha seems to be one of the only normal women here. She treats me like I'm just another man. And even after seeing me crouched behind a potted plant, she's continued to be polite and unaffected whenever I bump into her. I'm grateful.

I had told Stuart, "You could find me a man to trade with. We should have thought of that in the first place. I could be like Cyrano de Bergerac."

To which, Stuart said, "Who?"

Seriously. My publicist had never heard of Cyrano.

"You know, the guy who had someone else take his place to declare his love to the beautiful Roxanne?"

"But you aren't declaring your love."

"No. But I could definitely use someone to hide behind."

Stuart just chuckled good naturedly and went on sipping his mimosa and eating his buttered English muffin as if I were joking.

A knock at my door tells me it's time to resume the dog and pony show.

"Who is it?" I shout, even though I know who it is.

"It's me, one of the many men who wishes they could take your place."

"Ha!"

I stand and unlock the door. Stuart walks past me.

"Well, we have a winner!" he announces brightly.

"For ... ?"

"For dinner with you tonight."

"Ah. Yes. I had nearly forgotten."

"Convenient. Well, you are going to meet a ..." he pauses and looks at his phone. "Cass Thornhill from Tennessee. She's twenty-seven, and she says she's a big fan of your books."

"Aren't they all?"

I sound spoiled. I'm not ungrateful for the fact that I have so many avid readers. I truly appreciate each one—from a distance.

"They are. They are all fans of Amelie De Pierre, and now of you, Pierre Toussaint. Their love and admiration has grown more than ever this weekend. I just heard that you are to be featured in the A & E section of the LA Weekly! It's just what we hoped for."

Is it? I guess it is. If the exposure leads to book sales, and book sales mean I can keep doing what I've come to love for a few years longer, then yes. I am glad to be in a publication, or to have the temporary media attention. Emphasis on *temporary*.

"So, be on your best, most charming behavior. It's only dinner. Then you can retreat up here for the night, and you'll only have tomorrow left to encounter fans. One final meet and greet along with other authors. It should be less intense with all of you there to field the interest of the readers. Though, you are the only man in the bunch. That makes you stand out—as it should. We'll have books for purchase to be signed, of course. Then you'll have the closing ceremony, and we'll pack up and leave."

I take a fortifying breath. I can do this.

"Lighten up, Pierre. They are women. You know, women? The ones you write about. The ones you write for? Maybe think of it this way. You could gather some material for your next book."

"I'm not going to engage in any romance with a reader."

"I know. I know." Stuart pauses, walking further into my room and looking out at the view of the harbor from my window. "But that's not a half-bad idea, you know. A little romance would be all the buzz. Great publicity if we spin it just right. Maybe a walk in the moonlight on the beach? A kiss before you head up the elevators? I'm not saying you take her to your room. Just some public displays that will be photographable."

This man. He's too much. And I'm used to Frenchmen. But despite our reputation, most of the men I know prefer a steady relationship to a string of inconsequential hook-ups.

Stuart smiles at his idea. I stare at him with a look of incredulity. I've never been the type of man to take romance lightly. I'm not casual about most things in life. My sisters tease me that I'm too serious in general. I am what I am. And that includes being a man who will not casually kiss some infatuated reader in the name of good publicity.

"No."

I don't say anything else. Growing up, Papa always gave that concise, one-word answer when he didn't want us to do something. Just, *no*. It carried so much weight because he didn't seem to need to defend or fortify the word. I'm hoping my tone feels as weighty and immovable as Papa's did.

It must, because Stuart lightly shakes his head, and then moves on to the next subject—what I'm going to wear and where I'm to meet this woman, Cass.

Stuart leaves as quickly as he came, explaining that he's going to catch some sun and possibly capitalize on his connections to me by engaging in conversation with some readers. I wonder what his definition of conversation is, but then I drop it. That's his business, and I'd probably rather not know.

I spend the rest of the afternoon with my laptop open, sitting out on my balcony, a warm breeze caressing my face while I craft the next section of my work in progress.

Only a day and a half left on the island and I can return to Harvest Hollow where people leave me alone to write in my home at the edge of the woods. At least, those towns-people did leave me alone before this trip. With any luck, they still will when I come back from this weekend of revealing my identity.

I lose track of time while I write, but I finally notice the sun dipping lower toward the ocean, and I feel the tug in my body of having sat for too long without standing to stretch. When I look at the clock on my laptop, I gasp. I only have twenty minutes to be ready for my date—or whatever this is.

Dinner. It's dinner.

This is my fan. It's the least I can do to be pleasant and engaging for an hour and a half over a meal. I think of authors I admire. I'd love the chance for dinner with one of them. But I wouldn't be thinking about anything but their writing prowess. So far this weekend, my writing seems to be the last thing on most of these readers' minds. Are they all really that lonely and desperate that they need to conjure up ideas about me that couldn't be further from the truth? Perhaps.

I quickly shower and change into a pair of khaki dress slacks, brown loafers, and a cotton button-up shirt. I forgo a tie. Stuart said I looked too stodgy this weekend. *We're on an island for goodness' sake. Wear some shorts, a floral shirt.* I'm not wearing shorts. The last time I wore shorts, a woman had her hands on my legs at the bar, rubbing on me like I was her pet poodle.

I make my way downstairs and out the front doors, following Stuart's directions to the cafe where I'm meeting Cass for dinner. When I approach the building, I see a woman matching the description Stuart gave me. She's standing next to ... is that Tasha?

It is. My heart rate calms. It's odd the effect she has on

me. As if she's an old friend. She looks a little different. Her hair is up, the curls tamed, and she's wearing a touch of makeup.

"Pierre!" Cass says, stepping toward me. "I have a little idea. I hope you don't mind. I am definitely a fan. Huge fan. My whole family goes hog wild for your books. We'd give up goo goo clusters just to read 'em. But eating goo goo clusters while reading is really the best now, isn't it? Anyway, I'm rambling like a preacher without a potluck to get to after service. My point is, I'd like to swap my spot at dinner with Tasha, here. She's really your biggest fan. At least of all the readers I know. And I didn't figure it was right to take a dinner with you when Tasha would appreciate it so much more. So, I twisted her arm. Not really. That would be awful, wouldn't it? I did have to do some fancy talkin'. But she gave in. Now all we have to do is get you to say yes too. What do ya think?"

I look at Tasha. She's blushing. She starts to speak, but I stop her.

"I'd be honored to have dinner with Tasha. Thank you, Cass. Are you sure you don't want to join us? We could eat together—the three of us."

"Oh, no sir. No. I couldn't do that. The winner was one woman. And besides, I promised my twin, Winona, I'd be back to join her and our other friends for dinner. I wouldn't want them up and arranging a search."

"No. We wouldn't want that," I agree.

"Is this okay with you?" I ask Tasha.

"It's great."

"Okay, then," Cass says. "It was a pleasure meeting you, Pierre. You two kids go have fun."

She turns and leaves me with Tasha, who is still quieter

than she's been since the day she dropped her books at my first signing.

"I have so many questions after that," I say with a wink at Tasha.

She giggles lightly.

What is it about her that draws out a wink? I don't go around winking at women. It can give them the wrong idea.

"Shall we?" I ask, pointing into the restaurant, and placing my palm on Tasha's back to guide her in ahead of me.

We give my name to the hostess and we're taken to a corner table by the front windows where we have a view of the beach and the ocean beyond. The sun dips low, kissing the horizon, casting pastel hues across the water as the sky turns shades of charcoal and deep lavender. The boats in the harbor are silhouettes.

"So," I say, handing Tasha a menu. "Cass is a friend of yours?"

"She is. We don't live near one another, though. She's from Tennessee. I'm from North Carolina."

I don't even hesitate. "I'm from North Carolina too."

"Really? What part? From your accent, I thought you might be from France. I didn't pick up a note of southern boy in you."

I chuckle. "Of course. I am French. I am living in a town in the Blue Ridge Mountains for this year while I am in the states for my book tour."

"Ahhh. Well, that explains it. Are you allowed to tell me what town? I promise not to stalk you."

She wags her eyebrows, and we both laugh.

"I might need to tell you in case someone else tries to stalk me. You could employ your diversion tactics again."

She smiles.

I tell her, "I live less than an hour from Asheville."

"That's where I live now—Asheville."

"Now?"

"I grew up in a town called Harvest Hollow."

"What are the chances?"

Tasha's brows draw together.

"I am staying in Harvest Hollow."

"Really?"

"Well, I'm out near the lake, so not right in town. But yes. That is my home town for the year."

"My sister still lives there. With my nephew, Nate. Maybe you have met her. She manages Cataloochee Mountain Coffee."

"I know the place. Good coffee. I know who your sister is. Heather, is it? And everyone knows Nate. I have taken my laptop there to write when my house feels too ..."

"Claustrophobic?"

I was going to say lonely. I'm not sure why. I haven't really felt lonely. After this weekend, the idea of a little loneliness sounds beyond perfect. Not right now. I'm actually enjoying our conversation, the view, Tasha.

"Yes. Claustrophobic." I turn my eyes back to the menu when I see our waitress approaching.

Tasha looks up, notices our server, and fixes her attention on her menu.

After we place our orders, Tasha rests her chin on her hand, her elbow perched on the table. So American. It doesn't bother me like I would've imagined it would. "I can't believe you know my sister. What a small world."

"I don't really know her. Unless a deep relationship can be built on telling someone you want a double espresso."

"I'm sure many relationships have been built on less."

"Quite true." I chuckle. "So you grew up in Harvest Hollow?"

"Yes. I graduated from Harvest Hollow High ten years ago. Go Bobcats!"

I chuckle. I've been exposed to the school spirit in Harvest Hollow already. Rival American football teams draw a crowd. The season will really pick up once we're back. Or ... once I'm back. Obviously, Tasha won't be with me.

"I went to UNC, Charlotte after high school. Then I settled in Asheville."

"And how did you meet Cass?"

"Well, I run a bookstagram account."

My face must look confused because Tasha clarifies. "On Instagram. It's an account where I share books. Book reviews, clips of my work, advertisements for my services."

"Your work? Your services?"

"Oh. I didn't mention I'm a call girl?"

Her face is dead serious. She doesn't break my eye contact. I don't know what to say. Is this thing I have heard about American women being forward true? Would she just say this so boldly?

"A call girl?" I echo.

Maybe something is being lost in translation, though I took English through my lycee years of secondary school. I'm pretty sure there's only one meaning for *call girl*. Maybe, though, she answers phone calls. Or does bird calls.

Tasha's lip twitches, then a smile creeps onto her face, followed by a full laugh.

"Your face! You thought I was serious? Oh my gosh. You did."

I laugh, half with relief, half at the joke.

"Well, that's a relief."

"Maybe it is, maybe it isn't," Tasha jokes.

"No. Believe me, it is."

She laughs again, a twinkle of mischief remaining in her eyes. "It's one hundred percent a relief. I'm actually an author assistant. But my main job is doing voice narration for books. I run a bookstagram account where I share my work and my love of books. Cass, Winona, and Daisy all live in Tennessee. Our other friend, Brianna, lives in Charleston. We all met through bookstagram. When we heard about this event, and especially that you would be here, well Amelie ... which is you ... we all decided to come to finally meet each other face-to-face. Before that, we've only interacted online.

"Hasn't your mother warned you not to talk to strangers online?" I tease.

"She has." Tasha smiles. "And she's horrified that I'm here with what she calls total strangers. My sister wasn't too thrilled either. But they aren't really strangers. We talk every day online. Funny, huh?"

"It's the way now."

"It is. And ..." she drifts off as the server arrives with our plates, setting the scallops and asparagus in front of Tasha and the filet mignon and glazed carrots in front of me.

Once the server has left, I say, "You were saying?"

"Um. Oh, yes. I was saying, I came this weekend to meet you."

"Well, you definitely met me."

She laughs and then covers her face with both her hands, peering out at me through her fingers. "I made a horrible first impression."

"Memorable."

She shakes her head lightly, pierces a scallop with her fork and bites into it, humming with appreciation.

"Oh. These are so good. You have to try one."

Before I can protest, she has one scooped up and plopped onto my plate. Then she stares at me, as if she's waiting for me to take a bite before she does anything else.

I gently poke the tines of my fork into the scallop and slice off a bite. It's quite good. I've grown up eating seafood in France—caught fresh that same day. This doesn't compare, but it's not bad. It's not overly drenched in butter as Americans are prone to do with their cooking. The taste of the meat comes through clearly.

"Good, right?" Tasha asks.

"Quite." I look at my plate. "Here." I cut off a chunk of my steak and put it on her plate.

I picture Rene. What would he say of me being so comfortable with this woman I just met mere days ago? He would be happy to see it. He'd tease me, to be sure. But he'd be happy. I don't relax around many people. Not fully, anyway.

"So, you record books?"

"I do. And I'm not telling you that so you'll hire me or anything. I want it to go on record that I tried hiding my profession, but you got it out of me anyway."

"By telling me you were a call girl?"

"I had to think quickly. It's not my strongest asset—thinking on my feet."

"I'd say you do pretty well. You saved me the other night."

"Oh! That woman. She was something else. Has it been better since then?"

"I wish I could say it has. But unfortunately, no. Women seem to think I am as romantic as the men I write."

"And you aren't?"

"Well, I don't think so."

Tasha studies me. She doesn't say anything for a while. The silence between us is as comfortable as the conversation. I'm grateful for that. After these past few days of celebrity status, it's nice to feel like a normal man, out to eat with a friendly woman. Nothing more.

9

PIERRE

Dancing is just a conversation between two people.
~ Harry Connick Jr. as Justin Matisse in Hope Floats

Over the course of our meal, Tasha has shifted the conversation to focus more on me and my novels. She's genuinely interested in my writing process. I tell her about the dare that led to my unexpected career, a little about my life in France, and then we discuss the current book I'm working on. She's an attentive listener. Not once have I felt as if she were fangirling, as they say here. Our conversation flows easily, and I'm more deeply relaxed than I've been since I left North Carolina.

I even tell Tasha about my sister, Marguerite, and how I think the two of them would hit it off.

"I've always dreamt of visiting France."

"If you do, I promise an introduction to Marguerite. Even if I am not there, I will arrange for the two of you to meet."

I don't know what's come over me. I keep my family and

friendships private, separated from my work. I somehow sense that Tasha respects my need to keep my personal life personal. Maybe it was the manner in which she went out of her way to help me in the hotel lobby. I have faith in her ability to respect my boundaries. Too bad she's not a publicist.

"That would be amazing. You don't have to do that, though. I would never want to impose."

"I'm offering. You didn't ask. And Europe is always better experienced with someone who has spent their whole life on our continent rather than merely seeing all the tourist spots. Of course, those sights are good too. But you see so much more when you can visit the people of the country, not only the popular museums and buildings."

"Well, maybe you need to have some time with the people of America, then."

"After this weekend ..." I cut myself off before I complete my sentence, realizing I was about to disclose my thoughts to Tasha as if she were a family member or a close friend like Rene.

She surprises me by saying, "After this weekend, you would like to run from all Americans and hide away somewhere we will never find you again. Am I right?"

I study her. "Not all Americans. No. But maybe most of the romance readers."

She laughs a full laugh. Then she lifts her drink and tilts the glass in my direction. "Here's to finding life-sized potted plants wherever you go."

"Tchin-tchin."

"Tchin-tchin?"

"It is like your word, *cheers*."

"Ah, well, Tchin-tchin."

We clink glasses and Tasha sips her drink, glancing at me over the rim.

The rest of the meal, our conversation drifts through topics ranging from popular outdoor activities in North Carolina, to what my tour will entail, and even how Tasha got into audiobook recording. Our server eventually stops by our table to offer us dessert. Tasha looks at me expectantly. I don't have much of a sweet tooth, but from the expression on Tasha's face, I think she may want to order something. I don't want to be the kind of man who says *no* when a woman craves some dessert. Being the younger sibling to two women has given me that much insight, at least.

We end up ordering a slice of chocolate mousse cake to split. It should feel inappropriate to share a dessert, but Tasha doesn't bat an eyelash at the server's suggestion, so I just go with it. When the dessert arrives, we take alternating bites, and then when our forks are near enough that we'd start touching the same spots, I gently push the dessert plate her way.

"You finish the rest. I'm full from the steak."

"Are you sure?"

She looks like she hopes I am sure, but she's trying to be polite about it.

"I'm quite sure. I'd rather watch you enjoy the rest than overfill myself on any more of that decadent dessert. You only had scallops." I pat my belly to emphasize how full I am. "Enjoy."

"It is pretty rich," she says, already aiming her fork for her next bite.

She takes it into her mouth and closes her eyes to appreciate the flavors. I watch her facial expression soften, her eyelashes nearly flutter on her cheeks, her tongue dart out to retrieve the errant smear of chocolate off her lips. Then I sip my coffee and look out at the scenery.

"We're going dancing tonight," Tasha says, poising her fork over her next bite. "Would you want to join us?"

"Dancing?"

"My friends and I found this little spot a few streets up. It's a low-key nightclub with live music. We thought we'd get away from the resort and have some fun since it's our last night on the island. If you're too tired, or you aren't supposed to fraternize with your readers, I totally understand."

Before her invitation, I had planned to head back to my room after dinner. I tend to need time alone regularly to be my best. I've been surrounded by people for the past three days on the island, that doesn't include a full day of travel to get here. But I'm oddly inclined to let loose for once and do the unexpected. It's been a long time since I've been out dancing.

"I could come dancing for a while. I might turn in early, but I'd love to join you."

"Great!"

Tasha doesn't seem surprised by my easy acquiescence. And neither of us say anything more. I appreciate the simplicity of her reaction. For someone who is considered one of my greatest fans, she continues to amaze me with her ability to make our interactions uncomplicated and comfortable.

The nightclub is small. A sign near the inside of the door reads, *Maximum Capacity 120.* Tasha's friends spot us as soon as we walk past the bouncer, a man wearing beach wear and seated casually on a stool. He doesn't ask us for ID, instead he simply waves us in, telling us to have a nice night.

The band plays a variety of music from island-themed

songs to current pop favorites mixed with the occasional slow song. We dance as a group, shouting to one another over the music when we need to say something. About a half-hour or so after we arrive, the band dedicates a slow song to Cass from Winona. It's a song I've heard, but the band's rendition is at a slower tempo. Michael Bublé's *Just Haven't Met You Yet* fills the room.

Cass starts laughing, pointing her finger at her sister and saying, "I'll get you back, Win."

Winona tosses her head back and laughs a full laugh. "You'll get me back by meeting the man of your dreams and making me the maid of honor."

She pulls her sister into her arms and twirls her in time to the music. When I look away from the two of them, Tasha is standing right in front of me, staring at me with an expression I can't decipher.

"Dance with me, Cher?" I ask her on a whim.

"I'd love to."

I extend my hand and she places hers in mine. I wrap my other hand behind her back and we dance alongside Cass and Winona. Daisy and Brianna sit on tall stools at the bar table we've been using, just off to the side of the dance floor. They smile on as the four of us dance our way through the song.

I can't remember the last time I held a woman in my arms, let alone danced a slow dance. When the music ends, Tasha thanks me. We step over to our table to grab our drinks and join her friends, who all have been treating me like I'm just another man, which I am. But after this weekend, their blasé approach is refreshing.

We dance some more, and after another hour, I am surprised when Tasha is the first to say she is ready to turn in for the evening. I had assumed I would be the one calling it a night before anyone else. As soon as Tasha makes her announcement, we all decide we're ready to go back to Alicante. I walk with Tasha and her friends, chuckling to myself at the idea of what Stuart would say if he could see me now, flanked by five women, coming home from a nightclub.

The six of us part ways at the elevators.

THE NEXT DAY flies by in a whirlwind: breakfast with Stuart, a morning book signing, and then the closing ceremony before lunch where I accept an award for my best selling novels. I mingle with readers until Stuart informs me our bags have been brought to the lobby and we're being shuttled to the boat that will take us to shore in thirty minutes. I've barely seen Tasha all morning amidst the blur of events. I did catch her eye as I walked off stage with my plaque after accepting the recognition for my achievements. She was smiling softly at me, as a friend does.

Stuart and I catch the boat, then we are met on shore by a private car we hired to take us to LAX. Stuart's Lexus is parked in long-term airport parking, so we part ways there.

He leans out the driver window and shouts, "I'll be in touch once you're back in North Carolina."

I'm pulling my suitcase toward the elevator of the parking garage, but I turn back to meet Stuart's eyes.

In a deadpan voice, I say, "I'm looking forward to it."

Stuart doesn't pick up on my tone, which is admittedly laced with sarcasm. Maybe he did pick up on it. To his credit, he smiles and waves at me before driving toward the exit. I make my way into the airport and through security without any delays.

My flight to Charlotte leaves at three. I glance around the seats at the gate and see Tasha reading something on her Kindle. I'm not surprised. We're both heading to the same state. I'd assumed she'd be flying into Asheville, since that's where she lives. I chose Charlotte because those flights were the only ones shorter than nine hours, with no layover. A car will meet me and drive me home after we land at eleven tonight, getting me in my door sometime around three-thirty in the morning. I take the seat next to Tasha, trying hard not to disturb her. She's so absorbed in whatever she's reading she doesn't notice me.

By the time they start calling us to board, Tasha looks up. When she sees me, she gasps.

"Pierre! I didn't know you were there. How long have you been sitting here?"

"Only un petit moment."

"That means little."

"You are correct, of course. Je suis content que tu parles français."

"I don't. Parles. I just have been learning a little recently."

"Recently?"

She blushes. It's lovely, as it always is when a woman's skin flushes with modesty or the slightest embarrassment.

"Yes." She nods. Her voice is quieter, her eyes flit up to mine and then she glances at the line of passengers preparing to board. "It was to impress you. Silly. I know."

"It is not silly. It worked. I am impressed."

"You don't have to say that. I just thought it would be cool to tell you, j'adore vos livres. Ce sont mes favoris."

"Well, you are right. To tell me you love my books is very impressive. Your accent is quite good."

"Google Translate is a good teacher," she says, blushing again.

"You must be careful with that trickster, though. Sometimes the way things are translated, well, they are not quite right. It can lead to ... well, it can be good to double check."

She stands, grabbing the handle of her carry-on and putting her Kindle neatly in the front pouch.

"That sounds like there might be a story there."

"One I would tell you if we had the time."

She smiles at me. "What is your seat number?"

"I am with the snobs. In first class."

"Ah. Well, I am with the normal people. The commoners —in economy."

We both chuckle.

"Can I ...?" I start to ask at the same time as she says, "Would you ...?"

"Go ahead," I tell her.

"No. You first."

"I was going to ask if you would give me your contact information in case I'm ever in Asheville."

"Oh. I was going to offer to give you my number. In case you need author services while you are in the states. Or whatever."

"Author services, of course. Yes. That would be good."

"No pressure," she says.

"I asked, remember."

"You did."

We take out our cells as we walk to join the other passengers. The line is moving forward bit by bit. I could cut ahead to the spot where first class passengers are able to go onto the plane without a delay, but I decide to linger with Tasha to get her information. I don't have many friends here in America. If I'm honest with myself, I don't have time for friendships this year. I have a writing deadline for this manuscript, and another book to start as soon as I submit this one. I'll be traveling whenever I'm not writing. Still, knowing Tasha is only an hour away, and that her sister and nephew are right in my town, it seems good to get her number. Even if she is only sharing it with me in the event I need author services.

Our flight lands on time. I see Tasha at baggage claim. I slept on the flight, so I feel refreshed. She looks a little disheveled, her wavy hair ruffled and taking on a mind of its own. Her eyes meet mine, so I walk over to await the luggage drop with her.

"How will you get to Asheville now?" I ask her.

"I was going to take an Uber."

I have a car picking me up. It's only prudent that Tasha accept a ride from me. There's no need for her to pay for an Uber when I'm headed in her direction. I offer her the ride, and after she triple checks with me to make sure she's not imposing, she accepts. She gives my driver directions to her house. We're not in the car five minutes before she falls asleep, her head resting on the back of the seat, her breath coming softly.

The drive to Asheville is around two hours in the dark of night with no traffic. I wake Tasha about fifteen minutes before we hit the Ashville town limits. We say a quick goodbye when we reach the front of her house. My driver takes Tasha's bags up to her porch for her, and then we pull away after watching her enter her home and shut the door behind herself.

I'm awakened five hours later by the sound of my phone vibrating on my bedside table.

"Allo," I answer in French before even checking caller ID.

"Allo, Pierre," Stuart's too-wide-awake voice sounds through my cell.

"What time is it?" I ask in my raspy morning voice.

"Here it's only six. There, I guess that's ... either eight or nine. What are you? Three hours or two difference from LA?"

"Three. Why are you calling me at six in the morning?"

I picture Stuart leaning out his car window in the parking garage telling me we'd talk when I was back in North Carolina. I didn't think he meant mere hours after my lungs started breathing the Blue Ridge Mountain air again.

"Have you seen it? You old dog, you. Well, of course you haven't seen it. You just woke up. Am I right?"

"I did. Seen what?"

I sit up on the edge of my bed and rub a hand across my eyes and then comb my fingers through my hair. I won't be falling back asleep now, that much is obvious. Maybe I'll nap later, after I do some writing and unpack.

"The photos. They're on social media everywhere."

"Photos?"

"Of you and that reader at dinner and then the two of you dancing. Then there's one of you and four women walking into the resort together, laughing."

"C'est dommage!"

"What's that?" Stuart asks.

"Nothing. Nothing."

Why tell my publicist that something he sees as a triumph made me feel momentarily sorry for myself—and Tasha? She's caught up in this now. Her photo is on whatever platforms Stuart is ranting on about. And he is ranting. He's barely stopped to take a breath.

"... and why didn't you tell me, you sly fox? You were out with four women? Four. And you didn't even call me to join you."

"It wasn't like that."

"Oh, you don't have to tell me. I saw the photos. You obviously have the most interest in the one with auburn hair. The one you're looking at longingly over a table. The one you danced with to the Michael Bublé song."

"What?!"

"Am I wrong?"

He's only too right—not about my feelings, but those photos captured my evening in vivid detail. How did these private moments of my night get spread on social media? It never occurred to me that someone would care about me enough to follow me and photograph me. And, looking at Tasha longingly? That's probably Stuart's projection onto the images. I wasn't looking at her longingly, though I did enjoy her company. But it ended there. Two friends relaxing together over a good meal. Two friends letting loose together on the dance floor.

"Hang on. I'm forwarding you a few links and some screenshots. Check your messages. They just went through."

I hold my phone away from my ear, staring at the images Stuart just sent. He's not wrong. If a person didn't know better, Tasha and I look like a couple out for a romantic evening, laughing over our food, her leaning near to scoop a scallop onto my plate, me watching her as her eyes shut while she eats her dessert, us dancing while I hold her and we sway to the song. I'm a romance author. I understand the basics of what makes for a good story, and these photos, taken out of context, could be easily misconstrued.

I start to clarify things with Stuart, but then I hold back. He's bound to be skeptical. I'll just hear him out, and then I can decide what I need to say or do.

"Hold that thought, Pierre. I have to take this other call. I'll be right back."

The line clicks and I sit, holding my phone, staring at the photos that make me look like a man in love.

THE NEXT FEW days are just what I needed. I've holed up in my house at the woods' edge, writing, eating and sleeping, only venturing into town for groceries once. And, yes, a stop into Cataloochee Coffee for a drink and a chance to tell Heather I met Tasha. She was as nonchalant and relaxed as Tasha had been at the resort.

I've resumed taking my daily walks through the woods behind my home, appreciating the changing season. The cooler morning air and occasional stray leaf falling from a tree remind me fall is here. I'm back in my home after an early morning hike, checking email with a cup of café au lait in my hand.

From: Stuart Martin, Rep U Up PR Services <stuartjmartin@rep.u.up.com>
To: Pierre Toussaint, Author <AmelieDePierre@ADPierreAuthor.com>

Hello, Pierre,

This is urgent. I texted you, and you haven't answered all morning. So, I called, only to get your voicemail. If I don't hear from you, I'm tempted to book a flight. We need to talk.

Don't freak out. We'll get this squared up. We were contacted by a book distributor in Canada. They want to have you come do some signings at their stores while you are in North America this year. We can easily add dates to your existing schedule. Bob and I started looking at your documents to get things in order for a trip to Canada. We checked your visa. I'm hoping we just have an old one on file. Contact me as soon as you get this email.

—Stuart

DON'T FREAK OUT? How can I not freak out? I take a breath, sip my au lait and respond.

From: Pierre Toussaint, Author <AmelieDePierre@ADPierreAuthor.com>
To: Stuart Martin, Rep U Up PR Services <stuartj-martin@rep.u.up.com>

Stuart,
My apologies. My phone was on do not disturb so I could focus while writing.
I checked what I have on file. My visa permitted me to enter the United States at the end of July. For some reason, it doesn't seem to grant me the status I had anticipated. How did we miss this? Advise me as to our next steps. I am doing my own research in the meantime.

My phone is on now.
—Pierre

Twenty excruciating minutes later, my inbox pings with an email notification.

From: Stuart Martin, Rep U Up PR Services <stuartjmartin@rep.u.up.com>
To: Pierre Toussaint, Author <AmelieDePierre@ADPierreAuthor.com>

Pierre,
Sit tight. Bob and I are working on a resolution to this hiccup. Bob will be in NC tomorrow. He'll connect with you once he lands. He's arranged to reserve a room in that old library in the town where you're living. You can meet there. I'll Zoom in.
We've got this. Sometimes solutions call for a creative approach to problem solving. I think you'll like what we came up with. Based on our time on the island, I'm betting you will like it very, very much.
—Stuart

10

TASHA

Because the expected is just what keeps us steady,
standing, still.
The expected is just the beginning.
The unexpected is what changes our lives.
~ Dr. Meredith Grey

I'm hopping out of the shower when my phone rings. I secure a towel around my hair and wrap another one around my body, tucking it in place while I grab my cell off the counter. Caller ID flashes an unidentified number with the label, *Los Angeles*. Being in the voice recording business, I'm used to receiving calls from New York and LA for work, so I answer, hoping this will be a gig.

"Tasha Pierson?"

"Yes?"

"This is Stuart Martin from Rep U Up. I am Pierre's publicist. Pierre Toussaint?"

"Yes. Hi, Stuart. What can I do for you?"

"Well, that's the perfect question, actually. Pierre needs your assistance in a matter. His agent, Bob Highfil, will be in Harvest Hollow today. He's reserved a room at, I guess what's the old library in that town. He'd like to meet with you and Pierre. Are you available?"

"Today?"

"At two o'clock. Or we could adjust the time if that doesn't work for you."

"No. Two should work. What, exactly, is this about?"

"I'd love to give you the details, but I want to save that for when Bob is present. Let's just leave it at this for now. Pierre, the author you respect and adore, has a need. You are in a position to help him with that need. We will compensate you well for your service to Pierre. You're the perfect candidate for this position."

"Okaaaay."

I can't help the unprofessional tone my voice takes. Stuart's being vague. I'm assuming Pierre either needs author services or a voice actress for an audiobook recording. Why wouldn't Stuart come right out and say that? And why would Pierre's agent need to fly all the way out here and drive into Harvest Hollow to make those arrangements? Maybe there's an NDA to sign considering Pierre has been hassled so intensely since coming out as the man behind his novels.

Heather saw the photos of me with Pierre before I did. She's not one to really spend time on social media, but apparently the town Instagram page, aka gossip site, @harvesthollowhappenings, went hog wild, reposting pictures of me with Pierre. Then Margie came into Cataloochee waving her phone around and announcing that I was all over

Twitter and Instagram with "that famous author who's living out past the lake." Not an hour later, Peggy Grady pulled my sister aside in a mock show of confidentiality, asking for details about me and Pierre.

Poor Pierre. His privacy and obscurity have been busted wide open.

It took Heather no time at all to call me in a frenzy. I had only landed the night before in Charlotte, reluctantly hitched a ride home with Pierre, during which I embarrassingly fell asleep in the backseat of his car, mouth agape, hair resembling a bird's nest. I collapsed right into bed sometime around two in the morning, stripping out of my travel clothes, brushing my teeth, and leaving everything else to wait for me the next day. It wasn't even seven-thirty in the morning when Heather called, waking me from one of the deepest sleeps of my life with her excited ramblings about me and Pierre. I had only texted her from the resort to tell her the big reveal—that Pierre was actually a man, the man behind the novels I adore.

I saw the photos. Yes. I saved them to my phone. They are amazing—literally the stuff of dreams. There are a few of Pierre staring at me while we ate dinner, some of the two of us dancing, and then more of him walking back to the resort with me and my friends. We look so comfortable together. Of course, the media went rampant with speculation about who I am and what I mean to Pierre. All that is bound to die down. It's not like he's Chase Stokes or Tom Holland. He's an author, famous because of the buzz around his coming out as the writer behind the name Amelie De Pierre. The media will lose interest shortly and move on to something more juicy.

Harvest Hollow's another thing, though. Now they've

discovered they have Pierre in their midst. And they know me, a local girl. And they're well aware the two of us were together. I'll deal with all that later. For now, I'm in Asheville, and no one cares who I am or whether I've hung out with an author.

"Don't worry, Tasha," Stuart continues in a soothing tone of voice that sets me on edge for some reason. "I promise you all your questions will be answered when we all meet today. Of course, I'll be Zooming in. I have clients here in LA I need to attend to as well, or I would have made the trip with Bob. He thought one of us should be there in person to finalize details. And, look at it this way, you'll get to see Pierre in person again. That's a good thing, right?"

It is a good thing. I enjoyed my time with Pierre. Not only did I get to meet the author of my favorite novels, but I helped him escape a crazed fan, spent a delightful dinner with him, and we even went dancing. And dancing with Pierre is an experience I won't ever forget. He held me so proficiently. That's the least romantic word in the world, I know. But I can't muster another to describe the perfection of what it was to be in his arms, led around the dance floor in time to the music. Pierre's hands were placed exactly where they should be, his grip just the right combination of gentle and firm. His leading wasn't pushy or sloppy. Pierre dances just as he moves through life: beautiful, command-ing, gracious, and captivating.

Of course, I kept all my reactions under wraps. After watching women nearly drop like flies at Pierre's feet all weekend, I made it my mission to put him at ease. It was obvious he needed a friend more than he needed one more rabid woman who couldn't contain herself at the mere sight of him. Or his touch. Oh, that touch. I feel chills just thinking of it now.

"I'll enjoy seeing him again. He's a good man."

That's a neutral reaction, right?

Pierre *is* a good man. The way he spoke of his family and friends back in France told me so much about his character. He's a private person with a deep love for the people nearest to him. What a catch. Only, he won't be my catch. I'll just treasure the near-friendship we developed over the course of the convention and leave it at that. And maybe I'll even do some work for him. It sounds like that's probable.

"Good. Good. Well, gotta run and all that. I'll let Bob know you'll be there. And, Tasha?"

"Yes?"

"Keep an open mind. Opportunity comes in all sorts of forms. This one is a good one for you and Pierre. Remember that."

Cryptic.

"Okay. Um. Yeah. Okay."

"Ciao."

The line clicks.

Was that even Stuart?

The call was so bizarre.

And who says ciao besides actual Italians? Do they even say ciao?

Something in me says that definitely was Stuart. And Pierre needs my support. That's a no brainer. If Pierre wants me to assist him in his author career, or even better, to give me the honor of reading an English translation of one of his novels, I'm all in.

I DIDN'T ANTICIPATE BEING BACK in my hometown so soon after my trip. The old library is in a renovated Craftsman home right at the edge of the historic downtown district, walking distance from Cataloochee. I park my car along Elm and walk across the lawn and up the wooden porch stairs. A few moms sit on the rocking chairs on the porch while their children play on the grass. I wave and smile at them before entering the building.

A cool fall breeze follows me into the open space filled with bookcases, a few tables by the front windows and a circulation desk they installed before I was born, when they first turned this house into a library.

I remember coming here as a girl, checking out books, reading with Mom on one of the benches on the porch. The familiar smells of furniture polish and old books warm my heart, making me homesick for the second time this month.

Mrs. Herring waves to me from the circulation desk. I walk over to her.

"Hi, Mrs. Herring."

"Oh, Tasha! It's so good to see you. What brings you all the way into Harvest Hollow today?'"

"I'm meeting Pierre Toussaint and his agent, Bob?" I realize I don't even know Bob's last name.

"Oh, yes. Bob is already here. Very prompt. He arrived five minutes ahead of when he said he would. Dressed all snazzy. I guess no one told him we're casual and outdoorsy around here. Goodness knows he couldn't take a hike in what he's wearing. Anyway, he's upstairs. Go on up. You can't miss him."

I thank Mrs. Herring and head across the old oak floor and up the staircase.

At the top of the stairs, the hallway has what used to be

bedrooms coming off it on both sides. In the first room I see, a single man sits at the head of a table. That must be Bob.

I knock on the open door to the room as I step through the doorway.

"Bob?" I ask, at the same time as the man says, "Tasha?"

We both chuckle nervously, and I take a seat.

"Is Pierre here?" I ask, looking around for him as if he'll materialize at the mere mention of his name.

"Not yet. But I'm glad you are here first. Let's get Stuart on the virtual call, shall we?"

"Shouldn't we wait for Pierre?"

"He'll be here."

Bob stands and shuts the door. He takes the seat adjacent to mine and opens his laptop. Then, he bends toward a briefcase on the floor at the side of his chair and pulls out a folder. He extracts a stapled stack of papers.

"This is an NDA. I hate to just pop this on you, but our discussion today will be potentially compromising to Pierre, and I need you to review and sign this before we go any further."

"An NDA?"

To say I'm confused would be an understatement. Bob seems nonplussed. His face is neutral. Unlike Stuart, who seems like he mainlines caffeine and never tells the full story about anything to anyone, Bob feels like someone you'd entrust to oversee your grandmother's estate. If he wants me to sign an NDA, I'll sign an NDA. I still need to read every word—twice. There are a lot of legal terms, but the gist of it is that whatever I see or hear while working for Pierre, I don't repeat. To anyone.

I sign and initial all the spots indicated, pausing a few times to look around for Pierre even though the door is shut.

After I've finished the paperwork, I look at Bob again, "Pierre still isn't here."

"He'll be here. Don't worry."

Bob doesn't say anything more, turning his attention to the laptop open in front of him on the desk.

"There's Stuart. Ready?"

Am I ready? Would it matter? How do I know if I'm ready when I don't even know what's happening?

"Heyyyy!" Stuart says as soon as Bob permits him into the Zoom call.

"Stuart," Bob says. "Tasha is here with me. I haven't given her any details yet. She's already signed the NDA."

"Good. Good."

I look at Bob. Does he look pale? Or maybe it's me. I feel pale. I should have grabbed a water bottle from my car to bring with me.

"Well, let's get started," Stuart says.

"Without Pierre?" I ask, glancing at Bob.

"He'll be here any minute," Stuart says. "I just spoke to him before you arrived."

"Oh. Okay," I say.

Nothing about this feels okay. I feel like Pierre should be here. Maybe I'm being paranoid. Signing an NDA for work done for an author isn't unheard of. I just wish I knew what was going on.

"So, Tasha," Stuart says, leaning back in a leather chair at his desk, lacing his hands behind his head so his elbows extend out to either side.

The wall behind him has framed certificates and some shelves with books and what seem to be curated props—the kinds of items a designer would place on an office shelf to make it look trendy or magazine-shoot ready.

"I'll cut to the chase. We're all busy people. Well, I'm busy. Bob's got a plane to catch back in Asheville. I'm not sure how busy you are, but I assume you have a life."

"I do."

Sort of.

"Pierre has run into a snag. A hiccup. A little problem. It's easily solved, but it is critical. Well, the situation is critical. But we're about to fix it—with your help."

This does not sound like audio recording. And it doesn't sound like author services. What could they think I have to offer that would help Pierre in a critical situation?

"So, we have a proposal," Stuart says.

Bob's hands are resting on the desk. He drops them into his lap and wrings them once before rubbing his palms down his trouser legs. When I look at his face, he avoids meeting my eyes and nods his head toward the screen, so I look back at Stuart.

"A proposal! That's a good one. Right, Bob?"

"Yeah. Right."

"Could someone tell me what's going on?" I ask.

"Sorry. Sorry. Yes. Right," Stuart says. "You see, our boy, Pierre. Well, he somehow ... Well, maybe he didn't do anything wrong. We're still trying to get to the bottom of how this was overlooked. Anyway, what I'm trying to say is that he didn't get the proper visa. He was allowed to enter the states. And that was all on the up and up. But he needed a P status —performer, entertainer. He needed to have one year's permission to remain in the US to complete his tour. We have bookstores and other venues lined up through next summer. Many are on contract. When a distributor in Canada reached out after our time on the island to ask if Pierre could come there ..."

I start to blank out on Stuart's words, even though he's still explaining Pierre's situation. Pierre's status as a visiting French citizen on US soil is about to change. He's supposed to leave. He's not allowed to stay here without the proper paperwork. Bob and Stuart want my help. I'm assuming Pierre wants my help too. I'm not an immigration attorney. My mind scrambles through details as my eyes scan the windows across the room. Trees rustle in the light breeze, leaves barely starting to turn colors.

A proposal. They are proposing? On behalf of Pierre? And he's not even here.

It's clear what's not been said yet.

Pierre wants me to commit a crime—to marry him illegally, just so he can remain in the US. I'm assuming that's what this is about. What else would they be asking? And Pierre doesn't even have the decency to be here to ask me himself? That doesn't seem like Pierre, though.

I feel like I'm in a washing machine, water and bubbles swirling around my head while the agitator pushes me along. Everything's very sloshy and twisted.

The door to the meeting room opens.

Pierre.

Thank God.

He looks at Bob, then at the computer screen, and then at me.

"What is Tasha doing here?"

He pauses, regaining his usual composure. "Hello, Tasha. I'm sorry. That was rude of me. Hello."

"Hi." It's all I can eek out through my still scrambled thoughts.

Pierre turns his attention back to Stuart. "What is Tasha doing here?"

Stuart speaks from his place inside the laptop. "We have a solution, Pierre. And you are going to be so glad we came up with this. Don't worry, Tasha already signed an NDA. Your secret's safe with her."

Pierre looks at me. Then at Bob. Then back at Stuart again.

"Tasha, please forgive my publicist. He is a bit ... overstepping at times. I would like a moment with my agent and Stuart alone. Could you wait outside in the hallway for one moment? Maybe browse some books downstairs?"

Pierre's tone is as cordial as ever, but his jaw is slightly tight.

He looks at Bob. "She's allowed to leave the room, yes?"

"She is, of course."

"She should stay," Stuart says. "I already proposed marriage."

Pierre's eyes go wide. "Zut! Mince! A quoi étiez-vous en train de penser?" He fires off what sound like French expletives and questions in a rapid-fire explosion that belies his normal calm, collected demeanor.

Can you blame the man? His representatives just disclosed his private struggles to a near-stranger, and then proposed marriage to her on his behalf. And by her, I mean me. And by marriage, I mean *MARRIAGE*.

Oh. My. Gosh.

They want me to marry Pierre.

They want this. From the look on Pierre's ever-reddening face, and the way he's still spouting his native tongue like a French tutorial on 2.0 speed, he doesn't want me to marry him. At all.

Not that I want to marry him. I don't. Obviously. We don't even know one another.

Stuart speaks, his voice calm and unaffected. "Pierre. Sit down. We can all talk this through like rational adults. Let's look at your options. I'm sure you will see that Bob and I are acting in your best interest when you hear our thoughts on this. Everyone, sit down."

Surprisingly, Pierre sits. I'm already sitting. So is Bob.

Pierre looks across the table at me and mouths. "I'm sorry."

I mouth back, "It's okay."

It's totally not okay. Not even a little. Who proposes marriage on behalf of someone else? And who suggests a federal offense as if it's just a day at the beach? But I want to help Pierre feel less like he's coming undone, so I assure him with my words and my facial expression.

Pierre shakes his head, running a hand through his hair, making it look deliciously disheveled.

What? I don't want to marry him, but he's still one of the most strikingly handsome men I've ever seen in my life. Ruffled or pulled together, it doesn't matter. His presence draws every eye in the room to him. He seems oblivious to his own appeal too, which only amplifies his sexiness.

Stuart covers the options as if he's talking about any subject on earth, not an illegal marriage of convenience. What is this, the 1800s? And this is Pierre Toussaint. Couldn't he just appeal the situation based on who he is? It seems like America would make an exception in his case.

Stuart narrows down the choices: stay in America to complete the book tour, capitalizing on the momentum Pierre built at Marbella Island, or head home to France, canceling over twenty events, disappointing readers, breaking contracts, and losing all they worked for by staging Pierre's "coming out."

When Stuart puts it that way, I see the importance of Pierre staying here in America. He explains his plan for us to marry, and then after the year is up, we can start to publicize trouble in paradise. We can blame the stress of the tour and Pierre's writing career on our difficulties. We can say I wasn't able to adapt to the new level of publicity and all the females competing for Pierre's attention. We can even say we wanted to live on different continents and couldn't convince one another to move. Within eighteen months of getting married, according to Stuart's plan, Pierre and I can initiate a divorce, and within two years, we'll be legally single again, free to move into our futures separately.

I'd be a woman who had been married once—a divorcée —the ex-wife of a famous romance author. It's a lot to take in.

Bob speaks up, finally.

"Pierre," he says. "You know me. While Stuart would probably suggest you marry his grandma, I'm not so rash."

"Hey!" Stuart says from the other side of the screen. "I resemble that remark." Then he pauses. "Actually, if I thought Immigration would buy the idea, I'd see if Grams would be open to the prospect. You'd love her, Pierre."

Stuart laughs at his own joke. He's the only one laughing.

Then he adds, "Those photos of the two of you set the stage for believability. We aren't just stabbing in the dark. Bob and I were up talking about this for hours last night. You two make sense. You both live in North Carolina. There's already public speculation that the two of you are an item. We just have to put an insta-love spin on this thing and convince the world you two couldn't keep your hands off one another. Not hard to do after seeing those photos, right? And then we announce your engagement. Once you're married, we apply for a green card. Then, as you say, Pierre, voilà."

"Voilà, indeed," Pierre mutters. Then he looks at me again, "Sorry, Cher. This is si horrible." He says the last two words in French, his accent soothing my nerves.

"It's okay, Pierre," I say, giving him what I hope is a comforting smile.

"Look at you two," Stuart says. "So believable! This is great!"

All three of us stare at Stuart like he's lost it. Because he has. He's lost it.

Bob speaks again. "Pierre, I know this isn't ideal. I was dead set against it. After all, there are the legalities. But over the course of the conversation, as unconventional as this option sounds at first blush, Stuart had me convinced. If you want to stay here in the states to write and tour, it may be the most expeditious and straightforward way to go about it."

"Um, hello?" I say.

"Yes?" Bob looks at me.

"Hi. Bride to be over here. Did you want to ask me if I want to go through with this? Or am I just a pawn in this plan?"

Pierre runs his hand from his forehead down to his jaw in one slow movement. He shakes his head. "Ah, Cher. How will I ever make this up to you, Tasha? It is horrible. Si horrible."

"It's not really you who needs to apologize," I tell Pierre, shifting my focus to the laptop.

"You want me to apologize?" Stuart says. "Fine. Fine. Sorry. I'm sorry I put you in an awkward position. Of course we want your input. This whole plan is a flop without you. But understand, Tasha. As I told you on the phone, it's not like we're asking you for charity. We want to compensate you well for your time and trouble. You would get, what did we say, Bob?" Stuart pauses, lifting papers on his desk and searching for something.

Bob looks at me. "Two hundred fifty thousand dollars. American dollars. Not French, to be clear."

"We French don't have dollars," Pierre clarifies. "We use the euro and the franc."

"Two hundred ..." I nearly choke. "Two ..." I take a breath.

"Yes. Yes," Stuart says. "Two hundred fifty thousand. Unless you want more. Of course, you'll move in with Pierre as soon as the wedding is final. We're hoping in a few weeks. He has to be married before mid-October. So, the sooner, the better."

I'm speechless. That kind of money would pay off my student loans and give me a sweet nest egg. I could stop renting and finally buy a place of my own.

Money you'd make committing a crime, Tasha, my conscience reminds me.

But I'm not robbing a bank, I answer myself.

But it's a federal crime. Fed-er-al, my inner Jiminy Cricket chirps.

And, with that kind of money, I could possibly help Heather buy the coffee shop, I remind my morally-superior inner insect.

I look over at Pierre. His face looks pensive. When our eyes meet, he has a pleading look on his face. Does he want me to go through with a fake marriage?

"Um. I'll need some time to think about all this," I say, never taking my eyes off Pierre's.

"Of course, of course," he says. "I need that too, actually."

Stuart says, "Great! You kids think. Maybe go off somewhere together—in public, preferably, where people will see you. Think. But don't think for too long. We need to get moving on this one way or the other." He pauses. Then he says, "I hear wedding bells! Isn't it romantic?"

Bob glares at Stuart. It's not a heavy glare, but he sends a message. We all say goodbye to Stuart after agreeing we'll get back to him with an answer within forty-eight hours.

Once we're alone with Bob, I ask, "I know I signed an NDA. But can I at least tell my sister? She's my sounding board for every important decision I've ever made in my life. I want to ask for her input."

"I understand," Bob says. "But due to the precarious nature of this situation, I'm afraid we have to ask you to keep this to yourself for now. I'm terribly sorry."

"It's okay," I say for the third, or fourth, or fifth time during this bizarre afternoon.

Maybe if I keep saying it, I'll believe it. Maybe it is okay. I mean, I could do worse than marrying Pierre Toussaint and walking away with two hundred fifty thousand dollars.

11

PIERRE

I may be running out of options,
but running out isn't an option.
~ Mark Lawrence

Bob wraps up the meeting, shaking my hand, then Tasha's, and then profusely apologizing to each of us in turn.

He doesn't lambaste Stuart. Instead, he says, "Well, I have a plane to catch in three hours. I think I'll head back to Asheville so I can grab a bite before my flight. I'll leave you two to … think."

He stashes his laptop into his briefcase and gives me one more sheepish glance before he heads out of the meeting room into the hall. I hear his footfalls on the wooden staircase as he makes his way to freedom.

I'm left standing barely two feet away from Tasha. We don't speak. I notice the color of her eyes more fully. Brown with a lighter, nearly caramel shade of brown where the iris meets the pupil. We're close enough that the now-familiar scent of her vanilla shampoo reaches me. Notes of warm spices mingle in, as if she just drank a chai or ate a fall pastry. It reminds me of the night we danced, how easy things were between us—before my stupidity complicated everything.

Tasha looks up at me, nervously at first, but then, her lips thin and she gives a determined nod of her head.

"We have some thinking to do."

"Would you like to ..." I raise my eyebrows in question, wondering if I should offer this after all. But the words are already out in the air between us. "... to talk? Since discussing things with your sister is not an option. I could be a neutral place to share your concerns. I'm a good listener."

"Neutral?" Tasha barks out a laugh.

Then she laughs some more, the obvious tension of the past hour finding some release.

I chuckle with her, watching her closely as she wipes a tear from her face and catches her breath after her lapse into understandable, momentary hysterics.

"I am not neutral, obviously. But I can do my very best impression of a man who couldn't care less. I will listen to your thoughts and advise you as if you were speaking of someone else, and not me, the foolish author who did not check his papers well enough. This is what happens when you leave the administrative details of your business to others."

"Not always."

"True. I am sure you would have checked the dates on my visa."

"I can't say for certain that I would have, but I'd like to think my attention to important details is reliable."

Tasha looks around, as if remembering only now that we are in the library, standing in a meeting room with noises filtering up through the old structure, we exist in a fishbowl. Considering the raw vulnerability of our circumstances, the exposure feels magnified.

"Would you like to take a walk?"

"A walk?"

"Yes. We could walk and you could bounce your predicament off me. We'll do a ... what is the term? Ah. Yes. A pros and cons analysis."

"That sounds so romantic." She laughs again. "First Stuart proposes to me while leaning back in his leather chair like he hasn't a care in the world and is merely brokering a business deal, and now you want to walk through town while we do a pros and cons analysis."

"Would you like me to suggest something more romantic?"

I don't know what makes me ask the question. Our situation isn't romantic. The look in Tasha's eyes makes her appear lost somehow. If I can do anything to take away that expression and the sentiment behind it, I will.

"Of course not. It's just ... I never imagined these being the circumstances around my first marriage."

"Of course you didn't. I'm so sorry. Stuart should have been more sensitive."

And not only Stuart. I am the one responsible for this situation. I delegated the details. But my immigration status is my responsibility. This is my life, not anyone else's. The list of people I could blame are only hired by me to organize my life and to help my books reach readers. They are not responsible for this mess. I am.

Tasha picks her purse up off a chair. I wonder if she's going to walk off, leaving me in this room—never looking back. I wouldn't hold it against her if she did. We only met less than a week ago, and here I am asking her to give up two years of her life. And for what? Two hundred and fifty thousand dollars? I haven't even directly asked her to help me. Stuart asked for me. True. I didn't know he was going to, but still, another man has asked her to step up and take on my problem. The fact that she didn't already run out of this room screaming speaks volumes.

Though, you don't scream in a library, do you?

I've been equally shocked by the way things unfolded, I haven't had time to consider what a fake marriage would entail if Tasha were even willing to agree to this charade. Leave it to Bob and Stuart to spring this kind of solution on me after they've already asked someone else to bear the burden with me. I'm a commodity to them. Or, maybe this is just another day at the office. Solve the visa issue for the French author. Tend to other clients. Go home and relax.

Tasha would have to move in with me if we wanted to make a marriage between us appear legitimate. My house in Harvest Hollow is comfortable. At least I have an ample second bedroom with its own private bathroom across the hall. With the best part of fall around the corner, Tasha would have a beautiful view of the woods from her bedroom window as the colors turn. She'd be closer to her sister and nephew if she moved here. But still, she'd have to live with me. What would her family and friends say? She would be required to pretend our marriage is real to the people who matter most to her.

It's really too much for me to ask.

Not to mention, we'd actually be married—something I secretly swore I'd never do after Camille and I broke up. I'll write romance. That doesn't mean I'll be in one. Not that a marriage to Tasha would be romantic. It would be platonic —friendly. An arrangement. Not an actual relationship.

But still.

It's marriage.

If my career weren't so critical to me and this tour didn't matter so much, I'd simply return to France and reschedule everything for a later date when I could arrange for the proper paperwork and permissions to be securely in place. But, as Stuart so wisely pointed out, we have momentum. My books are doing well. This is the time to ramp things up and become more of a household name when it comes to romance novels. His plan did just what it should. To shut things down now would snuff the flame we fanned at Marbella Island. Who knows what that would do to my career—a career I've come to love, cherish and rely on for my livelihood.

Tasha turns and looks over her shoulder at me. Her hair swaying around her shoulders as she does.

"Are you coming?"

"Oui. Yes. I'm right behind you, Cher."

We walk out of the library, me trailing only a short distance behind her. I nod to the library employees and then to the women on the porch. Their eyes flit from me to Tasha and back.

I follow behind Tasha until I match her pace. For a while, we walk in silence, the cooler air and occasional breeze a reprieve after the meeting we just endured. I'm biding my time, following Tasha's lead.

She walks along the side of the library, toward the town square. People are gathered here and there on the lawn or benches. The sidewalk frames the outside of the square.

"I ..." she starts at one point. Then she shakes her head and keeps walking. So, I walk alongside her, quietly studying her features when she isn't looking. Her nose is long and suited to her face, her cheekbones high, her lips soft and full. Her eyes are warm and kind, though right now, her brow is furrowed, revealing her unsettled thoughts and concerns.

"I want to help you," she says softly. "It's not that I don't want to help you."

"I know you do. We haven't known one another long, but already you have shown that you will step in to help me when I need it. This request is asking for a little more than tossing your keycard on the hotel lobby floor to deter an overeager fan, though."

"It is."

"So, ask me the questions you would ask your sister. Or tell me the thoughts you would share with her." I change my voice to a soprano. "I will do my best to be like a sister to you."

Tasha laughs. "You aren't a thing like my sister."

"No?"

"No."

"Try me," I say in a less high voice, but still with a note of femininity.

Tasha shakes her head, but then she takes a deep breath, letting it out slowly and looking at me.

"Okay. Pros. I'd be helping you. I'd end up with a big chunk of money I could use." She looks over at me, a light flush to her face. "That feels weird, to be honest. My sister might be in a position to take over the coffee shop in a year. I could possibly use the money to help her out if she lets me."

"That's good."

"And I'd be closer to her and Nate in Harvest Hollow. I can really do my work from anywhere. If I need to record at a studio, I can always drive back into Asheville for a day or two. My rental is month to month. I wouldn't be breaking a lease."

"All pros. You're convincing me this is good for you." I breathe out a relieved sigh.

I'd feel better if I knew Tasha was gaining something from this arrangement too.

"Cons." Tasha looks at me and then looks across the square toward the fountain.

I brace myself, not wanting to sway her decision unfairly.

"I don't really know you. We'd be living together. It could be awkward."

"Right. Like when I walk around trimming my nose hairs. Or the way I sing opera in the shower. And there's my troll doll collection. I have hundreds in the living room, on every shelf. And my cat posters. You can never have too many cat posters—with motivational sayings on them."

She laughs. I keep a straight face.

"You are kidding, right?"

I wink at her. She shakes her head at me.

"Even without all that, it would be an adjustment. Getting a roommate always is. And I grew up in Harvest Hollow. I'll be lying to an entire community. One I need to return to when this is over. Then there's the minor detail that this is illegal and I could go to jail or be fined. And you would get deported."

"Mmmmm. Those are some serious cons. Is that what your sister would say?"

"No! She would say, 'Are you crazy? Are you out of your mind? Do you even know this man? And besides, this is illegal! Do you want to get arrested and be a felon the rest of your life?'"

"Wow."

"Yeah. But to be fair, she didn't want me going to Marbella Island either. She said meeting my online friends was stranger-danger. So, she's a little overprotective."

"That's a beautiful thing. My sisters are overprotective too. It drives me crazy, but deep down, I appreciate it."

"Most of the time, Heather drives me crazy with her concerns. But I do love her for it."

I look over at Tasha, then I think back to the meeting with Bob and Stuart.

"Je suis un poulet mouillé," I mutter under my breath.

Tasha looks at me. "What does that mean?"

"Ahhh. I think the exact translation is, I am a wet chicken."

"You are ... a wet chicken?"

She pauses, resting her hands on her thighs as her face lights with laughter. When her head tilts up so she can meet my eyes, she asks, "What is that supposed to even mean, you are a wet chicken?"

"It means I am a coward. You know? Do you say it this way?"

"No," she says with a soft chuckle. "We say someone is chicken. Brawk Brawk Brawk." She flaps her arms to demonstrate. "Just not wet. There is a saying around here, *madder than a wet hen*. It means hopping angry."

"Ahh. Yes. Well, a dry chicken can be brave, no? But a wet chicken is rarely brave."

"I haven't been around enough wet chickens to know. But I'll take your word for it. And you aren't a wet chicken. You are a man in an unexpected situation."

"Who allowed another man to propose to you on my behalf."

"Well, if it bothers you, Monsieur drenched rooster, do the honors."

I pause, looking over at Tasha. Her hair is more wavy than curly today. She's got a playfulness in her eyes right now—they nearly dance when they meet mine.

We're both weighed down with the heaviness of the decision laid out before us, but she's taking it in stride. I nearly drop to one knee, right here in the middle of town. Only one thing keeps me from following through on that impulse. I'm not eager to marry. The opposite, actually. But I don't want Stuart's request to be the one Tasha ponders. The request for help should come from me.

"I want to give you time. Let's take the forty-eight hours we've been given."

Tasha looks at her phone. "Forty six and a half hours now."

"Ça sent le sapin!"

"Translation?"

"Ah. Sorry, Cher. I revert to French when I get emotional. This means, I'm smelling the casket."

"You're smelling the casket? Is that a wet chicken smelling the casket, or are you no longer poultry now?" she chuckles as if she thinks I'm ridiculous.

"We say it like the end is near. I can smell the fir tree

wood. Things are so bad I can actually smell the wood of my own casket."

"Oh. Delightful." Tasha gives me a side eye.

"Right?"

"Don't be dramatic, Pierre. This isn't your casket. Either I will say yes, in which case we will make this work. We'll be convincing, and I'll be all in. Or, I'll decide I can't do it. Then you will need to choose what's next for you. I'm quite sure it won't be a hardship finding a woman who wants to be your fake wife."

"Wow. Thanks." I look over at her.

"I don't mean it that way. I mean, look at you. We had to pull off quite the theatrics to keep women at bay on the island. I'm sure one of those fans would be glad to take you up on this ... *proposal*." She emphasizes the word, and I wince.

"So, I should search for the name of the woman in green?" I stare at her with my eyebrows raised.

"No! Of course not. Could you imagine?"

"I can. Whomever we pick has to live with me in my home. I don't want to have to install triple deadbolts on the inside of my bedroom door. And, I need to write. Much of my time is spent writing in my home. I need someone who will permit me to carry on with my life, not someone who will be scraping hairs from my brush for their scrapbook."

She studies me with a teasing look in her eye. "Maybe you should consider some murder mystery books after this."

"No. It is romance for me. I love writing romance. Mysteries are too ... je ne sais quoi ... too mysterious and dark. I like making people happy with my writing. To give them the HEA, you know? All the feels?" I bump Tasha's shoulder when I say that last sentence and she looks up at me, a slight pink to her cheeks.

"Yes. I know. All the feels. You do that well, Amelie."

"Touché."

We're quiet again, both lost in thoughts about my predicament and what will happen next, I imagine.

"I think Stuart and Bob scanned my options," I tell Tasha. "You are the best choice. They are right about that."

She looks away, toward the buildings across the street. I think I see another blush rise across her cheeks, but it is hard to discern from my vantage point.

"So, give this forty-six and a half more hours. Okay? Call me whenever you need to. If you have questions or need to sort things out some more. Please, just call. And we can talk again, maybe in two days—before we give Bob and Stuart the answer. I will go with whatever you say. You are under no pressure from me. This is not your problem to solve. I leave the decision up to you. And I want to give you some time to think it through thoroughly. I wish I could permit you to speak with your sister. The first thing I am going to do on my drive back to my house is call Rene, my best friend since childhood. I wish I could give you that same luxury."

"It's okay. I understand."

"For now, please know it is me, asking you to be my fake wife, to help me for this year that I need to stay in your country—but only if it is something you can do freely and willingly. Not if it will harm you or be a hardship. Okay?"

I smile at her.

She smiles back. "Thank you for asking me on your own behalf."

"I never would have left this up to Stuart. If I knew what he was up to, I would have beaten him to ... how is it said?"

"To the punch?"

"Oui. To the punch."

She smiles. "Punching Stuart. Now there's a thought."

We both laugh.

How did I find a woman who could be such a friend to me in a time of need like this?

She is remarkable.

Cass: Ohmmmmygossssh. Did you all see the pics of Tasha and Pierre?

Winona: You know I did. We live together.

Cass: Duh. I'm talking to the group. Tasha, we need to hear the scoop. Have you been holding out on us, girl?

Daisy: Yes! Inquiring minds need to know. Or is it enquiring? I always get those mixed up.

Brianna: It's enquiring. Just think of the National Enquirer.

Daisy: You totally solved a life-long spelling problem, Bri. I owe you a latte when we next see one another.

Brianna: If you come down to Charleston, I'll buy YOU a latte.

Daisy: Deal.

Cass: Back to the issue at hand. Tasha. Are you avoiding us? We want to know what's up with you and Monsieur Toussaint.

Daisy: Am I the only one who finds that name hot? Sorry Tasha. (Not sorry.)

Tasha: I'm here. Yes. Long story. There may be something brewing ... I can't say right now, but besides my sister, you four will be the first to know.

Daisy: How unfair is it that we live all scattered around the south. I wish we were closer. That time on the island wasn't nearly long enough.

Cass: Maybe it was long enough for Pierre and Tasha (wink, wink)

Winona: Right?! Tasha, you're killing me with this vagueness. Get back here with solid details soon.

Tasha: I promise. Just ... a lot to process. I promise I'll be back here in our DMs to share all the details as soon as I can.

12

PIERRE

We are best friends.
Always remember if you fall, I will pick you up
... after I stop laughing.
~ Unknown

On my drive to back to my home, I dial Rene. It rings three times before he answers.

"Allo."

"Allo. Are you still awake?"

"I'm not answering in my sleep, if that's what you are asking."

"Funny."

"What has you calling me at this hour?" he asks.

"I have a situation."

"A woman?"

"No."

"Not that woman in the photos?"

"Not exactly."

"Mmm. Then, it is the woman in the photos. I thought there was something there. You looked like you were hit by un coup de foudre."

"Rene. I'm serious here. There was no lightning strike with Tasha. I already told you, the pictures were not accurate. Please, listen. I have a real situation. It's serious."

"Sorry, mon vieux. Tell me. Je suis tout ouïe."

He's listening. Good. Finally.

"Merci. It is horrible. So horrible. I have been asked to go to Canada while I'm on these book tours. Scheduling a trip over the border prompted Stuart to look into my paperwork. That was when Stuart discovered my status is not as we had assumed. I am not permitted to stay in the US past the middle of October. I don't know how we all missed it."

"Quelle horreur."

"Yes. Exactly. Horrible. Like I said."

"What can I do?" Rene asks.

I would ask him the same thing if our roles were reversed. I wouldn't hesitate to do anything for Rene. I'd drop whatever seemed important in my own life to help him out of a difficulty if he needed me.

"Nothing. Unless you are secretly a US Citizen and you want to marry me."

"Je t'aime mon ami. Yes. I love you, my friend. But not enough to marry you, I'm sorry to break your heart. Also, I am a Frenchman through and through. Nothing could persuade me to downgrade my status to become an American. But I will forgive you this question because of my deep love for you."

I chuckle despite myself. Rene always does know how to make me not take myself so seriously.

"So, Stuart has a possible solution."

"Marrying the American?" Rene laughs hard—so hard I have to wait for him to regain composure before I speak again.

"Oui. That is it."

"What?! He wants you to marry the American? I was joking."

"Well, Stuart is a practical man. He and Bob talked this over. The photos of me and Tasha are believable. They even fooled you. And she is pleasant."

"What is she, a sample of cheese? Pleasant. You are a mess, my friend. She's beautiful. And she helped you get out of a pinch a few times that weekend on the island. Deny what you will, but I heard you talk about her. You couldn't stop saying things about her. And she made you laugh. What woman has made you laugh—in so many years no one has. I have had to carry that burden alone. Ay. *She's pleasant.* If that's all you can say, you don't deserve her help. *Pleasant.* La vache!"

"You are right, of course. I don't deserve her help. She is far too patient and kind, and it is ridiculous that I am even considering this as an option. Besides, you know me and my personal space."

"Your sacred privacy. Oui, I know."

"No one has even been in my house here but me since I bought it. I don't even have a housekeeper, despite Stuart hiring one. When she showed up, I paid her to leave. My home is my sanctuary."

"God forbid a woman enter your sanctuary. You are like a monk. No females are allowed near you. Am I right?"

"I only wish. But she is different. Pleasant."

"Ah. Yes. Please, do me and yourself a favor and lose that

word. It is an insult to the female race. *Pleasant.* As if you only barely tolerate her. She is exquisite. You know it too. I saw her hair. Where did she get that hair? It is not quite brown and not quite red. Ah. Do tell me, what color are her eyes? The photos don't reveal them well because she is staring back at you while you look at her like she is so much more than pleasant. She is no slice of cheese. She is like the fresh baked patisserie first thing in the morning, warm from the oven, inviting, soft, perfect."

I want to put my hand through the phone and choke my best friend. Why? Tasha is nothing to me. A friend, maybe. If I don't ruin that with this horrid request.

"Her eyes are brown," I relent.

"Of course they are brown. Like chocolat. Like warmth itself. Like the chestnuts we roasted in winter for the holidays as boys."

"What are you trying to do?"

"To wake you up, my friend. You are a blind man standing in front of a masterpiece. So, I must describe it to you so you will see even though you are blind. You are like a man who has burnt his fingertips. Now you cannot feel the softness, the sharpness, the many varieties of textures in life even if they touch you. Your nerve endings are dead. I am the acupuncturist for your heart. You need to feel again, my friend."

"I can see, and I can feel. She is lovely. Okay? We have possibly even become friends. Or at least we were developing a friendship." I sigh, the weight of my situation washing over me with renewed impact. "Now, what should I do? Should I call her and tell her she doesn't need to accept this option?"

"She knows?"

"Yes. Stuart asked her for me."

"Tu es un poulet mouillé."

"I am not a wet chicken. Though I said the same thing to her about myself only an hour ago. Stuart asked her without my permission. After Tasha and I met with him and Bob, we walked around town and talked. I asked her myself if she would consider doing this favor for me. I told her there is no pressure."

"Well, at least you got that right."

"But I should change my mind, yes?"

"Not necessarily. What would it mean if you did?"

"If I come home now, we lose the momentum of the tour. I would deeply disappoint many readers who are counting on meeting me at one of the book signings. I would also break contracts. It would cost us money, publicity, and exposure."

Rene is quiet. I wait for him, watching the scenery change outside my car windshield. The woods become increasingly dense as I approach my property here on the outskirts of Harvest Hollow. It feels as much like home as a place can feel. It doesn't provoke that nostalgic feeling of home that only one's childhood surroundings can elicit, but it's the next best thing—a sense of someplace belonging to you, and you to it—even if it is only for the time being.

Rene finally speaks. "Here is what I would do. I would keep the door open with Tasha. Let her decide. If she is amenable, you go forward with it. If she does not want to do this, you do not pursue any other option. You toss in the sponge and you come home. You will survive without this tour. Yes. It's far better if you can continue to fulfill your obligations and make the most of the momentum you have started. But I know you don't want to coerce a woman into enduring life with you. And you also don't have a range of people to choose from. She is the one. The only one. And, who knows, you might fall in love."

"I won't."

"Well, let's hope she doesn't fall for you, then. The poor girl. She would have a hopeless situation on her hands. Would she not? I would be forced to come rescue her—to bring her a Frenchman who could appreciate her and treat her with the admiration she deserves."

"Rene."

My voice holds a tone of warning.

"Why do you care?" he pauses. "Unless you care."

I don't answer. Rene is not living overseas, far from family and friends, facing a wave of popularity and publicity for the first time in his life. He is not as private a man as I am either. He would eat this mass attention up. I am not from the same barrel as he is. Besides, even when romance has not gone his way, he has been like a rubber ball, bouncing back into the arms of another woman, willing to date and try again.

I am more like a porcelain doll—like the English nursery rhyme about the egg, I fell and I am cracked into all the pieces. The king's horses and men can't put me together again. Not even Tasha could put me together again.

"I care about her, of course. You have female friends. A few, anyway. You know I can have a friend in her."

"Oui. I have friends who are women. But I don't hold them like that when we dance. No, mon vieux. Your eyes tell me that you are a man at war inside his own heart. A secret you keep from yourself has been revealed to me. I only hope you will wake up from your stupor while you have a chance with this American beauty. And tell me, does she eat like a Frenchwoman?"

"Of course not. She eats. Full bites. Clears her whole plate."

"I think I am swooning. She is perfect."

"Since when did you want anything less than a feminine woman?"

"Since I saw your *friend*."

"*My* friend."

"Ah. But she is your friend, no? So she can be anything to me."

"Go to sleep, you pig."

He chuckles. Then he is serious. "I will do whatever I can to help you. You know that. I know I can't do much. And, be careful. We haven't even talked about this being a crime. In some ways, that detail is a formality—until it isn't. You are only trying to serve the American people—your fans—by being there. You are actually sacrificing your comfort for this trip. It's not like you are trying to serve as a French spy on American soil." He pauses. "Are you?"

"No. I am not. And if I told you I was, I'd have to kill you. And I like you too much to kill you."

"That is good news for me. My charm works in my favor again. Whew." He chuckles. Then he adds, "Just be careful. Okay?"

"I will."

"And not so careful with your heart. It is stronger than you think."

13

TASHA

In the middle of the night,
if you have decided to do
something good for the world,
don't wait for the morning to come!
~ Mehmet Murat Ildan

It's been the most confusing, emotional, distracting day of my life. After Pierre and I took our walk around the town square, I resisted the urge to pop in to see my sister at Cataloochee. It felt weird being in Harvest Hollow and not telling her I was there.

Once I was home, I tried to put together some posts for Instagram about books I recently read. I couldn't focus, not even enough to write a review of a book I loved.

I had some calls from my agent. I returned her call. She's booked two upcoming recordings for me. That means reading through a book to prepare to record the female POV in two weeks. The other gig isn't until a month from now.

I need to clear my head enough to concentrate. An

author who hires me to do her newsletter and oversee her advertising and promotions sent me an email. Those tasks are menial enough, so I tackle that work.

It's well past dinner time when I finish, but I can't think of forcing myself to eat. My stomach is a bundle of nerves. So, I plop on my couch and turn on Netflix, hoping to find a movie that will take my mind off the decision I have to make in forty hours.

Of course, *The Proposal* pops on the screen. Is this an omen, a portent, a sign? I settle in to watch the movie, hoping it will serve up the answer to my dilemma on a silver platter. It seems so easy for Sandra Bullock to announce she's engaged. But, it's Ryan Reynolds, so go Sandra! Then again ... it's Pierre Toussaint. Go me?

Unfortunately, the stress of the day catches up with me and I fall asleep halfway through the movie. So much for getting my definitive answer from Hollywood.

I drag myself off the couch and pad down the hall, no closer to a decision than I was at two this afternoon.

My phone buzzes on my way to my bedroom.

Heather: *Are you now in hibernation? It's not like you to avoid my calls and texts.*

Yes. I've been avoiding my sister. I'm afraid talking to her, or even texting her, will trigger her intuitive sense about me. She'll pick up on the fact that I'm hiding a big secret, and I don't know what I'll tell her. As a matter of fact, one of the biggest stumbling blocks keeping me from saying yes to this whole charade has to do with Heather. I can't imagine how I will manage to lie to her.

For some reason, lying to our parents doesn't seem as

hard. I know. I know. But they've wanted me to find a good man and settle down for years. They'll be overjoyed to hear I've found someone—even if it's a whirlwind.

Heather won't buy it. I don't know how I'm going to sell her on this. She'll know I would have told her if I were falling in love. I tell her everything.

> Tasha: *Sorry! I've been super busy. Lots of work for my author assistant stuff. Catching up from the trip has consumed me. And I got two gigs, so I've been starting the prep for those. Let's connect this weekend.*

> Heather: *I'm not waiting that long. Something's up with you. Come out here tomorrow, or I'll get Jack to cover the shop and I'll be coming to you.*

I knew it. She's onto me. I don't know how she knows. She just does. And, as much as I ought to avoid her, I'm going to have to face her sometime. Besides, I miss my sister, especially now when I'm up against one of the biggest decisions of my life.

> Tasha: *I'll come there tomorrow. Save me a mocha.*

> Heather: *I'll do better than that. I'll save you an apple crisp muffin. It's apple season, and you know what that means around here.*

> Tasha: *Yep. While the whole world goes pumpkin-spice everything, we go apple everything. And I'm here for all of it.*

Fall is my favorite time of year. I love everything about North Carolina in the fall: the colors, the leaves on the ground, the festivals, the apples, the cool morning air, a fire in the fireplace for the first time after a long summer, the sense that everything just got dialed into the cozy setting.

Heather: *Love you Teeter-Totter. See you tomorrow.*

Tasha: *Love you, Sissy. Thanks for relentlessly loving me. You're the best.*

I set my phone down, curl up under the covers and eventually drift off. Just that short text exchange made me feel like everything will be alright—no matter what I decide.

It's pitch dark when I wake to the ringing of my cell.

I grope around in the dark on my bedside table and pull my phone in front of my face.

Pierre?

What time is it?

Twelve twenty-eight? Why is he calling me at this hour?

"Hello?"

Nothing.

"Hello?"

The call ends.

Weird.

I lie in the dark wondering if I should call him back. Maybe it was a butt-dial.

I'll text him.

Tasha: *Did you just butt-dial me?*

Pierre: ...

Pierre: …

Pierre: *Butt-dial? What is this butt-dial? I did not do anything with my butt.*
My laughter sounds louder in the quiet darkness of my bedroom.

Tasha: *It's a phrase. It means you accidentally call someone. Like if the phone is in your pants and you sit down so your butt makes the dial for you.*

Pierre: *No butt dial. My phone is by my head.*

I laugh again. Sometimes the things that get lost in translation are the funniest. I think of him calling himself a wet chicken and laugh again.

Pierre: *I called you. I don't know what I was thinking. I should have waited until morning. It can wait.*

I cradle my phone next to my heart. If Pierre called at this hour, he has something important to say. I'm up now anyway. I press dial before I can overthink it too much.

"Allo?"

"Hi. I'm awake. What did you want to talk to me about?"

"Well, I was thinking."

His voice is deeper, more rough and a little raw. It feels intimate, talking to him in the middle of the night, from my bed, while we're both in a drowsy state of mind.

"What were you thinking?" I ask.

"You don't have to do this. It's too much to ask. I appreciate you being willing. But I can't imagine it. Why would you break the law and agree to live with me for over a year? It's more than anyone should ask of another person. And you barely know me. I'm not easy to live with."

"Because of the cat posters?" I tease.

"It's so much more than that." His tone is serious. "I'm a private man. I spend most days alone. I have my family and friends in Avignon, but even they don't see me every day. I don't know if I'd be a good roommate."

"We'd be sharing a room?"

I try to keep the alarm out of my voice. I mean this is marriage, but we're not *really* getting married.

"No! No. Of course not. You would have a room of your own and a bathroom to yourself. What do you call that?"

"Housemate. You can say roommate, but housemate is better."

"Okay, housemate." He pauses, seeming to try the concept out. I'm doing the same.

"I'm a bit grouchy before my coffee," he says apologetically.

"What else?"

"I like things to stay where they belong. I don't tolerate messes around me."

"Mm hmm. What else?"

"I lose myself in my work. You could bang a drum over my head and I won't hear it. I'll ignore you a lot."

"Noted. Anything else?"

"I don't think so."

"So you are tidy, you need quiet in the morning, and you are focused when writing."

"Yes."

"I think I can live with that. I'm not always good about picking up after myself. But I can work on it."

"What else?" he asks.

"Um. I love watching BBC romance movies. And I do sing in the shower."

"I can live with that."

"And I am pretty obsessed with fall. Like you'll have a lot of cider and apples in the fridge, and pumpkin decor on the table, and I'll be cheery most of the time. I just love fall."

"The season?"

"Yes. Not falling down. I'm not a fan of that. Not at all."

"Well, as long as it's the season you're a fan of, I think I can live with that ... Chronically cheery might be an issue, but I'll do my best."

Pierre's voice sounds more relaxed, as if talking to me might have helped him settle whatever nerves he had. I smile at the thought.

"I promise to have a bad mood every so often just to balance things out."

Pierre laughs softly at my joke and it hits me. I only saw him standing across a lobby less than a week ago. And before that, I idolized him—thinking he was Amelie De Pierre. And now, six days after thinking he was a hot French professor, we're talking intimately in the dark of night like old friends. I'm crazy, right? What am I thinking? No one marries someone they've only known for a week.

But then he speaks, his accent soothing my nerves and reminding me of who he is. I swear, he could recite French tax laws to me—that voice. And not only the voice, it's the man behind the accent and words. I might have only just met him, but there's no doubt Pierre's a good man.

"I was thinking you could talk to my friend Rene," Pierre offers. "He knows what is going on. Maybe since you don't have your sister to talk to, he could be a sounding board for you. Though, Rene might try to talk you into marrying him instead ..."

"Why would he do that?"

"He's enamored with you. He saw the photos of the two of us. He's ridiculous. You will see this if you ever meet him. He's loyal and funny, and he will do anything for me. But he is a man who loves women. And he will charm you as if you are the snake and he is the man with a flute in front of the basket."

"There's an image." I chuckle. "I don't need to talk to Rene. I think I'm going to say yes."

My voice sounds like it's coming from somewhere else. I didn't even know I was considering saying yes. But lying here, talking with Pierre, just the two of us, the decision is a no-brainer. He needs my help. I am basically his only option. I want to help him.

"There's only one hitch," I say.

"Hitch?"

"Yes. A barrier, something keeping me from diving into this headfirst."

"What is that?"

"My sister. Even if I hide this from her at first, she will know. Obviously, she'll know when we get married. I'll be living there in Harvest Hollow. But it's more than that. She can read me like a book. If you and I were really in love, she'd know. I would have told her. She would be in on every detail. I share everything with her. Hiding something big from her is so out of character for me. I don't keep secrets from Heather. Bob doesn't understand. I might have signed an NDA, but Heather isn't just another person. It's way better if I tell her. She won't tell a soul."

"Let me talk to Bob."

"Okay. That would be great. I'm going to see Heather tomorrow."

"You'll be here? In Harvest Hollow?"

"Yes. I will."

"May I see you?"

"Um. Sure. Of course. I'll be hanging out with her at Cataloochee and then we'll go to her house, probably. I'm just coming up for the day."

"When you're free, call me."

"Okay. I will."

"Goodnight, Tasha."

"Goodnight, Pierre."

"And thank you—for saving me, again."

Tasha: Okay. So. Yes. Pierre and I have had a whirlwind sort of attraction. And we're ... well, we're getting married.

Winona: Whaaaaaaaaaa?

Cass: Ha ha. Seriously, Tasha? We were just implying that you might be dating him now. No need to get all dramatic on us.

Daisy: Oh my goodness! It's just like a romance novel! Girl meets guy. They fall into insta-love and get married. I'm swooning hard over here. Suh-wooooo-ning. Get me some smelling salts. Plus: Pierre. It's Pierre. As in, your fave author. Could this get any more swoonworthy?

Cass: Daisy, do I have to come over there and pour cold water over your head? They aren't getting married. Tasha is yanking our chain. Right, Tasha?

Cass: Tasha?

Tasha: Not joking. We know it's fast, but sometimes you just have to make a decision. When you know, you know. And it's clear I'm the one for him and he's the one for me.

Daisy: This is awesome! Do we get to come to the wedding?

Cass: I'm going to message you separately, Tasha. I believe in love. I mean, I've read 136 romance novels so far this year, and it's just October. But marriage? Why the rush? Nope. Not asking that here. Forget I typed that. I'll message you.

Brianna: Just catching up on messages. ARE YOU SERIOUS? MARRIAGE!!!??? What is going on? In my mind people only get married this fast for three reasons.

- First came baby in the baby carriage.
- He needs a green card.
- You lost your ever livin' mind.

So, which is it?

Tasha: Love. Sometimes people marry for love.

Brianna: So, it's number three. You lost your mind. Love is the best reason to marry. But rushing this so quickly? It's not right.

Cass: Well, I guess I don't have to privately message you. Bri just dropped the truth-bomb I thought I'd be gently sharing with you privately.

Tasha: Please trust me. This isn't a rush. Yes, It's fast. But Pierre is amazing. I'm sure of what I'm doing. I really want your support.

Winona: You have my support. I'll give you enough support to make up for Cass and Brianna.

Tasha: Thanks Win.

Brianna: I met him. That accent would convince the Queen of England to commit highway robbery. And those eyes, his hair, the way he leans on things. Why is the way he leans on things so sexy? I guess I get it. If you marry him you can just watch him lean on things all day. The sooner the better on that.

Cass: Bri, this is her future husband you're talking about. You don't get to say he's sexy. Even if he is sexy.

Brianna: Sorry, Tasha. I won't say your husband is sexy anymore. I'm just saying I get it now that I think about it.

Tasha: Thanks, Bri. And yes, he's pretty captivating. I'll give you that. Sorry to spring this on y'all so abruptly.

Cass: We love you, Tasha. We're just looking out for you.

Tasha: Love you too. Thanks for looking out for me. I'd do the same if the situation were reversed.

14

TASHA

Home is a shelter from storms—all sorts of storms.
~ *William J. Bennett*

The state highway climbs uphill after I leave the outskirts of Asheville behind. My view shifts from the tree-lined road to a more rural landscape, with the Blue Ridge Mountains framed in the distance. Farms with split-rail fences line the side of the road. And then, when I hit Harvest Hollow, everything familiar brings me back in time. It's like I never left home.

The old brick buildings and the craftsman and Victorian homes aren't merely historic structures to me. I had play-dates with friends in some of these, trick-or-treated at others. The neighborhoods and shops all hold memories of my childhood and teen years, preserving them like a three-dimensional scrapbook.

I turn onto Maple and find parking in front of Cataloochee Coffee. The shops are all in a row here. Cataloochee's storefront is painted a brick red with a matching awning. The store name is painted on one of the front windows in a mustard yellow. A lone bistro table sits off to the side of the main door. A chalkboard A-frame sign announces: *We have the best apple cider and apple crisp muffins. Come on in and get your taste of fall.*

The shop smells like coffee and autumn and I want to snuggle up on the vintage sofa near the front window and never leave.

"Hey! She's here!" Heather shouts from behind the counter.

She sets down her towel and walks my way, engulfing me in a hug. I nearly cry from the relief that washes over me. I lean into our embrace and give my sister a squeeze, hanging on for longer than usual.

"Hey, what's wrong?"

"Nothing. Nothing. It's just good to see you."

"Well, I've been here. You're the one jetting off to island resorts, and then avoiding me when you get back. But enough of that. You're here. Let me tell Jack I'm taking a break. I'll get you a muffin and a mocha. Sit."

I do as she says, plopping onto the sofa and tucking myself into the corner, propping one of the decorative pillows behind my back.

I look around the familiar interior of Cataloochee. The walls are painted the same mustard yellow as the logo on the window. One small section of a wall near the counter has a mug rack that goes from floor to ceiling where regulars hang their ceramic mugs. It's just one more way this shop makes locals feel like they've got a place that belongs to them. In the back corner of the shop sits the roasting area. People fill tables and stuffed chairs throughout the space, relaxing, connecting, reminding me life goes on whether I marry Pierre or not.

"So," Heather says, taking the opposite corner of the sofa after setting my muffin and mug of mocha in front of me. "Tell me what's got you hiding from me."

"I'm not hiding. I'm right here."

"I'll get it out of you. You might as well cut to the chase. You know I'm not giving up until you spill the beans. Let's see. Does it have to do with those photos of you and the hot author?"

"What makes you think that? I told you those pictures didn't tell the real story. He's just Pierre. Maybe we're becoming ..."

I stop myself. If I'm supposed to be falling for him, I'd need to put a spin on this. I take a long sip of my mocha and sputter cough. That's what I get for trying to hide behind my drink.

Heather studies me like a botanist examining a plant under a microscope. She's quiet, but her gaze is loud, searching me for clues as to what's up.

"Okay. Okay." I relent too quickly. "Pierre has a situation. He needs my help. I'm going to support him. You can't tell a soul."

"Have I ever shared your secrets with anyone?"

"No. You're my safe place." I easily admit the truth. She knows it anyway.

"And you're mine. So what's up? Are you in danger? Blink twice if you are. I'll sneak you out through the back door. We can hide in the family cabin until the threat passes by."

She's giggling lightly and it makes me smile.

I blink twice anyway.

"Seriously?" she stage whispers.

"Not really. I'm just definitely in over my head."

"What's going on?"

Heather's face shifts from playful to concerned.

I lower my voice and look around, as if someone in here would care about Pierre's immigration status. But, despite the growth of our town over the years, we've still got our share of local busybodies. I don't want anyone to know Pierre's situation—which is about to become my situation too.

"His visa, or whatever it is they call it, is expiring. He's got this year-long tour planned to do book signings and meet readers in person. They even want to expand the tour to Canada. None of that can happen unless he gets his papers straightened out—which he can't do in time. So ..."

"He needs to get married?" My sister guesses so quickly, my head spins. Her eyebrows nearly meet her hairline. She's whispering, but her expression is shouting.

"Yep."

"You've known him, what? A week? Don't tell me you're considering this."

"Okay. I won't tell you I'm considering this."

One of the regulars walks toward the front door and says, "Bye, Heather. Have a great afternoon."

She turns her attention away from me and smiles warmly at the man. "See you, Floyd. Have a great time fishing. I hope you catch a bunch."

"Oh, you know it. The large and smallmouth bass are biting like crazy this time of year. I'll bring you some if I catch what I think I will. I've got a great recipe for pan-fryin' them with a lemon garlic sauce. You can thank me later."

"You're makin' my mouth water."

Floyd winks at my sister and walks out.

"Too bad he's near retirement age," I tease her.

"The last thing I need is a man—of any age. My seven-year-old man keeps me busy enough."

"The right man wouldn't be so bad."

"Yeah. Well, I thought Nate's dad was the right one. Look how that turned out. I'm pretty sure my picker's broken. But that is not what we're talking about. And don't you try to weasel out of this conversation. Marriage? Teeter. What are you thinking?"

"I'm thinking he's in trouble. He's a good man. I'm single. My life is flexible. He offered to pay me. Well, he didn't. His agent and his publicist did."

"Marriage. Are you hearing yourself right now? Plus, hello. This is a federal law. You'd be breaking the law."

"Sort of. But not really. I've been thinking about it. If I want to marry him and he wants to marry me, how is that really the business of our government? I mean, people marry for far less valid reasons all the time."

Heather leans back, her eyes wide and her mouth drawn into a thin line. "I can't believe you're thinking of seriously marrying a man you only met a week ago."

"I know this won't sound reasonable to you, but I feel like I've known him a lot longer. Also, I know him through his books."

"Oh, help me. Someone help me."

I sip my mocha, careful not to take a big gulp this time. Then I break off a corner of the muffin. It's warm and there are chunks of apple in each bite, plus it has this crumbly streusel topping. I pop the bite in my mouth, close my eyes and moan. It's so good.

"Do you always have to do that?"

"Do what?"

"Shut your eyes and moan when you eat good food. Wait. Did you do that at dinner with Pierre?"

"Um. Maybe."

"No wonder he wants to marry you."

I shake my head. "No. It's not like that. He's not romantically interested in me. I promise you that."

"And how do you know for sure?"

"I can just tell."

"What about you? Are you attracted to him?"

"I can't imagine who wouldn't be attracted to him."

"Ahhh ha! That's all the more reason you should not go through with this. You don't marry a man you're attracted to who isn't attracted to you. Talk about a recipe for heartbreak."

"I just think he's gorgeous. And charming. And sweet. I don't have feelings for him."

"Oh no. This is worse than I thought."

"What's worse than you thought?"

"Gorgeous? Charming? Sweet? Agh."

"Yeah. I see what you mean. That's awful."

"No. It is. Don't you see? He's the perfect man. You will fall. He won't. Oh, Tasha. Please tell me you will refuse to help him."

"I can't tell you that."

"Why not?"

"I already said yes."

As if on cue, the door to the coffee shop swings open, and in walks my future husband. Heather doesn't recognize him right away. I do, though. He's as beautiful as he was in the hotel lobby, though his clothes are more casual today: jeans and a polo shirt, paired with brown leather shoes. It's still a stark contrast to the outdoorsy vibe of most of the locals. But even if he were in Birkenstocks and Carhartt pants, he'd take up more than his fair share of space—in the room, and in my head. Maybe Heather's right. Maybe I am in danger.

Pierre walks toward the counter, still unaware of us on the sofa since it's tucked away near the front of the shop.

Heather follows my gaze. She whispers, "Ohhh. He's been in here at least weekly for the past month or so. Usually two or three times a week. He came in once to introduce himself officially after your trip. Yeah. I see it. He's definitely ... well, he's ... Okay. Okay. I get it."

I give her a scolding look. "Shhh. He'll hear you."

"Are you hiding from him?"

"Not at all. I told him I'd call him after I spent some time with you today. He wants to see me."

"Maybe he couldn't wait." She wags her eyebrows suggestively. Then she studies Pierre as he puts his order in with one of the baristas at the counter.

"How exactly does he get that look? It's like he's clean shaven, but he's still got that delicious light dusting of stubble."

"Stop drooling," I tease. "And, watch it. That's my future husband you're talking about."

Heather giggles at the thought, and I join her. She raises her hands in surrender. "I'm just noticing his grooming habits. You don't have to get all feral. I'm not after your man."

My man. Not my man. Not really. I steer the conversation back to more neutral ground.

Pierre hears us giggling and turns. He raises his hand in a wave. I wave back. He points to the barista as if to tell me he's waiting for his order. I smile back and nod.

"Okay. You two are cute," Heather says.

"We're not. Anyway, I think he uses a trimmer with a

stubble guard." I may have looked it up the first night in the hotel. Out of curiosity.

"Well, you're going to be living with him. Find out if you're right."

"What do you mean? You think I should just somehow make my way into his bathroom and check?"

"That's exactly what I mean. Women need to know. It's your civic duty. Come to think of it, men need to know. The future of our race may depend on this knowledge. Men need his secrets. That man has what all men should have—that innate appeal. And it's up to you to find out the behind-the-scenes intel."

"Well, when you put it that way ..." I pause for effect. "No. Absolutely not. I'm not snooping around Pierre's bathroom."

"You're no fun."

"And I'm also not supposed to tell you the marriage is a farce. I actually signed an NDA. But Pierre knows I'm going to tell you. I insisted you had to know. We can't tell anyone else. His friend in France knows, and his publicist and agent know. Other than that, it's you and no one else."

"What about Mom and Dad?"

I twist my lips and look at Heather from under my raised eyebrow. "You're kidding, right?"

"Right. Mom couldn't keep a lid on this if she wanted to. She can't even guard a family secret recipe."

"Exactly."

"So what are you going to tell our parents?"

"That I fell in love and it took me by surprise, but when you know, you know."

And right at that moment, as that sentence is coming out of my mouth, Pierre approaches the couch, drink in hand, his eyebrow raised and a smirky smile on his gorgeous face. I feel the blush creep up my neck and take over my cheeks. There's not a mocha in the world big enough to hide my reaction.

"Well, then. You'll have to tell them how you swept me off my feet as well," he says in that delicious French accent of his. His eyes don't leave mine when he says, "Tell them how I couldn't help myself. I simply had to propose to you. You were it for me."

Then he turns, and flashes a smile at Heather. "I think we have met, but in case you have forgotten me since I came in the other day, I'm Pierre. Your sister's fiancé."

15

PIERRE

When you are attracted to people,
it's because of the details.
Their kindness. Their eyes.
The fact that they can get you to laugh
when you need it the most.
~ Jodi Picoult, Sing You Home

There are few things in the world more beautiful than a woman with a blush on her cheeks. I tried to relieve Tasha of her embarrassment to the best of my ability. I'm quite sure Rene would have done a far better job of it.

"May I join you?" I ask.

"You better," Heather says. "I've got to get to know the man who has my sister saying yes to a shotgun marriage."

"Shotgun?"

Tasha shakes her head lightly. "It's an old term for forcing a man to marry a woman when ... well, it came from marriages that happened quickly for possibly compromising reasons." She looks at Heather. "No one is forcing anyone."

"I assure you, I am not forcing your sister. As a matter of fact, I tried to give her an out last night."

"Last night?"

Me and my big bouche. "Oui. I called her to tell her it is too much to ask."

"Well, at least you realize that."

"Heather," Tasha scolds.

"No. No. It is good. Your sister should be cautious on your behalf."

Heather gives Tasha a look I know all too well. She reminds me of my older sister. Then she turns her attention back to me.

"So, Pierre. You may be all ..." She waves her hand from my head to my toes, indicating what, I don't know. "But my sister is the most important person in my life next to my son, whom I think you've met before."

"The boy who is here in the afternoons or weekends?"

"Yes, Nate."

"He is charming. Delightful. Bright too."

"He is. But that's not what we're talking about right now. My sister is my heart. Do you understand me? We are very close. Not all sisters are. Some compete. Some don't get along. But Tasha is my best friend. If you mess with her, you mess with me."

"Oh my gosh!" Tasha says from her corner of the couch. "Pierre, I'm so sorry."

"No. No. I appreciate this. I'm sure my oldest sister would give you the same talk. It is good. You have a sister who loves you. She is only looking out for you."

I turn to Heather. "Tasha has been very kind to me

already. I am a man who spends most of his time alone, writing and reading. She has been the first real friend I've made in the states. I'm grateful to her. I would never hurt her intentionally."

"Good. I'm glad we understand one another." Heather nods her head succinctly. "Now, would you like an apple crisp muffin?"

"I'd love one, thank you."

Heather stands and walks behind the counter into the kitchen.

Tasha looks at me, barely meeting my eyes. "I really am sorry about her. I had no idea she was going to go all pit bull on you."

"I already told you, I appreciate it. She's being a good sister. And I won't hurt you. I will do my best to make this whole situation beneficial to you. Aside from being a grump in the morning and ignoring you, that is."

"Don't forget being a neat freak."

"Oh, yes. That too."

We both laugh.

"Did you have business in town?" she asks.

I didn't. I only came because I knew she would be here. For some reason that I can't discern, I wanted to see her. And now I have.

"Just a craving for coffee—this coffee."

"It's the best. I miss it when I'm in Asheville. I keep trying to tell the local shop to get Cataloochee coffee. They haven't listened to me yet."

"Well, when we are married, you can have this coffee every day if you like."

"Look at you," she says with a teasing glint in her eye. "Pampering your wife."

I laugh hard. "Trust me, no one will ever accuse me of being a good boyfriend or husband. But I will try to be good to you."

"I find that hard to believe—not unbelievable that you will try. I'm sure you will. I can't believe you wouldn't be known as a good boyfriend or husband."

If only she knew. But I will let her imagine I am better than I am. I'm not a bad man, I'm just incapable of the kind of romance I write so easily in books. On paper, matters of the heart are easy. In life, not so much.

Heather returns with a warm muffin. It is good—sweeter than the food I usually choose to eat, but quite delicious with all the spices of fall in each bite. Heather seems to grow less suspicious of me as we sit and talk over the next hour. I answer her questions about my life in France. She shares some funny stories about Nate, and tells me about her position managing the coffee shop.

Tasha sits back, sipping her coffee and nibbling her muffin. She closes her eyes at times, savoring the bites she takes. My eyes drift to her, watching her enjoy what she is eating. I can't help but think of how Rene described her. Yes. She is captivating—a masterpiece, he called her. But she is so much more. He hasn't met her, hasn't seen her kindness in action, watched her laugh, seen her blush. And, maybe he won't ever, if I have anything to say about it. The last thing I need is for my fake bride to fall for my very real best friend.

We finish our drinks and muffins. Heather tells us she needs to pick Nate up from school.

"Would you like to see my home?" I ask Tasha. "I thought you would like to know where I live and get an idea of how our situation would work."

Heather coughs loudly. "Well, that's my cue to go get my son. Come join us for dinner, Teeter."

"Teeter?" I ask.

"You never heard that," Tasha says, giving her sister a warning glance.

"I called her Teeter Totter when we were little. I don't know why I started it, but it stuck. Now our whole family calls her that nickname."

"Only my family," Tasha says, an imploring expression on her face.

"Won't I be your family when we are married?"

"Not that kind of family."

"Okay," I say. But I wink, restraining myself from using this nickname for now.

"So, come for dinner, okay?" Heather says to Tasha.

"Yeah. I'll come after I see Pierre's house."

"I'd invite you, Pierre, but I need some time alone with my sister after the bomb you two just dropped on me."

"I completely understand. I'll take what you call a rain check."

Tasha hugs her sister goodbye while I stand behind them, appreciating their bond. Then Heather surprises me by turning to me and wrapping me in a hug as well.

"Be good to her," she whispers into my shoulder.

"I will," I whisper back.

As absurd as this situation is, there is one thing I know for certain. I will protect Tasha. I will be good to her, even if that doesn't come naturally to me.

Tasha drives behind me away from the downtown section of Harvest Hollow, and then up through the neighborhoods near town, out past the lake, and up the hill toward my street. I turn, passing the first few properties.

When I veer onto my driveway and see her pull in behind me, a strange thought occurs to me. *I want Tasha to see my home.* I've never wanted anyone to see this house, let alone visit it. Not only do I want Tasha to see my home, but to like it and to feel comfortable here. I don't question myself.

I get out of my car and Tasha joins me as I walk toward the front door.

"This is lovely," she says as we step up to the porch. "A real log house."

"I like it."

"Well, that's good, since it's your house."

I chuckle. Then I open the door and wave my hand for her to pass me by. She steps in and the now-familiar scent of her shampoo surrounds me for a moment.

"This is the living room, obviously. And that's the kitchen and dining room. It's all in one space here."

She looks around, taking in the fireplace, and then looking out the windows that showcase the back deck.

"Oh! Look at your view! You have the woods right there. Do you just sit out on your back porch in the morning, drinking your coffee and dreaming up scenes for your books? You must!"

"Sometimes I do."

I smile watching her as she moves toward the windows, taking everything in with the enthusiasm of a child.

"You're going to really see the colors change in the next few weeks. You can already see a few leaves starting to turn. It's going to be so beautiful. You even have red maple and mountain ash. Those are two of my favorite local trees."

"I'm looking forward to it. Our trees also turn colors in Avignon. Along the river, and through town. I am sorry to miss it, but glad I will see these trees instead."

Tasha looks around some more and I watch her expression as she moves from place to place through the great room. She runs her hand along the bar counter dividing the kitchen space from the rest of the living area. Then she walks to the bookcase and examines the titles, tracing her fingers along some of the spines, and even reading certain titles out loud. I give her time to explore the books. They are the ones I chose to have shipped here—my companions from home.

She pauses at a thicker novel and reads, "Orgueil et Préjugés?"

"Oui, Pride and Prejudice. No self-respecting romance author would consider his library complete without it."

Tasha smiles. "You're just full of surprises."

When she seems satisfied with her perusal, I say, "Let me show you the bedrooms on this floor."

She follows me through the doorway to the hall where there are two bedrooms. One I have set up as my office, but there is also a pull-out couch in there.

"Tidy," she says with a wink when we step into that room.

"It's my only virtue, and even it may be a flaw."

"I wouldn't say it's your *only* virtue." Her tone is light and teasing.

"Here, let me show you your room."

I walk past her and open the door to the guest room. I've kept it shut since no one stays here. I had thought Rene would come on holiday and join me for a few weeks at some point. I never imagined I'd be showing a near-stranger this room so that she could occupy it while she pretends to be my wife.

"There's the bed."

"Ah. Is that what that is? I had been wondering."

"Well, now you know."

"And what is this?" she asks, walking to the dresser.

"I've never quite figured it out."

"I see."

"Do you like it? The room?"

"I do. It's perfect, really."

"There's a bathroom. Here."

I step into the hallway and Tasha follows me. I open the door and step back, allowing her to see for herself. The bathroom is a nice size with a tub that has jets and a rain shower head. There are two sinks and a vanity for getting ready.

"Fancy," she says as she walks out.

"My bedroom and bathroom are upstairs. The whole upper part of the home has been built as a master suite. If you want to see it ..."

"No. That's okay."

"Good. Okay. Well. That's the house."

"It's nice."

We stand in the hallway, staring at one another. I take in her features. Rene is getting to me, and I will scold him for it when we next talk. I didn't think of Tasha's beauty before he brought it up. Of course I noticed her, but mostly it was her embarrassment when she dropped her books, or the way her kindness caused her to step in and save me from that fan, or the thoughtful way she included me with her friends that night at the resort. I can't afford to be drawn to her now. I can't acknowledge her as a woman with a heart as beautiful as her face—not when we are about to be married. Attraction to her would muddy the waters. We can only be friends. Besides, I don't have anything more to offer, even if I weren't in this predicament.

Suddenly, my home feels small and I don't know what to do with my hands. I shove them into my pockets.

My wife.

What am I thinking?

"Pierre," Tasha says, walking away from me, toward the living room.

"Yes?" I follow her, breathing out a sigh as I go.

She sits on the couch, making herself seem more at home than I feel.

"Have a seat."

"Okay."

She studies me, her face relaxed. "It's going to be okay. You know that, right?"

I nod, even though I don't know how it will be.

"We might feel awkward sometimes. Who wouldn't? I mean, we're two acquaintances getting married." She shakes her head, but a soft smile is on her lips. "But it will be okay."

"I should be reassuring you, not the other way around."

"You don't need to. Once I decided to say yes, I settled on it. We're giving up a year of our lives, well, two years actually. You need my help. I can continue to do my work from Harvest Hollow. I'll be closer to Nate and Heather. You'll be able to complete your tour. We'll be housemates. We might even become friends."

"I'd like to think we already are," I tell her.

"Yes. I think you're right. We are friends."

And that's what we'll stay—friends.

16

TASHA

Sometimes, the best way to help someone
is just to be near them.
~Veronica Roth

I 'm reading *Love's Tender Kiss*, curled up on my sofa, making notes to myself as I go. It's no Amelie De Pierre novel, but it's not half-bad. We'll be recording in less than two weeks, so I need to have a feel for the characters, the plot, where to pause, and how to use my voice in different places in the story.

My phone rings. I recognize the number by now. *Stuart.* Ever since Pierre told Stuart I agreed to the marriage, I've been receiving calls from him several times a day.

"Hello, Stuart."

"Don't sound so excited, Tasha."

"I'll try to tone it down. What can I do for you?"

"Well, we've got a plan. You and Pierre need to get to know one another. You know, like what one another's favorite colors are, quirks, hobbies, interests, backstory. All the things real fiancés know about one another."

I can't help my sigh. It's not that I don't want to know more about Pierre. I love hearing about his life—about him. It's just all this third-party meddling by Stuart and Bob is already getting old. It will die down once we're married. At least Pierre assures me it will.

"What do you want us to do?"

"We've booked you a stay at the Old Edwards Inn in Highlands."

"Ooooh. That's a posh location."

"Oh. Wait. No. Sorry. Here it is. I'm staying at Old Edwards. You and Pierre are going to be at the Mountain Peak Treehouse Resort."

"Treehouse Resort?"

"Yeah. You stay in a treehouse. Like Tarzan and Jane." Stuart chuckles. Then he actually makes an "oooh oooh, ahh ahh," noise like he's a gorilla, and then he chuckles some more.

"Why aren't you staying in a treehouse?"

"Well, for one thing, you and Pierre need your privacy. And, for another, I'm not really the treehouse type. I'm more of the, *Sir, your hot stone massage is at two p.m.* type. Besides, my absence will give you all the privacy you need to really get to know one another. Consider this a crash course in dating your fiancé. Privacy will enhance you getting to know one another. And you'll have three whole days alone together, well, except for the photographer we've hired."

"Photographer?"

"You know what they say. If you didn't photograph it, it didn't happen. We've got one of the top event photographers in North Carolina meeting you at River's Peak to capture the moments."

"Capture the moments."

"Are you just going to echo everything I say?"

"Maybe. What exactly does capturing the moments entail?"

"You know. You and Pierre go about your weekend, and Godiva will follow you around to capture the moments: the two of you holding hands, looking in one another's eyes, kissing, going down the forest zipline strapped to one another. You know, the basics. All those convincing images will tell the world Pierre has found the love of his life in you. Your photos on Marbella set the stage. These will solidify the story."

Kissing? He did say kissing. I'm supposed to kiss Pierre? For a photo shoot that will convince the world of our ... love for one another?

"Did you say the photographer's name is Godiva?"

"Yes. Godiva Duckworth. Like the chocolate, and the waterfowl. She's British, but she lives in North Carolina now."

This keeps getting weirder.

"Have you heard of her?"

"I think I'd remember if I had."

"Right?! What a name. Anyway, she's won awards. You'll love her. She's going to really capture the moments."

"So you said."

"Okay. Well. As fun as this has been, I've gotta jet. Lots to arrange. Planning a wedding is exhausting."

"Planning a wedding?"

"Your wedding, Tasha. To Pierre. Catch up. I'll be sending you an email asking for a list of guests. We want to keep it small. You get ten—twenty people max. We need this whole sham to look legit. Of course I already have Pierre's people coming from France."

"His people?"

My head is swimming. I don't generally drink, but I think I could use something stiff right now, straight from the bottle. Or maybe one of those deprivation tanks where they submerge you underwater so you see and hear nothing at all. Are those even safe?

"Mom, Dad, sisters, his friend ... what's his name? Oh, yes. Rene."

Stuart's words snap me out of my fantasies about escaping into an underwater oblivion.

"Does Pierre know about you contacting his family?"

"It's all in the email. I cc'd both of you. I'm a busy man, Tasha. Pierre's not my only client. He's big. That's why I'm going to all these lengths. But I have a life."

Like I don't?

"Well, bonjour, Tasha."

I say, "Bonjour," before I even think better of it.

"Look at you, getting all French for your man."

I open my mouth to answer, but Stuart has already hung up.

THE ROAD to the Mountain Peak Treehouse Resort resembles the Road to Hana. We wind to the left and then quickly swerve to the right. And then left again. Right, left, right, left, tightly hugging the edge of the road as cars and trucks occasionally pass us coming down from further up the mountain.

I keep imagining us careening off the edge of this very steep cliff.

"This is beautiful, no?"

"So ... beautiful," I answer, gripping the safety handle over my door til the skin on my knuckles is taught and white.

I involuntarily lean toward Pierre as he takes yet another turn. My stomach takes a turn with the car.

"Um. Pierre. I don't feel too good."

"What? What's wrong?"

"I think I'm going to ..."

Pierre glances at me quickly and then looks back at the road, but he caught my meaning.

"Oh. Oh! Hold on, Tasha. I will pull over!"

Where? Where will he pull over? The steep road only has two narrow lanes with barely a shoulder. At some points there have even been traffic cones set out around a cluster of rocks which rolled off the shale cliff sides onto the road. I wondered when we went around the obstruction why the road workers didn't just sweep the debris and rubble out of the way. But I can't dwell on that thought for long. I'm fighting another big wave of nausea—and losing.

By some grace, Pierre finds a turnout. It only allows us to pull halfway off the main lane, but it's better than parking right on the road. I unbuckle and jump out faster than I imagined possible in my condition. I rush to the side of the road and look down. So far down. The hill descends away beneath me down, down, down, taking my breath away at a time when I need to breathe. I bend at the waist and feel Pierre's gentle touch, scooping my hair off my face and neck and holding it back while I lose the entire contents of my stomach.

Goodbye, McGriddle, hash browns, and caramel latte.

A sheen of sweat dots my brow, but I feel infinitely better until Pierre speaks, reminding me he just had a front row seat to me upchucking my breakfast.

"Are you okay?" Pierre asks in a soft, caring voice.

"Better."

Except I want to dive off the side of this cliff into the myriad of trees below us and never look Pierre in the eyes again. Thank goodness this isn't an actual romantic getaway. Still. I just puked in front of Amelie De Pierre, my favorite romance author—internationally acclaimed novelist. I lost my cookies while Pierre, the guy I think the world of, held my hair out of my face.

"Sit. Here. The cool air will do you good. I will be right back."

I do as I'm told, not at all too eager to get back in the car, only to drive up that winding road some more. Pierre returns carrying a cloth.

"Here. Put this on your forehead and neck."

I take the cloth from him. He's drenched it in cold water. I place the cool fabric on my neck. Then I discreetly dab at my lips and around my mouth. I fold that side in and place the cloth on my forehead. Pierre squats and then sits down, right in the dirt next to me. He's wearing jeans today, but they look like they've never been worn. His tennis shoes seem equally preserved. He's got a brown T-Shirt on, sporting the logo of Cataloochee Coffee. Nice touch. If he were trying to win my heart, he'd be doing a great job. Not that he'd have to work that hard.

"Thank you," I say weakly, forcing myself to look him in the eyes.

"That road was treacherous. Do you get carsick easily?"

"Not usually. Though, now that I think of it, I was the one

the family had to pull over for on more than one car trip. I also should mention I'm afraid of heights."

"Heights? Like this mountain?"

"I love being in the mountains. Looking down cliffs, not so much."

"Staying in treehouses?"

"We'll see. I think I'd rather be on the ground."

"I'll keep you safe," Pierre teases with a wink.

"When a branch gives way and the whole structure crashes down, what will you do?"

"You really do have a fear of heights."

"Yep."

"Oh no. Stuart also arranged for us to go ziplining."

"So he told me."

"You don't have to go."

"I do. I don't want my fear to define my life. I'll just push through it."

"I think we're connected to the same contraption when we go down the line."

"Please, don't say the word contraption. It makes me think of small screws that could pop loose, sending us plummeting to our death after we flail through the sky, helpless to save ourselves."

Pierre lets out a full laugh. He even places his hand on his abs as he bends in laughter. He gasps for breath. "Wow. That's really ... I don't know what to say. I'm pretty sure that won't be our destiny. But at least Godiva will capture our last moments and display them on social media."

At that, I laugh. "Yes. She'll be capturing all the moments."

Pierre and I smile at one another, the familiar comfort we seem to have always had settling between us.

"Do you feel ready to brave the rest of the road? My GPS tells me we only have fifteen more minutes left of the drive. We'll keep the windows cracked and I'll drive so carefully. Maybe you can sip some cool water?"

"We have to go the rest of the way eventually. I think I can make it."

Pierre stands in one fluid motion. He extends me his hand and I take it. When he pulls me up, I'm tugged forward, landing chest to chest with him. His hands grasp my upper arms, keeping us both from toppling. Pierre runs his hands down my arms in a gesture of comfort. My skin tingles, and then I make the mistake of looking into his eyes. He's got a concerned look on his face, his brows drawn up, his eyes searching mine.

"Are you okay?"

"I am. Sorry about that."

"No problem." He rubs his hands up and down my arms again, giving me a tender look, and then he turns to head back to the car. I grip the wet cloth in my hand a little more tightly, and then I run it across my forehead and cheeks, which suddenly feel overheated despite the cool fall mountain air.

We make it the rest of the drive without any other embarrassing gastric disturbances on my part. Yay, me! Pierre made the fifteen minutes stretch out to twenty-five. I think a vision-impaired, nearly-napping senior citizen would have driven faster than he did. I appreciate his overcautious approach, though.

We park at a building that has, *Welcome Guests*, burnt into a pine plank over the door. Inside, everything is decorated in what I'd call a Mountain Lumberjack Plaid theme. The curtains are red, white, black and green plaid. The sofa cushions match, as do the throw pillows on the side chairs. A few wooden carved statues of black bears and racoons are set in various spots around the room. Even the lamps are made of bear statues. A big elk head is mounted over the stone fireplace.

"Welcome. Welcome," an older man says as he walks out from another room and takes his place behind the knotty pine reception desk.

I look behind him and notice a "collectible" print of mallard ducks flying over a lake. I say it's a collectible only because of how worn and aged it is.

"Hello," Pierre says. "We're checking in for the weekend. Touissant."

"Ah, yes. Mister and Missus Too-sant. Welcome. We've got you in the Lofty Pine."

He hands Pierre a map of the property and draws a line to show where our treehouse is.

Lofty. That's just a play on words for a treehouse dwelling. Right? We won't really be *lofty.* I hope.

"Here's your key. We've got all the amenities up in your treehouse. Full kitchenette. King bed. Jet tub."

The man looks at me, then back at Pierre, then he wags his eyebrows.

I look around and make eye contact with one of the bears and then the elk.

Pierre thanks the man and slips his hand behind my back, coaxing me to head out the door. I don't mind his touch as much as I probably should. It feels anchoring and comfortable. I actually could get used to Pierre's hand on my back. I wouldn't complain a bit if he wanted to spend the weekend with his hand right there. I mean, of course he'd have to release me to brush his teeth, shower, and get ready for bed. But otherwise, if he wants to touch the small of my back in that protective, warm way, I'm so here for it.

But I shouldn't be. Pierre and I are in such a weird situation. I'm his fiancé, but we're barely becoming friends. And he's focused on his tour and writing. It's best if I guard myself against the thoughts that seem to be begging me to indulge in the sweetness of his touch. He doesn't need a fangirl. He needs a friend.

"Have a great stay. If y'all need anything at all, just come down here. We're open at six and we shut the office at around six or seven in the evening depending on how we're feelin'. But we're over in High Hemlock if you need us. Sometimes the TV's up a little loud. That's my wife's doin' I'm afraid. She loves her shows and she's a bit deaf in one ear. But if you keep knockin', we'll come out eventually."

Pierre thanks the man again.

In the car, Pierre looks over at me. "Let's go find our tree-house, Jane."

"What?"

"Me Tarzan. You Jane." He makes the declaration in his beautiful French accent. It sounds so refined and un-Tarzan-like. Unless Tarzan were sitting in a cafe wearing way more than a loin cloth. And now my mind is picturing Pierre in a loincloth, sitting at a bistro table, sipping cappuccino, eating a pastry. Bad mind. Bad, bad mind.

I involuntarily let loose with a giggle.

"What's funny? My joke?"

"Yes. Your joke. It was very funny. Way funnier than when Stuart said it to me over the phone."

"He said it to me too. I had to look it up. I know of Mowgli in Jungle Book. I never had seen Tarzan."

"Well, let's hope we don't have to swing on a vine to get into our treehouse."

"I think there are bridges," Pierre assures me.

"Not much of an improvement," I mumble.

We park in a spot under a wood carport with the name of our treehouse over our designated space. To our left is a staircase going up, up, up to the bridge leading off to a platform that has other bridges extending to treehouses. These are not houses attached to structures on the ground. The houses are supported by thick beams and trees. Lofty is an accurate description. My stomach threatens to flip again. I take a steadying breath.

17

PIERRE

Sometimes what you're looking for comes
when you're not looking at all.

~ Unknown

I look over at Tasha. She's scanning the bridges and treetops like a man standing at the edge of an airplane doorway doing his first parachute jump. I remember my twenty-first birthday when Rene talked me into taking a jump with him. He's always been the one pushing me outside my comfort zone, but jumping alongside me to make sure I am never alone in my risks.

"Are you okay? I can tell Stuart we want to stay somewhere else. We can leave. Stuart's not the boss of me."

Tasha chuckles. "You've picked up some of the funniest American phrases."

"I heard Nate say that to your sister the other day. He put his hands on his hips and said, 'You're not the boss of me,' and Heather told him, 'I actually am the boss of you. Now get busy.' I had to hold in my laughter, and I finally covered it with a cough when I couldn't help myself." I pause, smiling at Tasha. "Your sister's a great mom."

"She is."

I want to ask where Nate's dad is, but I'll wait. Right now, I have to get Tasha comfortable enough to go up those stairs and across two bridges so we can settle into our treehouse.

"How about I walk up and across the bridges, carrying our bags. You can watch me. If I fall to my death, you don't have to follow me. If I survive, I'll come back and I'll walk with you."

"That sounds like a deal."

Her voice is so serious. I had expected her to laugh.

I'm about to grab our luggage when I'm cut short by a British woman shouting our names. "Pierre? Tasha?"

I turn to see a woman I assume is our photographer. She's carrying a professional looking camera.

"Hello! I'm Godiva! I thought I saw you pull in. Let's get a shot of you two arriving. Tasha, can you just sit back in the passenger seat, and Pierre, you open her door. Then, Tasha, you step out and look Pierre in the eyes. Feel free to linger there, staring at him, considering your fiancé and the fact that you have a romantic weekend ahead together."

I wonder if Godiva knows we aren't really engaged. I'm guessing Stuart hired her to take our photos under the pretense that we are actually engaged and in love.

Tasha's already walking toward the car, so I dutifully follow her. She shuts her door. I open it, extending my hand for her to grasp while she stands. Her palm slides against mine, soft and warm. Tasha ends up right in front of me— like she was on the roadside, only we aren't pressed together like we were then. Her brown eyes capture mine and I smile at her. She smiles back up at me. Her face looks believable, like she's a woman engaged to the man she'd want to marry. The thought plays with my mind a little. I push it away like a fly buzzing around soup.

"Good. Good. Now hold her other hand, Pierre, while you shut the door behind her."

I do as I'm told, enfolding Tasha's other hand in mine. She looks at me nervously, so I smile a comforting smile at her. I bend in and whisper into her ear. "After this, I'm feeding you lunch. We just have to make it across two bridges."

She giggles nervously and a slight blush colors her cheeks.

"Oh, this is pure gold!" Godiva nearly shouts. "Kiss her cheek, Pierre."

Kiss her cheek? Well, we kiss cheeks all the time in France. It's just another cheek. Just another kiss on another cheek. Why does it feel like more?

I lean in and place a soft kiss on Tasha's cheek. Her eyelashes flutter closed and then she pops them back open and lets out a nervous laugh.

"Don't worry, Cher," I tell her in a soft voice meant for her only. "I kiss my grand-mère the same way."

"I bet."

I look over at Godiva. "That's enough for now. Tasha and I need to get settled."

"I got plenty of good shots. Thanks, you two. I'll ring you in a bit. We'll want some sunset photos and then we'll talk about tomorrow. I'm staying in Whispering Walnut."

She points in the direction that must lead to her treehouse.

I nod to Godiva, thanking her briefly, and then I grab the two bags I had pulled out of the trunk. I carry them up the stairs, along the first bridge. At the platform, I take the bridge labeled, "Lofty Pine."

I let myself into our room, and then I return for Tasha.

"I survived. That means you can come with me."

Tasha takes a deep breath. I grab the cooler and bag of food I brought with us out of the trunk. There's a restaurant on site, but it's not open nightly. The website actually said, "We serve dinner most nights." That sounded a bit sketchy. The nearest town is a half-hour down the mountain. I'm not eager to traverse that road again, especially not for restaurant food. Besides, I love to cook, so I planned our menu for the weekend.

"Would you rather go ahead of me, or behind?"

"I think behind you."

I nod, shifting the cooler slightly and making my way to the stairs. I can't grab the hand rails since my arms are full, but I won't ask Tasha to carry anything. She needs to be able to hold on with both hands. I hear her behind me as I step up the stairs. We make it to the first bridge. It's sturdy, solid, and permanent.

"I'm looking at your back to keep from thinking about how high up we are."

"It's a good strategy. Are you hungry?"

"I think I could eat."

"Good. I have lunch planned once we are in the room."

The next bridge is a bit more tricky. It's a swinging bridge.

"Let me cross first so my movements don't jostle you."

"Okay," Tasha answers in a shaky voice.

I rush across the bridge, set the cooler down in front of our door and turn. "Keep your eyes on my face and walk. Pretend you are just walking down the street."

"A wobbly street."

I smile. She's looking at me, focused and intense. Her face exudes a beautiful vulnerability.

Rene. He's sneaking in again. This seed he planted cannot grow. I'm not in a position to feel anything but gratitude and friendship for Tasha—especially since she is being paid to be my bride. But I am a man, and I'm not immune to a beautiful woman, especially one who has extended me such unexpected kindness. When the sunlight filters through the trees showing off the auburn highlights in Tasha's hair, contrasted with the delicate porcelain skin of her face, I notice. I kissed that cheek. I can't forget the way her skin felt against my lips or the way her eyelids fluttered shut in response to our connection.

"Good. Good. You're nearly here."

Tasha takes the last three steps quickly, and the bridge sways violently. But, she's on the porch in front of our door, landing merely a few feet away from me. I want to grab her into a hug to celebrate her making it. Instead, I put the key in the lock and push the door open.

Tasha takes a look around. There's one king bed and a smaller sofa. A kitchenette is off to the side of the room with a block island that doubles as an eating space. In the middle of the far wall, there's a doorway leading to the bathroom. Otherwise, the sitting area and sleeping area are all right here in the same room.

"It's ... cozy." Tasha looks back at the bed and then at me.

I've written romance novels long enough to know about the one-bed trope. A man and woman who are not in love end up with one bed between the two of them. Oh, la vache! What are they to do? Well, what can they do? They must share the one bed, of course. Will one of them take the floor?

No, of course not. What if they are nearly strangers? No. It matters not. They will sleep in this bed together, as if they are forced against their wills. And before you know it, they are wrapped around one another like a twisted bread knot. Voilá, marriage is around the corner. Absurde.

"I will take the couch," I tell Tasha.

"Oh. You don't have to. It's kind of small."

"I'm fine. I like small couches. So much. They are my favorite. I feel like a child, curled into bed." *A child? Really?*

"You like to sleep on small couches?"

"Oui. Even at home, sometimes I just leave my bed and go to the living room so I can sleep on the small couch."

"You do this here? In America?"

"Yes. I wake and choose the small couch. It is a thing with me."

She giggles. "We call it a love seat."

"I understand why. This name fits the couch. I love it—the love seat."

She laughs. "You're full of it, Pierre."

"I'm not. Why do you question my love of the love seat? I love this love seat. Watch how I love it."

I walk to the couch, size it up, lie down, and tuck my legs a little so my whole body will fit on it. Is it comfortable? Not even a little.

"I'm in love," I assure her.

"You are ridiculous."

"Ridiculously in love. Now. Let me feed you, my bride to be."

Tasha turns away, but I see the blush again. I hope I am not making her nervous.

"Can I help you fix anything?" she asks.

"Oui. Yes. The salad. I have cake salé to go with it."

"Cake for lunch? Now you're speaking my language."

"No. It is called cake salé. It is like a savory or salty cake. I made the ham, spinach and cheese type. It's like a bread with chunks of these savory ingredients in the dough. Sometimes we add olives. We occasionally eat this dish for lunch, or as an appetizer, or even breakfast."

"It sounds delicious."

"It is. And that is our word too. Délicieuse."

She copies my pronunciation exactly.

"Do you speak French?"

"I don't. Remember, I studied a little to impress you? But then I dropped my books at the signing and ruined my first impression."

"Not ruined, Cher. I knew you were in shock. You expected Amelie, and you got me instead."

"I'm glad I did. I mean, glad you are her."

Our eyes connect and I hold her gaze for a beat. Then I pull the cooler over to the refrigerator and start unloading food. I tell Tasha what to do with the items in the grocery bag, and she puts everything away in the cabinets over the sink.

After Tasha freshens up, we wash our hands and fall into a comfortable rhythm preparing lunch together. It's been a while since I've cooked with anyone. Usually it is Rene or my family, or our friend group. It feels oddly familiar to be cooking with Tasha. She prepares the vegetables and we take our plates with the savory bread and salad to the table on the balcony outside our room.

When we first step out, I can tell Tasha is too distracted to notice the height of our treehouse. I try to divert her attention with conversation.

"So, do you have the questions Stuart sent us?"

"I do. On my phone."

"Let's start quizzing one another over lunch."

Tasha takes a seat, and then she looks down, gasping when she notices the height.

"Would you rather eat on the couch?"

"On your love seat?"

I chuckle. "Oui. My love seat."

"No. I want to eat out here. It's beautiful."

Tasha examines the beams supporting the porch. Her eyes scan the structure, lingering on places where one piece of wood meets another.

"Okay. Let's get to the questions." Tasha pulls out her phone and asks the first question. "Tell one another about your childhoods—where you grew up, who your friends were, your experiences at school, your family members. The more details, the better."

I'm surprised I know many of these details about Tasha already.

"I feel like I know about your family and where you grew up," Tasha says.

"I was thinking the same thing."

I fill her in a little more about my years in school. She does the same. Then we tackle some of the other questions between bites of our lunch. The cake salé is delicious. Tasha agrees. Her salad is also quite good. We relax over the meal, sharing stories with one another, laughing and even growing more serious at times.

We're about to take our dishes back into the kitchen to wash them when my phone buzzes with a text.

Stuart: I saw the photos Godiva took of your arrival. Good stuff. You'll need to do more than peck Tasha on the cheek. After all, this is your fiancé. You two will kiss at the wedding. We can't have that looking like your first kiss. You need to look practiced.

I feel myself gulp as if swallowing a whole chestnut.

"Everything okay?" Tasha asks.

"Yes. It's just Stuart."

"What did he want?"

I hand my phone over to Tasha.

She reads the text and looks up at me. "Oh. Well. Yeah. He has a point."

"We don't have to make a big deal of it. We've both kissed someone before. Right?"

"Right. Yeah. I've kissed plenty of people. Well, not plenty. It's not like I'm running around kissing people. Of course, I'm not. I've had boyfriends. I'm sure you had girl-friends."

"I have had a few, yes."

"So we'll kiss. No biggie."

"Tasha?" I reach over across the table and set my hand on top of hers.

She looks down at our hands and then back up at me.

"I told you this might be too much to ask. You can still back out."

"No. No. I don't want to back out. I mean, we can kiss. We're adults. We'll just kiss. Right?"

She sounds nervous. Which is making me unexpectedly nervous.

We can kiss, of course. I already kissed her cheek. I feel that kiss on my lips now as I think of it. Her soft skin, the way her eyes fluttered shut. I'm not sure she's even aware she responded that way. Maybe I'm imagining her response.

She was probably only closing her eyes to avoid feeling embarrassed or having to face me during an intimate moment.

"It's okay," Tasha says. "We'll kiss. It will be simple."

"Should we kiss for the first time in front of Godiva?"

"Um. No. I don't think so. I get the feeling she thinks we're actually in love and engaged. Knowing Stuart, he didn't want to tell anyone about our farce if it wasn't necessary."

"I thought the same thing," I say. "I think she believes we're just your average engaged couple."

"Well, we'll have to act like one, then."

I nod.

We clear our dishes in silence, the looming pressure of our first kiss lingering between us like a living entity.

I soap the dishes and rinse them. Tasha takes them from me and dries them, returning them to their spots in the cupboards. She's about to hang her towel on the oven door. I know I need to catch her off guard. It's better if we don't overthink this. We can course correct later, refine our technique. I'm a man. I can make a move and kiss her. Rene would have kissed her a week ago—and not only for show. That thought spurs me forward. I don't want Rene kissing Tasha—ever.

This kiss is for the good of our performance later. Like Stuart said, we need to be convincing. At least, this is what I'm telling myself as I move across the kitchen toward Tasha.

She places the towel on the bar and turns, letting out a soft gasp when she sees how close I am. I smile at her without saying anything. Words complicate moments like this one. Instead, I lift my hand, brushing her hair away from her cheek. She averts her eyes, a coy expression on her face. She is inviting me, despite her sudden shyness. I understand her nerves. But I bypass them, taking her invitation, mustering enough courage for the both of us.

I allow my fingers to trail along her cheek. She closes her eyes again, leaning her face into my palm. This is our moment. I need to make a move. I study her for just a fraction of a second, the softness of her face, the way her hair falls in waves down to her shoulders, the fullness of her bottom lip.

Her tongue darts out briefly. She is ready. Whether I am or not, I need to kiss her. This feels like more than an assignment, but I don't have time to consider all the warring thoughts in my head. I cup Tasha's cheek, tilting her head so that I can angle my mouth over hers. When our lips touch, all thoughts vanish from my mind. Tasha's hands lift, holding my head. Her fingers rake through my hair as she returns my kiss. I lean in, wrapping my arms around her back and tugging her toward me. Our kiss takes me by surprise. I thought we would kiss quickly and separate. Instead, I'm pulled toward her, aware of the way our mouths fit, the feel of Tasha's fingertips grazing the skin on my neck, my senses filled with her all-too-familiar scent.

Tasha snaps away suddenly. She's ruffled and slightly dazed.

"Okay! Good. That's good. I think we kissed and it was … great." She's looking at me and then away from me. Her eyes return to mine. "Good. Right? It was a good kiss. For the purpose of convincing people. I think we're convincing. Don't you?"

I'm tongue-tied. Unable to find a single word to say. I simply stand in the kitchen looking at Tasha, a woman I've come to appreciate and care for over the past few weeks. But this? Our kiss was a complete blindside. I feel like I've been run over by a truck. A truck I want to chase down and ask to run over me again and again. That kiss awakened something in me I thought was dead, or at least dormant. And I can not allow myself to want more.

"I agree. It was good. Sufficient. Well done."

Sufficient? Well done? Well done?

What is this? A performance evaluation?

"Yes. Well done," Tasha agrees.

"Okay. Good. Well. Would you like to take a walk?"

"Yes. A walk would be great."

Tasha darts toward the front door as if the cabin is on fire. I linger behind, my hand going to my mouth like it has a mind of its own. I brush my fingertips over my lips in the same way a high school girl would after her date dropped her off.

I'm in a daze.

That kiss was my undoing.

I need to call Rene.

18

TASHA

For it was not into my ear you whispered,
but into my heart.
It was not my lips you kissed, but my soul.
~Judy Garland

Oh me, oh my. I didn't see that kiss coming. I might not have seen it, but I felt it from the top of my head to the tips of my toes. I could brush off the way my body reacted to Pierre, pretending the lingering kiss and the way I responded to him was solely because I got caught up in the moment. That might be plausible.

After all, it was a really, really good kiss. No. Really. We're talking, definitely the best kiss of my life—sensual, passionate, but somehow tender and filled with something I don't even want to think about in case it is completely one-sided.

But it wasn't just the kiss. It was Pierre. I wasn't sleep walking. I was fully aware of who was kissing me every nanosecond of that encounter—from the approach he made toward me to the moment I finally pulled away as if I had been electrocuted. I may as well have experienced a shock from a wall socket. I still feel the buzzing across my skin, even though our kiss ended several minutes ago.

I didn't hold back, either. I leaned into his hand, allowing myself to revel in Pierre's caress to my cheek, the careful way he tilted my head, the gentle brush of his lips, the way we both succumbed to something I don't think either of us saw coming. I took it all like a greedy beggar, unsure when I'll ever kiss Pierre again. Of course, I should have kept things chaste and simple. But I can't bring myself to fully regret indulging in that kiss. Not when my lips are still humming with recollection.

I don't even notice the jiggling of the bridge under my feet or the nearly twenty yards of air between me and the solid ground below. I'm too focused on putting distance between me and Pierre and that kitchenette where I allowed all my walls to crumble.

What does he think?

Sufficient. Well Done.

That's what he thinks.

This is a formality to him. A job. An extension of his career.

Does he like me? I know he does. We have a friendship. Or we did, before we kissed one another like there's no tomorrow. He kissed me too. And why? Maybe that's just how he kisses. He is a romance author, after all. Maybe he doesn't know how to modify his passion. I'm one to talk. I didn't restrain anything either, not until the realization hit me like a bag of bricks. We have to live together for a year. After that kiss, how will I look at his mouth again without thinking of what it's capable of?

I should have known better. I've felt drawn to Pierre from the first moment I saw him. How can I carry off being his fake wife if I'm developing very real feelings?

"Tasha?" Pierre's breathy voice snaps me out of my spiraling thoughts.

He runs across the first bridge and then onto this second one.

"Wait, please."

I don't answer him. I'd like to bolt like a frightened deer off into the woods, away from the hunter in hot pursuit of me. But I have to face Pierre sooner or later, so I may as well get it over with.

I really need to call Heather.

Pierre's breath comes in short bursts when he reaches me at the top of the staircase. His eyes are full of compassion and concern—not exactly the look a woman wants from a man she just kissed senseless.

"Are you alright?" he asks, point blank.

"Dandy."

Dandy? Really?

"Dandy?"

"It means fine. I'm fine."

Pierre eyes me suspiciously. He's not buying what I'm selling.

"How are you?" I ask.

Maybe flipping the tables will shift the spotlight off my awkward reaction to that earth-shattering kiss.

"I'm wonderful. Never better."

"Hmmm. Really?"

"Oh yes. Really. I'm here in these beautiful woods. I had a delicious lunch followed by a kiss with my fiancée. Now we're about to take a hike to explore the surroundings. I couldn't be better."

There's a brightness to his voice that's either a cover for something or a tease. I can't tell if he's being sincere, or if, like me, he's trying to compensate for the massive awkwardness left in the wake of our kiss. I'll just roll with it.

"Great. Me too. I'm fantastic. Très fantastique. The mountains in fall, a good lunch, a great kiss. C'est bon."

Pierre chuckles. Okay, maybe I went a little overboard in my enthusiastic presentation of how okay I am.

"Your French. It ... well ... m'excite."

"What is mix-eet?"

"No. M'excite. And it is something I will not translate for you."

"Why not?"

Pierre looks around, neatly evading my request, "Ah. There's the trailhead I saw on the map. Let's go."

And just like that, we've swept the smoochy elephant with all her gigantic feelings under the rug. Pierre bounds down the stairs like a teenager. I follow him like a senior citizen scheduled for a hip replacement, clinging to the railings on both sides of me. When my feet hit the ground, I feel like bending down and kissing the earth. Kissing. All I think about now is kissing.

"You made it." Pierre looks at me proudly.

His sensitivity to my phobia doesn't help shore up my resolve to make light of the kiss or my emotions.

"I made it! Let's go exploring."

The trail leads away from the center of the tree house property where there's a fire pit surrounded by Adirondack chairs. We walk along the dirt path, lined with tall trees, all in various shades of yellow, orange, red and magenta. Fall hits a little earlier at the higher altitudes, making me all the more eager for the trees on Pierre's property to show their fall display.

We walk in silence for a while, and then we talk about a bunch of meaningless subjects. We finally pull up Stuart's questions and dive into the section he labeled "Favorites." We toggle back and forth sharing favorite colors, foods, times of year, memories, people, music. By the time we're back from our nearly two hour hike, my legs are pleasantly burning and the kiss we shared after lunch is long forgotten.

Okay. It's so *not* long forgotten, but we've put it to bed. To rest. To something that's not a bed but means it's not on our minds. You get it. And now, all I picture is Pierre curled up like a giant boy in a man's clothing on the loveseat, saying how comfortable he is and how he can't wait to sleep on that tiny piece of furniture. If I can find a way to switch with him so he gets the bed, I will.

I yawn as we approach the stairs to the bridges leading back to our rooms.

"Tired?" Pierre asks.

"A little."

"Why don't you nap while I get some writing in, and then we can meet Godiva for our photo shoot at sunset. We can eat dinner when we return, unless you like to eat earlier."

"I'm fine with a later dinner."

"That's very European of you." He winks. Then he adds, "You might as well rest while you can."

For some reason, traversing the bridges doesn't freak me out as much as it did when we got here. I'm still keeping my eyes up and ahead of me, but I'm not shaking with nerves. When we get to our cabin, I curl up on the bed and Pierre grabs his laptop, heading onto the porch where we had lunch so he can write.

I wake to him smoothing a hair off my face, his voice a murmur. It's a surprisingly intimate gesture that would catch me more off guard if I weren't half-groggy from a deep afternoon sleep.

"Hmmm?" I say, rolling over and stretching.

"We should get ready for our photo session. You were sleeping so peacefully, I hated to wake you."

"I'm fine. I feel good. Give me a minute and I'll be ready."

I stand, making my way to the bathroom. While I attempt to tame the unruly waves of my hair, I shout out, "Did you get much writing done?"

"Some. It is a slow burn, this one. These characters are killing me."

"Now you know how we feel as your readers. You torture us!"

His laughter filters through the bathroom and I have a fleeting glimpse of what the next year of my life might be like. Though Pierre warned me he would be ignoring me regularly, so far he's been nothing but attentive—a complete gentleman. Only when he kisses does his self-control slip just the slightest and a far more uncontained side of himself breaks free. I look at myself in the mirror, noticing the flush on my cheeks. I really have to stop dwelling on that kiss.

Stuart sends a text to Pierre telling us where to meet Godiva. We end up driving and taking another hike to an area called Graveyard Fields where the fall foliage is going crazy. There are two waterfall hikes. We take the lower one, which is a shorter walk in. Godiva has us pose in front of the waterfall, arms around one another's waists, then turning to face one another, looking into each other's eyes.

"Let's have a waterfall kiss!" she shouts from her spot about fifteen feet away from us.

"Under the waterfall?" I ask, turning my gaze from Pierre's eyes to Godiva.

"No. Though, that would be spectacular. Are you game?"

Pierre and I both say, "No!" simultaneously, which causes us both to laugh. I'm barely aware of the click of Godiva's camera while I look at Pierre, his features even more beautiful under the effect of his amusement.

"Okay, you two. Let's have a kiss for the camera."

To my surprise, Pierre wags his eyebrows at me, lightening the mood and dispelling my nervousness.

"Are you ready for a kiss?" he asks softly, his hand already traveling up to my hairline and dragging down along the side of my face.

I fight the urge to lean into his touch like I did in the kitchen, even though I feel like a kitten ready to purr.

I nod, and Pierre leans in, smiling as he approaches my lips. I close my eyes, letting him direct the kiss. He cups the back of my head, drawing my mouth nearer to his. Then I feel him, his lips on mine, softly moving in a slow, tender caress. I melt into him, responding like I did in the kitchen, only feeling more comfortable this time. The familiar sensations of being in his arms and having him kiss me make me forget where we are and who is watching us. I lift my arms, looping them behind his neck. Pierre lets out a low sound from the back of his throat—it's somewhere between a growl and a hum. I grip his head and his shoulder, running my fingers through his hair.

What are we doing?

I realize the kiss has escalated again, and then I think of

Godiva. I can't just snap away, looking flustered. What would I do if this were real—if we were actually engaged?

I pull back slowly, allowing Pierre to drop his forehead to mine. We're both breathing a little heavier than we were before the kiss. His eyes search mine, and a smirk unfurls across his lips. Those lips. I smile back at him.

"C'était un baiser assez incroyable ma chérie."

"Hmmm? Translation please?"

"No. I cannot translate that for you."

Our heads remain resting close together. Pierre's hands rest behind my back in a way that feels very much like a boyfriend would hold his girlfriend. My thoughts and feelings tumble together like rocks at the bottom of the waterfall.

"Please, translate."

"Okay. But you must not make fun of me."

"Never."

He laughs lightly and gives me a side-eye. "I think you do like to tease me sometimes."

"True. But I won't make fun of this. You have my word."

"It means, that was some kiss."

I feel the blush creep up my cheeks. So, he notices we kiss well together. Him saying it was quite a kiss doesn't mean the kiss signifies something to him. The kiss isn't anything but a part of our façade. This charade we are executing on his behalf requires some kissing. I'm not complaining, regardless of how dangerous our kisses are to my heart.

Godiva breaks through our private moment, "These are amazing!"

She holds up her camera as she approaches us, showing the screen on the back of her camera to us while she scrolls through image after image of Pierre and me, looking at one another, touching one another, and kissing. He's right. That was some kiss. Seeing it from a third-person vantage point makes it all the more real.

We kissed.

And in two weeks I'm going to marry Pierre Toussaint.

19

TASHA

It is a risk to love.
What if it doesn't work out?
Ah. But what if it does?
~ Peter McWilliams

The next morning, I wake to Pierre, sleep-rumpled and sitting with his laptop and a cup of coffee.

"There is coffee. Would you like me to get you a cup?"

"I can get my own," I say, stretching my arms and rolling over onto my back.

I'm in no hurry to get out of bed. The view is amazing anyway. Not only the view out our treehouse windows, but the view inside. Pierre is a sight to behold, as always. But seeing this less polished, more private side to him feels more intimate than our kisses. It's like I'm getting a glimpse at a part of his life no one else sees.

"I know you can get your own cup, Cher. I am asking if you would give me the pleasure of getting it for you."

"Oh. Well. When you put it that way ..."

"Do you like it sweet and creamy? Or are you truly a French woman in an American's body, liking it black and strong?"

"It should taste like ice cream."

He snickers lightly. "C'est un crime."

"Cream?"

"No. Not cream." He changes his pronunciation to the American version of the word. "Crime. It's a crime."

Pierre shakes his head, the smile on his face causing dimples to appear under his unshaved stubble. Those dimples are a crime. They are definitely making me want to do illegal things right now.

"A crime? Adding cream and sugar to coffee?"

"Oui. But I will indulge you, my little criminal."

Oh my gosh. He needs to stop. How am I supposed to remain neutral when a man who looks like that—sounds like that—makes teasing jokes and brings me cups of coffee in bed? I won't. I'll cave. And if I cave, I'll ruin everything. We are in this as friends—partners in a business deal to ensure he can stay in the states to fulfill his obligations to his readers and his publisher. It may be a marriage on paper, and we may have to kiss, but this is merely a contract. He said so himself.

Pierre walks to me with a mug of heaven in his hands. I sit up, fluffing the pillow behind my back, take the mug and sip, closing my eyes to savor the layers of sweet, nutty flavors. The lightly bitter bite at the end causes me to open my eyes. Pierre is standing at the edge of the bed, studying me.

"Hey, creeper," I tease.

He clears his throat. "Is the coffee the way you like it?"

"Perfection."

"Good. I aim for perfection." He winks.

And, unlike most people, he seems to hit that mark too.

"I aim for imperfection," I say with a wink of my own. "It's a far more achievable goal. I hit it nearly every time."

I swear I hear him mutter, "I disagree," but his back is turned and his voice is muffled.

"Are you ready for this ziplining?" he asks.

"No. I will never be ready. But I will do it anyway."

"I admire that about you."

"Thanks."

His soft smile confirms his words. I'm not one to let fear dictate my life. If I were, I wouldn't do what I do for a living —the income is too unpredictable and fluctuating. But I love recording books and I love supporting authors, so I risk some less profitable seasons simply so I can pursue my passion. And, when I move back to Harvest Hollow, I'll pick up some shifts at Cataloochee to supplement my income. Heather can use the help, and it will be good to see her more often.

Pierre and I dress and meet Godiva at the zipline. A tall tower with a platform at the top has been built around a tree so that the tree grows right up through the middle. Pierre and I are the only people here, with the exception of the guy working the zipline. He greets us at the bottom of the platform, introducing himself as Animal. Yes. Like the crazy Muppet character.

"Animal?" I repeat.

"Yeah. I'm a beast on the zipline and rock climbing. Plus, I play drums. Some friends gave me the nickname in junior high and it just stuck."

I'm dying to ask his real name, but I get distracted when he holds up our harnesses, explaining how to put them on and handing me one to slip into. This series of nylon straps will be the only thing coming between me and my plummet to death.

"Are either of you hesitant to do this?"

Pierre doesn't out me, but he does give me a look of compassion that nearly threatens to buckle my knees on the spot. I'll need the harness today just to hold me together, apparently.

"I'm afraid of heights."

"Wow. Okay. Well, that's admirable. You do know this involves heights?" Animal says with a wink.

Pierre steps closer to me. Our shoulders brush.

"It is why we chose the tandem option."

"Good call, man. She's gonna be basically on your lap the whole ride."

I will *what*? Be in his *lap*? By some odd miracle, fear of heights just became my second greatest concern. How am I supposed to ride on Pierre's lap without clinging to him like a spider monkey? I will surely suffocate him by the time we reach the end of the ride. Not only that, I will die of sheer mortification.

"Good," Pierre says, appearing completely unfazed by this information.

We go through the rest of the orientation, putting on our helmets and gloves while Animal spouts out terms like, "passive arrester system" and "capture block," and I feel a little lightheaded. Pierre must notice. He places his palm on my lower back and I can't help but lean into his support.

He bends toward me and whispers, "I've got you, Cher. You just sit on my lap and enjoy the view."

Oh, sweet baskets of lavender from Provence. How will I make it through a year of his thoughtfulness without climbing this man like a tree? My self-control has an expiration. I don't know what it will be, but I'm afraid at some point I'm going to pop like a champagne cork and all this pent up longing will explode between us. Like all explosions, this one has danger written all over it. I need help. And distance. And someone to pour cold water over my head.

After we've been instructed as to what to expect and how to partially control the speed of our ride, we are strapped into two seats. I'm not exactly sitting directly in Pierre's lap as I had imagined. I'm in my own seat, but it's positioned right in front of his. I have handles to hold onto over my head. One has a brake for slowing or even stopping. Thank goodness for small mercies. I feel Pierre behind me, his legs touching mine as if I'm in his lap.

"Are you good, Cher?" Pierre shouts up to me.

"I'm good!" I say.

Good is relative. I'm doing an out-of-body, completely pretending I'm not here, about to dangle over the treetops, suspended by a few metal clips that look better suited to hold a chip bag closed than to keep me from falling. I take a deep breath.

I feel Pierre's warm hand on my shoulder. He gives a firm, comforting squeeze.

"I'm proud of you, Tasha."

As much as I secretly love him calling me Cher, hearing my name come across his lips with such affection and tenderness does something to my belly. A swarm of baby butterflies awakens from their cocoons and starts practicing flight right behind my belly button and across my abdomen.

They're bumping into one another and flitting around, giving me the warmest tingles.

"Put your hands on your handles and hold on," I shout back, like a dufus.

Pierre chuckles. "I might ride down with my arms out like an airplane."

"Don't you dare!"

He chuckles again. "Maybe I should keep my hands here?"

He places his hands back on my shoulders, calming and exciting me simultaneously. I don't tell him to remove them. He doesn't release me.

Animal checks if we're ready. I'm quiet, leaning into Pierre and his grip on my shoulders.

Animal says, "Okay. I'm going to push you on three." Then he counts, "One, Two, Three!" and I feel the momentum of him propelling us forward as the platform slips away behind me and the rush of air meets my legs. I clench my eyes closed, pretending I'm just sitting in Pierre's lap somewhere closer to the surface of the earth.

"Are you closing your eyes?" he shouts from behind me, giving my shoulders a little squeeze.

"No!"

"Open your eyes, Cher. You are safe, and it is beautiful. Don't miss this."

I peek one eye open. We're moving quickly over the canopy of forest below us, reds, yellows, and oranges mixing with the ebbing green of the leaves. It is beautiful. I take a big gulp of air and lean back.

"That's more like it," Pierre shouts.

He never releases me the whole way down. I nearly forget that I've got the Go-Pro camera on my helmet, capturing the whole ride. My body tingles from the heady combination of fear, adrenaline, and Pierre's assuring touch.

At the end of our ride, a platform looms in the distance. I instinctively raise my legs, tipping myself further back toward Pierre as we approach the landing spot. Pierre tells me to hit the hand brake to slow us, so I do. When we land I let out a whoop—mostly of relief, but also thrill and the huge sense of accomplishment that comes with overcoming a fear.

A guide unclips us and helps us out of the seats. I turn and before I know what's happening, Pierre grips my waist, holds me up and spins me. My arms fly around his neck to stabilize myself. He draws me into a hug and I let him. When I glance across the platform, Godiva is there, chronicling every second of our spontaneous celebration.

Pierre turns and sees Godiva, and then, perhaps to give her more material, he brushes his mouth across my lips in a tender kiss. When he pulls back, his face is flushed. His eyes meet mine.

"You did it, Cher! I'm proud of you! That was amazing!"

"It was," I admit. "Completely amazing."

The kiss. Oh, and the ziplining. That too.

20

PIERRE

Men always want to be a woman's first love ...
What [we women] like is to be a man's last romance.
~ Oscar Wilde

Tasha is at my home this afternoon. She called, telling me she was stopping by to bring me some apple strudel her mother made. I love that she announced her plan rather than asking if she could come. I want her to be free to come here. It will be her home in eight days. She may as well start to feel comfortable coming and going.

When she arrived, I insisted she stay and eat strudel with me. I generally don't eat between meals, but when she showed up, fidgeting on my doorstep, I had the inexplicable urge to invite her in—to find some way to make her stay for a little while.

Her answer to my invitation was, "If you insist," but her actions contradicted the feigned protest in her words. She walked right past me toward the kitchen. I smiled, watching her from behind, allowing myself to indulge in a moment of fantasy where she was my real girlfriend and I was allowed to approach her when she visited my home. I would come up behind her and wrap my arms around her, setting the strudel on the counter and drawing her in for a kiss. Maybe we would eat strudel eventually, after I had thoroughly kissed her.

I am aware that I am what Americans call a "hot mess express." I've heard this phrase in the coffee shop, and Stuart has used it a few times.

My kisses with Tasha on our weekend getaway had the effect Prince Phillip had on Sleeping Beauty. Only, I am the one who has been asleep. It had been ages since I kissed a woman. I have been channeling all those feelings and thoughts into my novels, avoiding romance in real life like a plague with the potential to annihilate me. When Tasha kissed me, going soft in my arms, responding with her lips to mine, something dormant awoke, and now that part of me is like a petulant toddler at nap time, refusing to return to a resting state.

I am awake to her—alert to every movement, every nuance of her beauty, every vicissitude of her emotions and thoughts. It is a problem. A hot mess express of a problem.

And last night we had to sit holding hands on a loveseat in her parents' home while we told them about our engagement before joining them for dinner. Even holding Tasha's hand made me hyper aware of her. She leaned into me at times, squeezed my hand at others, absently allowed her fingers to brush over my knuckles. It all elicited feelings I had sworn I'd never entertain again. But I never counted on meeting a woman like Tasha.

The Piersens were surprisingly calm and encouraging. I really thought they would balk at our timeline. Our engagement has been rushed. If I were her parents, I would be more than skeptical. But Tasha's mother said she thought prolonged engagements just caused people unnecessary stress. She commended us for knowing our minds and cutting through the fluff. Her dad even said something about how they never thought they'd see the day when Tasha would settle down and find a man she could tolerate.

I teased Tasha all the way back to her home after we ate dinner with her parents. *Can you tolerate me?*

She teased me right back. *Barely. Especially when you poke fun at me about my parents.*

I assured her I already loved her family and was grateful they were so accepting of me. We both skirted the fact that we're lying to them. The longer I spend time with Tasha, the less our arrangement feels like a farce.

Would I marry her in less than a week? No. I would not. But I would ask her to dinner, take her home, and kiss her goodnight. And I'd do that again and again until, maybe one day we both became convinced we could make a future together.

Now, with her sitting across from me in my kitchen, fork poised over her plate of strudel, I have to do something. This is my moment.

"I almost forgot." I stand and move from the kitchen to the living room, opening a drawer and removing the box Heather helped me acquire this week. "I have something for you."

"For me?" Tasha's face scrunches up until her eyes land on the box. "Oh!"

I smile at her and fall to one knee.

"You don't have to get down on one knee. This is a formality."

"I still want to do this right."

"Okay." The blush I've come to crave creeps across Tasha's cheeks, but she doesn't avert her eyes from mine.

"Tasha, my friend. You have become the one person I can count on to be honest with me here in the states. You support me without any hidden motives. You have made me laugh more than I thought I could. Will you do me the honor of being my wife—until Stuart do us part?"

She laughs at my last words, giving me the reaction I had hoped for. This could be awkward. I want to make it less so.

Tasha surprises me, reaching out and cupping my face in her hands. "Pierre, I have loved you for years—well, of course I thought you were a woman then." She pauses to wink, her hands remaining on my face. "Now that I know you, there is nothing more I would want to do than to say yes to being your wife on paper—until Stuart do us part."

She smiles at me and it takes a Herculean effort on my end not to lean in and kiss her rosy lips. I imagine brushing my mouth across those blushing cheeks, moving my lips to hers, and holding her to myself while she nestles against me and I run my hands down her wavy hair to express everything bottled up in my heart.

Instead, I distract myself by clasping her hand, opening the box and pulling out the ring to place on her finger. The blue aquamarine stone is flanked by two smaller diamonds. It's not a traditional engagement ring, but it suits Tasha. Once the ring is on her finger, Tasha pulls her hand out of mine, holds it away from herself, turning her wrist back and forth so the light catches on the gems.

"It's beautiful. How? How did you know to pick this one?"

"I may have had some help from a local coffee shop manager who doubles as a ring consultant."

"Heather helped you? You asked her?"

"Of course. A man is a fool if he doesn't solicit the help of his future sister-in-law."

"Sister-in-law." The look on Tasha's face is nearly as awestruck as it was when she first saw the ring. "This makes it all feel so official."

"It's official. We're going to enter a contract together."

"A contract. That's good. I like that. I promise to be the best fake wife you've ever had."

She giggles and I smile at her, loving the levity between us.

"I have no doubt. And I promise to be the best fake husband you've ever had." I gaze at Tasha—the way she's looking back at me with such kindness and the unexpected intimacy we've come to share. My heart swells. "Wait. You haven't had another fake husband before me, have you?"

"Definitely not! I don't think I could take going through this twice."

I shake away the urge to offer her another out. She's made it clear she's determined to go through with this. I'm equally determined to make marrying me something she never regrets.

"Let's finish our strudel," I suggest.

I settle into my chair. Tasha holds her ring up again and admires it. The gesture fills me with pride. I didn't realize the nerves I had anticipating whether she would like it or not.

We're back to eating in a matter of moments, as if I hadn't

just put a ring on her finger. But I see it there, perched on her hand, a reminder of the week to come and the hurdles ahead—facing our interviews at Immigration, getting my green card approved, and the year of living together. Not to mention what it will mean when she and I decide to part ways. My heart clenches at the thought. If I feel that way now, how will I feel after having her under my roof for a whole year?

"Stuart says your family will be here from France in three days," Tasha says after she swallows her last bite of strudel, licking her lips and blotting them with her napkin.

"I saw his email. That is how I found out he had approached my family to invite them to the wedding. Of course, I called them immediately after reading his email. I wish Stuart would have let me tell my family before he called them. It was beyond awkward having to explain why I didn't tell them first—why they had to hear my big news through my publicist. They know I am a private person, but even for me, this level of secrecy and indirect communication is uncharacteristic."

"How do you feel about them making such a big trip for our fake wedding?"

"I don't have a choice. Of course they will come. They want to support me. And to meet you. Besides, I truly miss them. It will be good to see them, even under these circumstances."

"What do they say about us? They've never even met me, and here you are planning to marry this strange American woman. They must have some reaction."

"My sisters are saying I am crazy. They are quite sure I have lost my mind. My father has not said a thing. And Rene knows the truth. My mother says you must be something special to have won my heart. She said she knew if I ever fell again I would fall fast and it would last forever. "

"Again? Have you fallen in love before?"

"Eh. Maybe it was something. I don't know now if I would say it was truly love. I think I have never really been in love. But I have absolutely had my heart broken."

"Me too. I'm pretty sure I've never been in love. I don't think I have, anyway. But I have had my heart broken." Tasha pauses, looking out toward the woods. "Isn't it a rite of passage as a human being? We all have our hearts broken at one point or another."

"I guess you are right. Except Rene. He is the heart-breaker, not the one whose heart is broken."

"Maybe Rene has not yet met his match. One day he may meet a woman he wishes he could win and she may not return his affection. Or maybe he will be broken in another way. I think it is something we all endure one way or another, but maybe that's just the romantic in me."

"Ah. Are you a romantic?"

"Guilty. Heather teases me relentlessly."

"She is not a romantic?"

"No. She had her heart broken in a way that is hard to come back from. I hope she does someday—come back from it. I have told her many times that the key is not to let rejection and grief define you."

I hum, considering Tasha's wise words.

"I think I did let rejection define me. I never wanted to go through that kind of agony and humiliation again, so I promised myself I would never get so serious with a woman in the future."

"That's pretty absolute."

"Rene would tell you how he tried to talk me out of my staunch resolve. He can be very persuasive."

"I'm looking forward to meeting him."

"No. You aren't."

Tasha smiles, chuckling softly at me as she stands to take her plate to my sink to rinse it.

"I will get the dishes. Leave it."

She disregards me and turns on the faucet, running my scrub brush across the plate and then opening the dishwasher to place it in the rack.

"You must remember, Rene is a charmer," I warn Tasha as she returns to the table to take my plate.

I hold onto it like a stubborn child. She cocks an eyebrow at me, not releasing the grip she has on the dish. I relent and allow her to clear it for me. I'm so used to living alone and doing all these things for myself. I realize she will be here in a little over a week, eating meals with me, rinsing dishes, and loading the dishwasher daily. I don't hate the idea as much as I would expect to.

"Are you afraid Rene will steal your wife from you?" Tasha teases.

"No. Don't be ridiculous. Frenchmen are mostly one-women men, even the flirts like Rene. He will respect that you are mine."

I brush some crumbs off the table into my cupped hand and walk the debris to the trash can, avoiding Tasha's searching expression. It feels odd to say she is mine, since she isn't. If we were dating, I would be exclusive with her by now. But that is irrelevant. Tasha doesn't need to know how much she has come to mean to me. The kisses we shared last week confused things enough.

She is doing me a favor as a friend. I remind myself of this fact daily.

Do I think Rene would steal her? He wouldn't. But he will overshadow me. How can he not? He's charismatic, engaging, outgoing, and has a way with women. He's the antithesis of me. He could easily win Tasha's heart—and she'd have to turn him down because she's strapped to me.

TASHA ACCOMPANIES me to the Asheville Airport a few days after our visit over strudel. I haven't seen her since that afternoon. I'm busy writing and she is preparing to record a book. I pick her up at her apartment on the way to the airport.

The terminal building is small, with the baggage claim at the end. My family has traveled sixteen hours with two stops to get here from the Provence region of France. I feel a little guilty, but assuage myself with thoughts of how they will enjoy themselves visiting America. It will be good for us to see one another after a few months' separation.

"Are you nervous?" I ask.

Tasha wipes her hands down her jeans.

"Yes. I'm nervous. Isn't that crazy? I have the same nerves I would have if we were really engaged and I was meeting your parents for the first time. Only, top that off with the fact that I'm lying to total strangers." She giggles nervously. "Seriously, though. I want to make a good first impression."

"I hope you understand that my family might seem a little stand-offish. It's only the French way. We are like the coconut. Our shells are hard, but at the center, we're soft."

"What are Americans like?" she asks. "I mean, what do you think?"

"We say you are like the nectarine. Soft on the outside. Easy to get to know. You hug strangers. Tell everyone your secrets. But inside, there is a shell around the softest parts."

"That's relatively accurate."

"So, don't take my family personally. If you encounter the coconut shell, it's not you, it's them."

"Spoken like a true romance author."

My eyes are drawn away from Tasha to the sliding doors where Rene is leading my family out through the double doors of the baggage claim. I jump from my seat and rush to greet them. I approach my mother first with *la bise* to both cheeks, left, then right. Then I greet my sisters and father in the same way, leaving Rene for last. He pulls me into an embrace and claps me on the back while we kiss one another's cheeks. And when he releases me, he sees Tasha. She is standing back from us a little, allowing me room to greet my family.

"Ah, Tasha. Bonjour," Rene says, wagging his brows just the slightest and giving her a smolder that rivals the cartoon character in that American children's movie, *Tangled*. Then he pulls out the French. "C'est un plaisir de rencontrer une si belle femme."

He reaches for Tasha's hand and kisses it, his lips landing unbearably close to the ring I gave her this week. Give me a break.

Tasha blushes just the slightest, smiling at Rene, and then she looks at him and says, "Merci beaucoup," in her seemingly well-practiced French accent.

I step toward her, instinctively putting my arm around her waist. She looks up at me with a smile.

"Do you understand what he said?" I ask, purposely

placing my mouth close to her ear so my words are only between us.

"Oui, Pierre. J'étudie le Français." She smiles at me, her words soft and quiet.

"You are studying French?"

She blushes and leans into me as if to hide herself even though our conversation is private and no one but the two of us and possibly Rene heard our exchange.

"A little. I'm just starting to study," she says. "I think Rene said it was nice to meet such a beautiful woman."

"That is exactly what he said." I glance at Rene who is sizing me up and then looking at the spot where my arm encircles Tasha's waist.

I introduce Tasha to each of my relatives. She says, "Bonjour" to each person. I didn't even coach her in that cultural expectation. I am very impressed. I also realize I should have given her more pointers. But maybe it is not necessary since she is doing fine so far.

Each member of my family says, "Nice to meet you," in English. I'm grateful they are making an effort.

I reach over to help my mom lift her suitcase. This is the moment my so-called best friend chooses to give Tasha the customary French greeting. Two kisses. One to each cheek. In some regions of our country they give four kisses, and with the way Rene is uncustomarily lingering on each of Tasha's cheeks, I can be glad we are from Provence–Alpes–Côte d'Azur. Tasha leans in further than is usual while greeting Rene. Her lips land nearer to his ear. He and I exchange a look when she pulls back.

He mouths, "Elle est adorable," to me.

I roll my eyes and then give him a stern look. Tasha is adorable, but he doesn't need to notice or mention it.

Then, for good measure, I mouth back, "Elle est ma femme."

Rene chuckles. I've never staked a claim with him before. It feels barbaric. But Tasha is my future wife. In five days, we will be married. Rene needs to keep that firmly in mind.

21

PIERRE

French people do like good fighting,
they like it better than anything.
~ Gertrude Stein

"The weather here is so much like Avignon. I feel we are almost at home." My father is making coffee in my French press.

When I woke up this morning, my father was already in my kitchen. It's six hours earlier here than in France, so essentially it's noon to him. He's up and functioning without any sign of jet lag, even after a full sixteen-plus hours of travel yesterday.

I bought a bag of local beans this week from Cataloochee and ground them fresh this morning. We'll see what my father thinks.

"What is for breakfast?" my mother asks, coming into the

kitchen fully dressed in a soft sweater and pressed pants. "Do you have a pâtisserie in this town?"

"We have a coffee shop. They carry baked goods baked fresh at Harvest Hollow Bakery and a few specialties made by a woman who works in the bookshop. There's apple muffins and apple tarts, apple dumplings, apple cider whoopie pies, apple coffee cake, apple cider donuts, apple strudel ..."

"What is it with all the apples?" my sister, Colette asks, coming in behind Mom.

My kitchen is starting to feel very crowded, even though there is plenty of room for us here.

"North Carolina is the seventh highest in apple production of all the states in America. I learned that this month—from more than one local. It's practically all the people in Harvest Hollow talk about once fall hits: apple season, apples, and the Harvest Festival. We can go this weekend, after the wedding. I thought we'd go to the festival and the Farmers Market this weekend."

"Aren't you taking a honeymoon?" our middle sister and chief troublemaker, Marguerite, asks as she saunters into the kitchen, also fully dressed in fall clothes that look far more dressy than the usual attire I've gotten used to seeing around Harvest Hollow.

"We are postponing a honeymoon. I've got writing deadlines and my tour, and Tasha is preparing to record a book. We went away two weekends ago anyway."

"But, the honeymoon ..." my mother says with an imploring look on her face.

My father sidles up to her, embracing her and dipping her as if they are on the dance floor. Then he kisses her in a way that should make all three of us blush, only we've grown up with their affectionate displays, so we are immune.

"The honeymoon never ends, coco," my father says to my mother in a very romantic tone.

"Okay!" Marguerite says. "Enough. Children are present."

Maybe we aren't completely immune.

"You should be following your brother's footsteps," Mamie says to Marguerite. "Getting married. Having grand-babies for me."

"I am not having grand-babies," I amend. "At least not right away. I'm touring America."

"Then you and your beloved will relocate to Avignon, no?" Rene joins the conversation, entering from upstairs where he slept on my pullout couch in the master suite.

His face is full of mischief. But my family seems not to notice.

"Ah, bonjour, Rene," my father says.

Each family member greets Rene. Rene greets them back. It's a thing with us. Bonjour all day.

"Will you return to Avignon?" my mother asks, picking up where Rene left off.

"We aren't sure. The subject is one we will take up later."

"You might not come home?" Marguerite sounds appalled. "You can't be serious. You won't live in America. You are a Frenchman."

"I will decide that with my wife."

The room should go silent, only we love an argument. So it goes on, everyone chiming in with their opinion as to what I should do and why. I am so grateful Tasha is not here. This might overwhelm her.

The debate continues. I could walk out of the room and it might go unnoticed amidst the friendly tension and exchange of ideas. They're talking about my future, but now the conversation has taken on a life of its own and I am all but irrelevant. The discussion grows more heated with each person stating their reasoning and then another contradicting or agreeing. Even when they feel or think the same thing as someone else in the room, their comments sound contradictory. A wave of homesickness washes over me. Few cultures argue and debate like the French. It's our beloved hobby—our national sport. We love deeply, speak passionately, and argue with finesse.

No solution or outcome is achieved after a good twenty minutes of this lively tête à tête.

I suggest, "Does anyone want to drive into town to get pastry with me? My fiancée's sister manages the coffee shop."

A chorus of "Oui," goes up in the kitchen. Everyone is obviously curious to meet Heather. Maybe I should call ahead to warn her. Of course, we will be far more contained in public than we were in my kitchen. Here in my home we are among the closest friends and family. There we will be surrounded by strangers.

We drive into town, my family taking in the scenery as we pass the lake, then wind through the roads leading into town, and finally make our way down Maple, finding parking in front of a building in the historic downtown district of Harvest Hollow.

"Comme c'est pittoresque," my mother declares.

Her tone is even. It's as if she can't help but acknowledge the quaintness of Harvest Hollow, even though she wants me to move home when my year in America is over. I wish I could assure her I will be coming home with my wife. But Tasha and I will separate and then we will divorce. I will return to the life I knew in France, only it will be with a heart full of holes that Tasha has created without intending to. They are the spaces I'm imagining only she can fill.

When did this ambush on my heart take place? I have not been guarding myself well enough. Now I am a man who feels so much. A man who would do anything Tasha wants me to do. A man who cannot stop thinking of her.

When we walk into Cataloochee Mountain Coffee, heads turn. This time of year, tourists are more frequently seen around town, mostly coming here for our world-famous apples, but also for the fall events and the changing color of the trees in the Blue Ridge Mountains.

I'll admit my family and I definitely look out of place in our effortlessly classic, slightly-elegant attire. This region of North Carolina is known for rivers and hiking trails. People dress ready to engage in some outdoor activity. My family looks like they habitually shun dirt in favor of an iron and steamer.

"Pierre!" Heather shouts out from behind the counter toward the back of the store.

"Hello, Heather," I say, leading my family past the watchful eyes of the locals.

After introductions are made all around, Heather offers us some baked goods on the house. I try to insist on paying her, but she refuses.

"Beautiful and generous," Rene quips, loudly enough for Heather to hear.

"Handsome and dangerous," Heather answers. "Don't worry, my sister already warned me about you. Rene, is it?"

My sisters break into full laughter at Rene's expense.

"Oh, Cher, I am not dangerous. She is mistaken. I am a connoisseur of beauty and a man who knows something exquisite when he sees it. I am like a pussy cat."

"Hmmm," Heather hums thoughtfully, a blush rising up her cheeks that reminds me of the same shade Tasha's face turns when she is embarrassed.

My mother steps up to the counter, thanking Heather graciously and then suggesting to me that we take the pastries home where we can enjoy them together for breakfast.

Mon père turns to me, "You should invite your fiancée to join us, no?"

Rene nudges me as we walk out of Cataloochee, "Are American women immune to me?"

He is nearly pouting.

I chuckle. "No. Only these two, I'm afraid. Tasha is committed to me." I don't have to elaborate that her commitment is one of a friend helping another friend in his time of need.

"And, her sister ..." I lower my voice. "Well, I don't have the story, but she has a son and she is single, so I think her shields are up where men are concerned."

"But I do not think your fiancée is immune to you," Rene says with a playful wag of his brows. "And you are most definitely not immune to her."

"What do you mean?"

My family has walked ahead of us. They are eyeing the items in the General Store next to Cataloochee, huddled together in front of a window, waiting for me to unlock my car while Rene and I fall back a little behind them for a private conversation between friends.

"I watched you yesterday. I see how you look at her."

"I don't look at her in any special way."

I hope I don't. I have been working so hard to conceal my burgeoning feelings from Tasha.

"I've known you my whole life," Rene says in a serious tone. "You can't lie to me. If you believed you could, I don't think you would have even told me you are getting married under a pretense. You might be able to fool your family, but you are not going to ever be able to fool me."

I nod my head. Then I glance at my family. They are taking their time, moving along the front of the store, pointing at the displays behind the windows, in no hurry to leave.

"I do feel something for Tasha. You are right. She surprised me. We had to kiss for the photographer. Stuart wants these photos for publicity, to help convince the world of our story—a whirlwind romance that resulted in a speedy engagement and marriage."

"You had to kiss her. Poor you. What a hardship."

I laugh at Rene's teasing. "Not a hardship, believe me. It was the best kiss of my life. And the first kiss I've had in years. It made me ..."

"Desire her?"

"Yes. But more than that. Tasha is remarkable. What woman makes this kind of sacrifice for a man? And she's funny, easy to be with. At first, I thought we merely had a friendship developing. But now that I have kissed her ..."

"You feel more."

I nod.

Rene hums. My family tires of their perusal of the shop. They start to head our way.

"You need rules," Rene says just before Colette is within earshot.

"Rules?"

"Yes. Rules." At a much lower volume, he adds, "Tasha's going through with this pretense as a friend to you. You are catching feelings. That is unfair to her. Rules will help you keep the lines where they need to be."

22

TASHA

Learn the rules like a pro,
so you can break them like an artist.
~ Pablo Picasso

"I have called you two together for an important reason. As you know, your wedding is in less than twenty-four hours. So we have to get down to business."

I look from Pierre to Rene.

Pierre's family is reluctantly exploring Harvest Hollow for the next two hours. Rene told them they needed to give the three of us some privacy. He can be bossy when he wants to be. First, he called me to come to Pierre's, saying it was urgent. Then, when I arrived, he practically pushed Pierre's parents and sisters out the door, telling them to stay gone until the sun starts to set.

We have a girls' night planned with my mom, Heather,

and Pierre's mom and sisters. It's not exactly a bachelorette party, but it's something—something I'm not exactly excited about.

"You sound so serious," I say with a joking tone, trying to lighten the mood.

It's serious enough that Pierre and I are about to commit this felony, though it doesn't feel like it should be illegal to offer him this opportunity. His motives are good. I'm being paid to help him.

"I am serious. You do not know me well yet, Cher. I can be, as you Americans say, flirty. But I am also serious when the occasion calls for it. And we have some business we need to get to."

"Business?" I look at Pierre.

"He wants us to set rules."

"Rules?"

"Oui, Cher," Rene says. "Rules. Guidelines to protect you two for the coming year."

"Oh. Yeah. Okay. That sounds good. We probably should have thought of that ahead of the night before our wedding."

"This is what I am here for. Leave it to me. I've thought of all the rules you will need."

"You have?" Pierre and I ask simultaneously, glancing at one another with smiles as soon as the synchronized words are out of our mouths.

"Look at you two. You need these rules. So, let's get started."

Rene sits back. "Pierre, you have paper, no? And a pen?"

Pierre stands, going to a drawer in his kitchen, grabs out a legal pad and pen and returns to the table with them.

"Okay." Rene taps the pen on the pad of paper. "Rule number one: No kissing unless it is required for publicity."

"Of course," I say.

Pierre's voice nearly tumbles over mine. "Naturally."

"So, we're all agreed?"

"Why would we kiss when we aren't in public?" I ask, trying to keep the note of disappointment out of my voice.

It's not that I thought we'd be sitting around Pierre's home making out at night. It's just, the declaration of this boundary reinforces the reality—Pierre and I are in a contract, a friendship, me helping him. Rene is probably right. We need these rules to be spelled out.

"Exactly, we won't have any reason to kiss in the house. Or even in town, unless it were for publicity, as you say," Pierre says, further reinforcing my awareness of where we stand.

"Great." Rene gives a quick bob of his head, and then writes the rule on the pad of paper in front of him.

His face looks like he's thinking about something. I'd love to know what.

"Rule number two: No catching feelings."

"Catching feelings?" Pierre asks.

"It's an American phrase," Rene explains. "It means you don't start falling in love with one another. This is a contract for the benefit of your business. Tasha, you are being reimbursed. You two are about to enter a business arrangement. Feelings would make things unnecessarily complicated and messy."

"Right," I agree.

Too bad I'm already catching feelings. But Rene is spot on. I need to smoosh my feelings like a bug. They will only ruin my friendship with Pierre and cause problems in the year to come.

"Oui," Pierre says. "No catching feelings."

He and Rene exchange a look. It feels like a private, wordless conversation.

Rene looks at me. "Rule number three: No dating other people while in this fake marriage."

"Duh." I sound like a petulant teenager.

Isn't it obvious we are committing this year exclusively to one another?

"This is obvious," Pierre says.

For some reason, his assertion calms me. Not that I thought he'd be running around dating other women, but hearing him say he won't feels assuring. Maybe Rene's not completely off base with this list of rules.

"Tasha," Rene says, looking straight in my eyes. "I can't promise I'll save myself for you, Cher, but if I am single when you divorce, I'll gladly be your rebound."

I giggle. I can't help myself. Rene is funny.

Pierre glares at his best friend. Rene ignores him.

"Rule number four: No touching unless you are in public."

"No touching at all?" Pierre is incensed.

"Why would you touch her? She is merely an employee."

"Not an employee in the strictest sense of the word."

"You are paying her, no? She is providing a service. This is the definition of an employee."

"What if I accidentally touch her?"

"That is acceptable. Wait. Tasha, is that acceptable?"

"I'll allow it," I say with a small smile toward Pierre.

Rene writes the rule on the pad. I study the list in front of him.

"Rule number five: No nicknames or affectionate pet names."

Like, Cher? I love when Pierre calls me Cher.

"Is that rule really needed?" I ask.

I guess the nickname is partially responsible for drawing me to Pierre, so maybe Rene is right. I would feel less of a magnetic pull if Pierre didn't glance at me with tenderness and call me Cher.

Pierre sends me a playful look. "I think she likes it when I call her Cher."

He noticed? I feel my face heat.

"Besides," Pierre adds. "I don't think I can stop myself from calling her Cher. It's what we say to women. You call her Cher."

"I do. But I am not in a fake marriage with her. I am not putting my heart or hers in jeopardy when I say it."

Putting our hearts in jeopardy? Is Pierre's heart in jeopardy? No. Of course not. Rene is speaking in hypotheticals— being cautious.

"I don't like this rule," Pierre says, crossing his arms over his chest.

"All the more reason you need it. Rules are not for liking, they are for your good."

"Fine," Pierre concedes. "No more Cher."

I feel like screaming. But I sit quietly by while I kiss the word Cher goodbye. Rene is right, the word has played with my heart.

Rene takes a breath, as if we are wearing him out. "Rule number six: You must wear clothing at all times. And you must not leave undergarments in public areas of the home."

My eyes snap to Rene, but he will not meet my gaze.

Pierre spouts off what I think is an expletive in French. And another. "What are you even saying?" He glares at Rene. "Of course we will be dressed. My word."

Rene chuckles. "These things should be spelled out. What if Tasha likes to parade through the home in her ..."

"I don't," I cut in before Rene can finish that thought.

"It's fall. The air is cool. We will be bundling up. This rule will not go on your list," Pierre insists.

"I think it is a good rule. Without it, you have no guideline for dress code in the home. Things could get very out of hand."

"They won't," both Pierre and I say at once.

Then we look at one another, and I can't help but blush.

Rene writes the clothing rule down. He shakes his head and goes on to the next. "Rule number seven: No giving sweet compliments."

"Like what?" Pierre asks, a note of irritation in his voice. Is he regretting asking me to be his fake wife now?

Rene plows on, undeterred. "Like saying she looks beautiful. Or her saying you look handsome. No telling her she smells delicious. No leaning in to sniff her, either."

"Ridiculous," Pierre says, nearly growling.

"Ridiculous rule, or ridiculous to ask you not to smell Tasha? I can smell her from here. She is like a fragrant flower bed, like a fresh day in fall or spring when the air is crisp and you want to stroll along the Rhône, hand in hand with your beautiful, delicate, flower of a woman. So, what is ridiculous?"

"You. You are ridiculous," Pierre says. He's the most unrestrained version of himself I've ever witnessed. I can't say I hate it. He's passionate and a little grouchy. But he seems to be grumpy about being told not to sniff me. I nearly giggle at the thought. Did he want to smell me?

Okay. That is too funny.

I bend my head and study my hands in my lap to cover my smile.

"I am ridiculous?" Rene is the picture of innocence.

Pierre shoots Rene a look. When Pierre's gaze turns to meet mine, his countenance changes. "Tasha. Do you like this rule?"

"I don't know if I like it or dislike it. I don't really know if we need it. It's not like you're running around telling me I'm beautiful or sticking your nose in my hair." I giggle a little, unable to contain my reaction to the thought of Pierre planting his nose in my hair on purpose. "I think you've got this covered without the rule."

"Quel fou," Rene mutters as he grabs the pad and scribbles the rule onto the page. "Être entouré d'une telle beauté et ne jamais dire un mot."

"What did he say?" I ask Pierre.

"He said I'm a fool to be surrounded by such beauty and never say a word." Pierre shakes his head. "He doesn't understand I'm not the flirty type of man he is. I can appreciate a woman without making a display of myself."

Does he appreciate me? In the way a man appreciates a woman? I am confused, which is not really the optimal state of mind to be in the day before my wedding.

"Okay. Bon. I don't think we need anything more," Rene declares, setting the pen across the tablet. "You are protected now."

"Thank God," Pierre mutters.

"Thank God you are protected?"

"No. Thank God we are finished with that torture."

Rene laughs a hearty laugh. It seems nothing can deflate him. He leans across the table and claps Pierre on the back.

"You were a good sport, mon pote. I am finished torturing you now. You will thank me later."

"Hmph. Maybe."

"Okay. Well. Your parents and sisters will be back in less than an hour. Let's get ready. We have plans for you tonight."

"For me?" Pierre looks shocked.

"Oui. It is the last night you will be a bachelor. We are taking you on the town. There is a place I found called Tequila Mockingbird. We will go there with Tasha's father and your father."

"Please tell me you aren't getting him drunk the night before our ceremony."

"No, Cher. I wouldn't do that. Perhaps a glass of wine or two. That is it. You have my word."

The Rules for Tasha & Pierre

1. No kissing unless it is required for publicity.

2. No catching feelings

3. No dating other people while in this fake marriage

4. No touching unless you are in public.

5. No nicknames or affectionate pet names

6. You must wear clothing at all times. And you must not leave undergarments in public areas of the home.

7. No giving sweet compliments

Cass: It's your big day! I wish we could be there, Tasha.

Tasha: Me too. But I understand. This was short notice for a big trip from Tennessee to North Carolina. Besides, we decided on family only.

Winona: And his best friend.

Tasha: Because he's the best man. Heather's my maid of honor. We're keeping it simple.

Cass: I'm still in shock. Send lots of photos, okay?

Brianna: I'm so excited for you! Eat up every moment of this special day!

Daisy: I'm sending all the good wedding vibes from over here in Charleston.

Tasha: Thank you, Daisy. Thanks—all of you. I'm so grateful for you.

Brianna: Let's plan to meet up after the wedding dust settles.

Tasha: Well, he does have a Tennessee tour date. Maybe I'll see you all then. I could possibly come along.

Cass: No maybe about it. Send us the date. You can stay here.

Cass: Wait. What am I saying? You will want to stay with Pierre, of course. Ignore me. But for sure plan to come when he's here.

Tasha: Gotta run! Time to get ready for the ceremony. Love y'all.

23

PIERRE

Love starts as a feeling, but to continue is a choice;
And I find myself
choosing you more and more every day.
~ Justin Wetch

Rene pulls my tie and pats a hand on it after straightening it for the second time in the past ten minutes. We are standing on a grassy lawn at the back of an orchard on the Harvest Hollow Farms property. The clearing where we will hold our ceremony is set apart from most of the farm where fall activities are taking place. Families parade through the orchard about thirty meters away from us, picking fruit off trees and plopping the apples into buckets they were given at the seasonal barn store near the entrance of the farm. A hayride drives by at a distance. Squeals of laughter ring out from the corn maze a few fields over.

"You look handsome, my friend," Rene says.

"So, there is no rule about you saying that to me? Are we allowed to tell one another we look handsome?"

Rene simply laughs. "I am not in danger of falling head over heels in love with you."

"No one is in danger of that."

"I would not be so sure. I feel the connection between you and Tasha. It is like a living thing, an energy that fills the space when you two are within five feet of one another—no, even ten or twenty feet. But as you say, I am a hopeless romantic. Ironic, is it not? Your best friend is the romantic, while you make an enviable living writing romance books."

"A romantic should never write romance. Leave it to the pragmatics. We balance love with pain."

"Ah, Pierre. Love is pain. Is that not what they said in the movie *The Princess Bride*?"

"Only because Westley was a man under the delusion that he had been scorned and replaced. Also, why are we talking about this on my wedding day? I'm at the altar waiting for my bride to appear any minute and you're talking about love and pain."

"You brought up love and pain. I merely brought up the suggestion of a possibility that your bride might fall in love with you."

"Psht." I give Rene the brush off, and then my head turns.

Tasha has given me no indication that she feels anything more than fondness and friendship for me. Yes, our kisses might have felt charged, but a deep relationship isn't built on kisses filled with a passing chemistry. Not that the attraction dimmed for me after we kissed. To the contrary, ever since I kissed Tasha, she has been the only thing I can think about. I redirect my thoughts regularly, but they invariably drift back to her.

I look out at the faces of our guests. There are only nine chairs filled for our ceremony: four for my family, two for Stuart and Bob, two for Tasha's parents, and one for her nephew, Nate. The seats are all set in one row, separated so that there is a semblance of an aisle between them.

Rene and I stand in front of hay bales. It's the best the farm could do in terms of creating a makeshift altar on short notice. All of their arbors and arches are being used for the harvest festival in town this weekend. The pumpkins adorning the stacks of hay are a nice, festive touch, albeit casual. But they suit the occasion, considering this is a rush-job of a wedding, cloaked in a string of lies.

Conversation hushes when Heather begins to walk down the aisle toward us. The young man seated on a bar stool with a guitar in his lap starts strumming after Heather is more than halfway down the nylon runner that I'm assuming is supposed to look like real satin. He's playing a tune that feels more like a country barn dance than a wedding processional.

Heather smiles at me—a knowing smile. I'm grateful she and Rene are the two standing up as witnesses, best man and maid of honor, since they are the only two people besides Stuart and Bob who know the truth about my situation.

I watch Heather take her place across from Rene and me.

My attention is drawn to Tasha, standing at the end of the runner, dressed in white, her gown clinging to her curves, edged in lace, and falling to the middle of her calves. She's wearing a dressy pair of boots to stave off the chill in the air.

Tasha's hair cascades down past her shoulders in big curls. Her eyes look incredible, even more pronounced than usual. Her lips have a deep tint to them, somewhere between red and the color of my favorite burgundy wine. She's carrying a bouquet of autumn colored flowers with fall leaves tucked into the arrangement.

When our eyes meet, my breath hitches, and not because we are pulling off a charade.

It's her.

Tasha.

My eyes lock with hers, and I half hope she can read all my emotions on my face. The other half of me hopes I'm not an open book.

She's stunning. And kind. And funny. And sweet. And she means more to me than I ever thought a woman could. I'd do anything for her, and here she is doing everything for me.

A string of memories assaults me. I see her at the book signing, in the hotel lobby, on the dance floor, at the airport, sleeping in my car on the way back from our flight, the first time she saw my home, making her way across the swinging bridge. I envision her laughing, thinking, pondering, smiling. And then I remember our kisses. A tear tracks down my face and I know I can't reach up to swipe it or I will draw more attention to the fact that Tasha's affecting me this way.

She walks on her own, a choice she made, asking her father to remain at her mother's side. She had said, "Mom will need you more than I will." I glance at her mom, she's wiping a tear from her eye, gripping her husband's hand like he is her anchor.

I should feel like the charlatan I am, but I'm not play-acting right now. My eyes lock on Tasha's and I'm looking at a vision, a woman I've grown to admire and care for. And I have feelings swelling up in my heart that I have never felt before. There is no other woman in the world for me. I want her to be mine.

Tasha makes it to my side and I extend my forearm to her. She grasps it, looping her hand under my arm so she is tucked beside me.

"You are beautiful, Cher. So beautiful. Breathtaking."

She smiles up at me.

I glance over at Rene and he mouths, "The rules."

I mouth, "It's our wedding."

He shakes his head, but he has a half-smile on his face.

Tasha leans in and asks me, "Are you doing okay?"

"I'm great. Thank you for everything, Cher."

Rene looks at us and whispers, "Rules number four, five, and seven."

Tasha giggles. Then she leans into me. "You look handsome in your suit too."

I smirk at Rene.

The pastor delivers a short speech about love and marriage. I can't focus on most of his words. My arm is so aware of Tasha's touch. I keep glancing at her, wanting to memorize this day. We may separate after a year—we will, of course—but I will always have the memories of what she looked like and how her eyes softened when she glanced up at me, here at our hay bale altar.

A wind blows through the clearing, carrying dried leaves, catching wisps of Tasha's hair and brushing them across her face. I lift my hand and tuck the strands back, away from her cheeks, allowing my fingers to drift down her neck before I face the pastor again.

Rene shakes his head at me as if I'm a lost cause. I probably am.

The pastor asks for the rings. I reach for my pocket, and

there is a loud sound like a gunshot, followed by a thunking sound not too far away from us. I give Tasha a quizzical look. Then there's another shot, and a splat. These sounds continue. Repeated loud booms and splatters. The guests murmur among themselves. Finally, the young man with the guitar shouts out, "It's the apple cannon! Just carry on."

Explosive sounds, followed by the impact of shattering apples continue in the background the rest of the ceremony. The pastor recites our vows and Tasha and I repeat after him in turn.

I take you to be mine ...
To have and to hold from this day forward ...
For better and for worse ...
For richer and for poorer
In sickness and in health ...
To love and to cherish ...
Till death do us part.

And then the pastor turns his attention to our nine guests and says, "Ladies and gentlemen, it is my honor and privilege to present to you, Mr. and Mrs. Toussaint!"

He completely butchers the pronunciation, saying Too-saint, but I couldn't care less.

Everyone cheers.

I look at Tasha. She is smiling up at me, not appearing like a woman pulling off a farce, but like the woman I have gotten to know and treasure as a dear friend. The woman who causes me to have feelings I've never felt before.

The pastor says, "You may now kiss the bride."

I knew he would say this. I had prepared myself—or so I thought. But when the words come out of his mouth, I feel my pulse quicken, my palms go slightly damp, and my tongue feels suddenly dry. I just uttered vows. Vows Tasha doesn't know I'll keep if it kills me. Not keeping her as my wife, of course, but I will be here for her in any way I can, long past our arrangement. Not because I have to, but because I want to.

And now, the most stunning, captivating woman, who is officially my wife on paper, is waiting for me to kiss her.

I turn my attention fully to Tasha, cupping her cheek and looking her in the eyes—those beautiful, brown, doe eyes. Yes, the people who matter most to us are watching, but I tune them out and focus solely on Tasha. She may think this is for show. After all, Godiva is here, chronicling our wedding to spread the evidence on the internet. A swarm of videography drones and a mass of paparazzi could hover around and crowd us right now. All I would see is Tasha's eager expression. She's the sole object of my focus and attention. My beating heart threatens to hammer out of my chest with longing for her.

I lean in and brush my lips over hers, holding her face so that she doesn't break our connection too soon. She doesn't pull back. Instead, she loops her hands behind my neck and pulls me in for a deeper kiss.

Rene lets out a sort of cat-call and then a whistle. The people gathered cheer. And the young man with the guitar starts playing ... What is that? La vache! It's the French National Anthem.

Tasha and I slowly separate. Her eyes are soft and fixed on me. I smooth my palm down her cheek, over her shoulder, trailing the back of my hand down her arm until our fingers are intertwined. I don't know when I will be allowed to touch her again, or kiss her, or even call her Cher, based on our rules, so I plan to take full advantage of this moment between us.

Tasha reaches over and rubs my lips with the pad of her thumb.

"You had my lipstick on you," she says, a sweet blush rising up her cheeks.

"Always caring for me," I muse, mostly to myself.

"We're married," she says softly so only I can hear her.

"Yes, Cher. You are my wife."

She shakes her head in disbelief, smiles up at me again, and I lead her down the aisle. Our families, my agent, and my publicist, throw handfuls of fresh fall leaves in a shower of oranges, reds, and yellows over our heads while we run by. Tasha warned me she's absurdly obsessed with fall. I hope she will always remember our wedding day when she thinks of her favorite season in the years to come.

After we take photos with our family and attendants, we drive from the farm to the Harvest Festival where we wander around in our wedding attire with our guests. Locals stop and stare, many of them wishing us congratulations.

Most of the people we bump into don't seem shocked at Tasha marrying me. They must not be aware of the brevity of our engagement. Her life has been under less local scrutiny while she lived in Asheville.

My family trails behind us, looking out of place, and obviously assessing every aspect of the makeshift carnival rides, games like bobbing for apples, and the dunk tank where people are paying tickets and attempting to drown the high school principal, Felicia Fudrucker—locals call her "The Fud." Marguerite and Tasha link arms and chat like old friends as we walk through the festival grounds. I knew they would get along—seeing the ease of their connection with my own eyes does something to me.

"Let's stuff a scarecrow!" Tasha says, rocking on her heels and looking back at me like an eager child.

My mother's eyes momentarily bug out of her head, but she reins in her reaction and follows along as I indulge my bride.

The rest of the afternoon, I carry a scarecrow and pull a red wagon full of pumpkins, gourds, and a harvest wreath Tasha picked out at the craft booths and the pumpkin patch. I could be annoyed. Some men would be. I'm not bothered —a fact which should concern me. Tasha's planning on filling my home with fall vegetables scattered on previously clean surfaces. She's going to hang the wreath on my door, and I have no doubt, the scarecrow, whom she named Bert McStuffins, will be posted somewhere where he can greet us daily.

Godiva snaps shots of us on the tilt-o-wheel, at the pumpkin toss, and in the petting zoo as if we were Brigitte & Emmanuel Macron.

Rene saunters up to my side, a smug look on his face. "I never thought I'd see the day my best friend towed a wagon full of zucchini and carried a stuffed farm hand around a festival for his wife. I will believe anything now."

I smile at him. It's my wedding day. Probably the only wedding day I'll ever have. Not even his teasing will deflate my contentment.

After hours of indulging ourselves in American fall traditions, we're standing near the lot where all the cars are parked. Everyone is starting to drag from the intensity of a day filled with a wedding followed by a harvest festival.

I suggest, "Why don't we let Heather and Tasha head

back to Heather's home, and then my family can come with me back to my house."

"Unheard of!" my mother says before anyone else can speak.

"It's your wedding night," Colette says softly. "I'm pretty sure it's bad luck for a couple to sleep separately on their wedding night. If anything, we should leave the house so you can be alone together. Really, Pierre, your wife deserves a honeymoon."

"She absolutely deserves a honeymoon," Marguerite agrees.

"I didn't want a honeymoon," Tasha says, coming to my defense.

She steps closer to me, looping her arm through mine in a show of solidarity.

"You want one," Marguerite says. "Every woman wants a honeymoon. You're only being considerate of my workaholic brother. It's not right. You should come before his work. He knows time off is as important as work. Family first. It's the French way."

"Really," Tasha insists. "I don't want a honeymoon right now. I have a book to record next week, and another one scheduled shortly after that. If I really wanted a honeymoon, Pierre would give me one."

I would. I should have insisted on it. Though, what would we do on a honeymoon? We aren't really married. Well, we are, but not in our hearts, where it matters. This marriage is on paper only.

"We should get a hotel," my father offers.

"You should have your home to yourselves," Marguerite says. "It's your wedding night."

"You have the upstairs suite. It is private," Colette says.

"Why don't we put Maman et Papa in a hotel? Rene can get a room as well. Then Marguerite and I will stay downstairs in the guest room where we have been sleeping and cook for you—like servants on your honeymoon."

"I can stay in the other guest room," Rene offers. "I, too, want to serve my friend on this special night."

I shoot Rene a look, hoping no one sees me. He should be helping me avoid this situation, not co-signing it.

"Oui. C'est bon," my mother says.

It's good? It's not good. This means Tasha and I will have to sleep in my master suite together. We will have to carry on like we are newly married in front of my sisters for the next twenty-four hours.

"C'est définitif," my father says.

It's final. When Papa says something is final, it's final. Ah well.

I look at Tasha, flashing her a weak smile.

"This is so sweet of you," she says to my sisters. Then she turns to me and gives me a wink.

Always coming to my rescue. How will I ever begin to repay her?

24

TASHA

The wedding night is not
the end of your married life; it is the start!
~ Ngina Otiende

We drive to Pierre's house in relative silence after dropping his parents off at The Maple Tree Inn and Suites at the edge of town. His mother and father both kissed me on my cheeks, then kissed each member of the family before heading up to their room. Colette says she'll bring them their toiletries and a change of clothes after we all get settled in at Pierre's.

My husband's home. Our home for now. But really, it's his home and I'm a paid houseguest—one with a crush that is growing like a dangerous wildfire.

The way he looked at me when he said our vows, the tenderness and passion I imagined I felt from him when he kissed me, the fact that he carried our scarecrow around, pulling that wagon full of pumpkins for me ... it's all adding up to him being beyond perfect. I already thought he looked like a dream of a man when I saw him in the lobby of Alicante. Then, I found out he's the author behind the books of Amelie De Pierre. And now, I know him—this kind, thoughtful, alluring man whose personality is as attractive as his looks.

He should have some glaring flaw, some defect of character, or at least a giant mole with hair blossoming out of it and a rank stench.

That would help. It really would.

Instead, the more I get to know Pierre, the more I like him, and the more irresistible he is to me. But we have a common goal. And we have rules. I'd like to burn those rules in the first fire we set in the fireplace this fall. Or maybe I should have them tattooed inside my eyelids. I need them, and I loathe them.

"We must make this night amorous," Rene says from his spot in the back seat.

I'm in the passenger seat and Rene is flanked by Colette and Marguerite in the back. The ease with which the three of them banter and tease one another shows me he's been in this family long enough to be more like a relative than a friend. He's in. I'm still on the periphery.

"Amorous?" Pierre asks, glancing in the rearview. "I think I'll cover the amorous elements. You just make yourself scarce."

"Quelle chose ridicule à dire."

"It's not ridiculous," Pierre answers. "I'm the husband. I will bring l'amour."

I can't help but think of Pierre bringing the l'amour. Um. Yes, please. Bring it, Pierre. But all he'll be bringing is a clean set of sheets into his master suite so one of us can sleep on the pullout couch up there. No l'amour for this girl. That wasn't our deal, even if his kisses still linger on my lips and his vows still ring through my ears and heart.

The French starts flying between Rene and Pierre after Rene calls Pierre ridiculous. They had been speaking English, for my benefit, I'm sure. Now the conversation is becoming more heated. Not angry, but more intense and rapid and impassioned.

I try to keep up. It's going too fast. I only catch a word here and there. But I speak body language, since that's relatively universal. Pierre is putting Rene in his place. Why is Rene suggesting an amorous night anyway? He knows this is a farce. He helped us write the rules. Is this for the sake of making Pierre's sisters believe we are really married? I would think Pierre could tell them the truth. Not that he should, but even from the little I've seen of them, I think they would keep his secret.

"Let's have dinner, the five of us," I suggest, pivoting so I'm facing the three in the back seat.

"What? No!" Colette says. "We will cook for you, something delicious. We will pour the wine. Then we will duck into our rooms and the two of you will have a lovely meal together alone, as husband and wife—one you will remember for years to come because it is your first night as a married couple. Afterward, you can sneak upstairs ..." She trails off, wagging her eyebrows suggestively at me. "In the morning, Marguerite and I will go into town and get you pastries and coffees and we will serve you breakfast like we are the servants in your honeymoon hotel. You can even eat in bed. Oui. You should. Pierre can feed you chocolate croissant."

She says it like shoe-ku-lah kwah-soh. It's beautiful. Makes me want to have Pierre feed me pastries every morning in bed. Oh, who am I kidding? I didn't need any help wanting that to happen.

Marguerite looks at me with a pleading expression on her face. "Please. This is the least we can do since you will be so far from us after today. It would be so much better if you were in Avignon. We could be like real sisters."

What can I say to such a sweet offer?

"Okay. If you insist. But what will you eat?"

"Don't worry about us. We will eat. And we will feed Rene, even though he is a menace and a hopeless flirt."

I chuckle. Rene gives me a wink. This man. He really is unflappable.

Pierre has gone silent, obviously aware as to when fighting his sisters is futile. We park the car in his driveway and he pops the trunk to pull out the scarecrow and pumpkins. I'm still in my wedding gown and Pierre is in his suit. I want to put on sweats.

My sister had a friend of hers park my U-haul with all my stuff in it here this morning so I could move in after Pierre's family left. Key word there? *After.* But now, I'm preparing to spend a night with my new husband in his room, carrying off a farce for his sisters' benefit.

"Where should we put Bert?" Pierre asks, holding the scarecrow at arms' length as if it might bite him if he got too close.

"Can we put him outside the front door?"

"Of course. Whatever you wish."

"Whatever I wish?" I ask, feeling emboldened by all this talk of amorous nights and morning croissants in bed.

"Within reason ..." Pierre winks.

That wink. It's going to be the death of me.

Here lies Tasha Pierson Toussaint, killed by the winks and unrequited love of a Frenchman.

Pierre plants Bert McStuffins outside the front door. Rene says something taunting to Pierre which I can't make out because he says it privately and in French. As a result, Rene is tasked with lugging our pumpkins and gourds into the kitchen from the car.

I excuse myself once we're inside to go upstairs, lugging a suitcase from the U-haul up to Pierre's bedroom as if it will be the room I move into after today. It won't, and I need to keep that fact squarely in mind.

I change into yoga pants and a baggy T-shirt that says *Call Me Your Personal Assistant since Full-Time, Multitasking Ninja Isn't A Title*. One of the authors I work for got it for me last year. When I arrive back in the living room, my hair in a messy bun, and my feet bare, all four sets of French eyes land on me. Both Marguerite and Colette scan me from head to toe, obviously trying to hide their opinion of my attire— and failing miserably.

Rene speaks up, as usual. "Wow. You're moving right into the comfortably married zone."

"What?" I ask.

"You look beautiful," Pierre says, walking over to plant a kiss on the top of my head while he wraps an arm around me. He's still in his suit and tie.

"Do you want to get comfortable?" I ask him.

"Of course," he says. "I will put on something less ..." He doesn't finish his sentence.

He walks toward the hallway, leaving me with his sisters and Rene.

I know French people tend to dress more chic and pulled

together than we Americans do, as a rule. I could go change into something more dressy.

"Should I change?" I ask Marguerite.

"Nonsense. I love your comfortable choice. It shows you are at home with my brother. He obviously is smitten with you. And now you are going to relax and start your life together. You should wear whatever you feel good wearing."

Smitten with me? Pierre is not smitten with me. At least we know we are convincing if his own sister believes he is in love with me.

"Thank you," I say. "Can I help you prepare the meal?"

"No. Of course not. You should go upstairs with your husband. Be alone together. This is your wedding day. Pretend we are not here. Go enjoy your husband. We will call you down when the meal is ready."

"Okay," I say feebly.

I can't even look Rene in the eyes as I walk out of the room, into the hallway and toward the staircase that leads to Pierre's room. *Enjoy my husband.* Gah!

I knock gently on the door to Pierre's room. We haven't really been alone since before the wedding. I miss him. Isn't that crazy? How did he become a person I would miss after only a little over twenty-four hours' separation?

"Come in," his deep voice sounds from the other side of the door.

I crack the door open only a little at first. "Are you decent?"

"Mostly." He chuckles softly.

I walk the rest of the way in. Pierre has pressed jeans on. That's it. He's not wearing a shirt and his feet are bare. Why is that such a turn on? Bare feet? I think I'm losing my mind. His glasses are off, set aside on a dresser. He looks ... well ...

let's just say I cross my arms across my chest to keep myself from lunging from the doorway to where he's standing.

If we were really married right now, things would be so different. We'd be falling into one another's arms. Maybe we would be somewhere far from here on a real honeymoon. But I can't think about that. I really can't afford to imagine what Pierre would be doing to me if I were his wife.

Yes, Cher. You are my wife.

No, Pierre. I am not. Not really.

Pierre walks to a closet at the side of the room and pulls a shirt off a hanger, pulling it over his head. I watch. How can I not?

"Is this casual enough? If I leave it untucked?"

My mouth is so dry it takes me a minute to answer him. "Uh. Yep. Yeah. That's great. Perfect. Casual as can be. You betcha."

He chuckles again.

"Sorry about my sisters. I wish I could tell them the truth, but Stuart is adamant that I need to keep our situation between you, me, Rene, and Heather."

"I understand." I walk further into the room, looking around more fully than I did when I came up here to change. "I wish we could tell them too, but I know we shouldn't. I just feel badly leading them to believe what's going on between us is real."

"But I do like you, Cher. That is not fake," Pierre says, a warmth in his eyes that makes me turn to look away from him so I can gather my bearings.

"This room is huge," I tell him. "I didn't expect it to be so big."

"Yes. It covers the whole second floor, so it's quite large."

His bed is in the corner, with a navy comforter spread across it and tidy matching throw pillows propped up on the knotty pine headboard. Two bedside tables flank the bed. On the same wall is a window and then a dresser. On this side of the room, near the door, there's a desk, a wooden filing cabinet, and a comfortable looking sofa. My suitcase is tucked neatly to one side of the door, ready for me to take it downstairs tomorrow.

"This will be my bed," Pierre says, following my eyes to the couch. "You will sleep in my bed tonight. It's more comfortable."

You will sleep in my bed tonight. Talk about words I never imagined in a million years I'd hear Pierre Toussaint say to me.

"Okay," I say. "I can take the couch bed, though."

"Nonsense. I am a gentleman. Please. You take my bed."

"Okay," I repeat, feeling suddenly shy.

"I am sorry, Tasha. I know this is awkward. You had to kiss me. You are having to pull off a lie to my family, and to your parents, and to so many people you grew up with. I don't know what to say."

"It's okay. I want to help you."

And the kisses are not a hardship, believe me.

"So, we are kicked out of the downstairs?" he asks.

"Apparently. They want us to be alone now that we are married."

"My sisters. They mean well. And Rene. He does not mean well. He's full of mischief."

"He's funny."

"Don't fall for his charm. It is like a lure on the end of a hook."

"Really?"

"Not really. But still, you should not fall for him or his charm."

If I didn't know better, I'd say Pierre was jealous, or protective.

I do know better, though.

"You looked beautiful today," Pierre says, surprising me.

"So did you." I smile awkwardly. "Handsome, that is."

"It was a good wedding. Minus the apple cannon," he smiles warmly and my heart feels like it could burst.

I giggle lightly. "It was a day to remember, I'll give you that."

"Yes," he says, looking me in the eyes. "A day I will never forget."

25

PIERRE

I wake up wanting to talk to you,
I go to sleep thinking about you,
and I dream about
you holding me the way only you do.
~ *Unknown*

That t-shirt and leggings Tasha is wearing are going to be the death of me. We had a lovely dinner. Simple. French. Homemade. Onion soup with a crusty bread on top and the cheese melted over the toast. Dijon chicken that was moist and flavorful. Green beans almandine on the side. Crème brûlée finished off the meal. My sisters went through all the trouble to make dessert from scratch—a two and a half hour process including refrigeration. After Tasha and I ate our food by candlelight at my dining table, we were ushered upstairs where we're now awkwardly preparing for our first night as husband and wife.

"Don't mind us!" Colette's voice carries up the stairs after only a few minutes of Tasha and me retreating to my master suite. "We'll just watch the TV and be so very quiet down here."

"Oh. My. Gosh," Tasha says, "They think we're going to ..."

I chuckle. "Sorry, Cher. My family is French. We speak maybe more openly about these things. My sisters are getting too much fun out of teasing us. Imagine your baby brother finally getting married. They are harmless, though."

I look over toward my bed where Tasha is re-fluffing my pillows before climbing in. Her back is mostly toward me, but I can see that her neck and cheeks are pink with a blush that makes me want to pull her into my arms and gently pepper kisses along the smooth column of skin below her ear.

I clear my throat and continue making the pullout sofa bed. Once we take our turns in my en suite bathroom, we crawl into separate beds and I turn out the lights. The room sounds eerily quiet with the exception of Tasha's breathing, reminding me she is right there, in the bed across the room from this makeshift bed I'm in, wearing that baggy T-shirt and her leggings, her long hair splayed across my pillow, her body tucked under my covers.

"Pierre?" Her voice cuts through the dark.

"Oui? Yes?"

"Was today everything you needed it to be?"

What an odd question. Thoughtful, really, considering what she is enduring to make my stay in the United States possible.

"It was more than I imagined. A perfect wedding day."

She giggles softly. "A perfect wedding day."

"For you? Was the day what you hoped it would be?"

"It was a good day. Everyone seemed to enjoy themselves.

I think Godiva took enough photos to fill a spread in People magazine if she needed to."

"She was always snapping a shot of us every time I looked around."

"Are you happy, though?" I can't help but ask.

"I am."

"That's all that matters," I say honestly.

"Thank you for being so sweet."

I am not sweet. If she knew how many thoughts I have had today of breaking those *horribles* rules. *Je ne suis pas un homme honorable.* No. I am not an honorable man. It is only my thoughts of the year ahead that keep me twenty feet away from her right now, determined to stay on this poor excuse of a mattress while she sighs contentedly in my bed.

"You are welcome, Cher. Thank you ... for everything."

"I love how that word sounds when you say it."

Her voice is growing softer, more drowsy.

"What word is that?" I feel the smile on my face. Tasha makes me smile from my heart outward. "Cher?"

"Not Cher, though you were right when you told Rene that. I do like you calling me Cher. I like when you say evechree-zing."

I chuckle. "You mock my accent? On my wedding night. Oh, my heart. It is bleeding."

She laughs. "I'm not mocking. I'm appreciating. Your accent is sexy."

She giggles a nervous giggle. Then she says, "Okay. Pretend I didn't say that. Goodnight, Pierre."

"Bonne nuit, Cher ... Tasha." I say her name with all the affection I feel for her, the darkness making me bold.

"Bonne nuit," she murmurs, and then she is quiet. Only minutes later, I hear her breathing slow into a sweet rhythm.

I don't fall asleep easily, tossing and turning, always aware Tasha is here, but not where I wish she were, tucked in my arms, curled up like two spoons in a drawer. My skin itches and buzzes with the awareness of Tasha's presence and the desire to be closer to her.

One night.

I can do this.

Though, after tonight, she will be in my home every day —and every night. I might go mad. I would talk to Rene about it, but he will invariably tease me. I will talk to him anyway. After the teasing he will be serious. And I need his support to keep me strong.

I finally fall asleep. I don't know when or how. I wake before the sun, having maybe gotten four or five hours of sleep at the most. The light at my window tells me sunrise will come shortly. It is one of my favorite times of day.

Tasha is sitting in bed with the light of her Kindle illuminating her face.

"Good morning," I say, stretching and standing from the pullout bed.

"Good morning. How did you sleep?"

"Eh. Fine. It was fine."

"That means it was awful, and you're just being polite."

"Perhaps. How did you sleep?"

"This bed is heaven. I slept well. But I do need your help with something."

Her voice sounds both mischievous and tentative.

"Anything. What do you need?"

"Well, you were talking in your sleep." She smiles.

"No. I wasn't. I don't do that. Were you imagining it? Dreaming, perhaps?"

"No. You were. I recorded you."

"La vache! You recorded it?"

"I'm not showing anyone. I just wanted to ask you to translate. Or ... I could go on Google translator if you prefer."

"Ahh. Well, play me this horrible recording."

I send her a playful smile even though I am embarrassed. I don't talk in my sleep. Not that I know, at least. Maybe I was so exhausted it caused this anomaly.

Tasha pulls her phone off the bedside table, scrolls a little and then taps something. My voice rings out from her phone. Too loud. Too personal. Too revealing.

Tasha, oui comme ça. Oui Cher, embrasse-moi. Tu es tout pour moi, ma belle épouse.

"Oh," I say. "Let's see ..."

"What were you saying? I heard my name."

My voice sounded drunk with longing in that recording. Of course, I was asleep. I can't be held accountable for what my dreams make me say. I could have just as easily dreamt I was being chased by a drooling, hairy, long-toothed monster named Tasha and I wanted to club it over the head. Only, my words tell me my dream was not about clubbing her over the head. Quite the opposite. How do I tell her I was saying, *Tasha, yes. Like that. Yes, Cher, kiss me. You are everything to me, my beautiful wife.*

"It was me saying I appreciate you being my wife," I say, hoping her lessons in French are not advanced far enough along to help her with this particular translation.

"Ah. Yes. I did hear that word, *épouse*. But did you also say, beautiful, like *belle*?"

I am about to attempt to try to fib my way around this revelation when there is a knock at the door followed by Marguerite's voice.

"Breakfast is served! Open up you lovebirds!"

Tasha's alarmed expression matches the one that must be on my face.

In barely a whisper, I say to Tasha, "Make noise!"

She looks at me with a confused expression until I point to the couch. Obviously, I have to shove it back so the bed is not on display. How would I explain to my sisters that I spent my first married night on a pullout. They would assume the worst.

"Ohhhhh! Pierre!" Tasha says in a loud voice, followed by a moan that I will never forget.

The shock on her face following her own outburst makes me nearly lose myself in a fit of laughter. I bite my cheek.

She covers her face with the blanket, peering over the edge at me, full of embarrassment. I press on. We can't stall. My sisters are right there outside the door. They already heard her, and the couch is still out.

"Once more," I whisper so quietly, barely a noise comes out of my mouth.

"No!" Tasha whispers back, obviously horrified at her choice of what *making noise* turned into.

"I have to shove the bed in. Once more, please," I whisper.

When she hesitates, I improvise. "Oui! Tasha! Oui!" Then I let out a groan.

I ram the first part of the bed in. It makes a thunking noise. Only one more section to collapse and we're home free.

Now it's Tasha's turn to look both mortified and as if she can barely keep herself from bursting into a fit of giggles. Tasha covers her already blushing face with a hand.

I prepare myself to shove the bed the rest of the way in and she obliges me by moaning out, "Yes, Pierre! Oh! Yes!"

I join her with some French that she will never get me to translate unless one day we are actually married. The thought nearly stops me in my tracks. Of course, we aren't ever getting married. She is here as my friend. One of the best friends I've had, surprisingly. But a friend is all she is, and all she will be.

Our eyes lock, laughter nearly brimming out of us, but we are both working hard to remain quiet—well, quiet after our intentional outbursts.

The couch is back in its proper spot, looking innocent and unused.

When I look toward the door, Tasha's eyes go wide. Then she averts her gaze. I hop into bed next to her, arranging the covers and looping my arm around her shoulder, drawing her into my side where she fits like she was meant to be there.

"Do not worry, Cher," I say quietly. "My sisters have grown up with our parents being very demonstrative in front of us. They are not batting the eyelashes right now."

Tasha looks up at me, her hands still in front of her face, her eyes only peeking through her fingers. "I'm so embarrassed." Her voice is hushed.

"Don't be. It was fun. My sisters won't even mention it. You wait." I don't give Tasha another minute to cultivate more anxiety or embarrassment.

When Marguerite says, "Is it safe to bring breakfast?" I shout, "Come in!"

The door cracks open and Marguerite says, "Good morning."

She winks at me and walks into my room with a tray in her hand. Colette follows behind, a knowing look on her face.

"I'm glad to hear you are having a honeymoon after all," Colette says.

Tasha leans her head into the crook of my neck, burying her face so she nearly disappears.

She softly whispers, "Kill me now. I can never face your sisters again."

I turn my head so my lips are in her hair. She smells delicious and I'm grateful for this chance—one I won't have after our guests leave. I know it's wrong. I should be respecting her boundaries, but, to be fair, she is the one clinging to me, burrowing like I am her only refuge in the world.

"Nonsense, Cher," I whisper into the crown of Tasha's hair. "They are happy for us. Look up. They brought pastries and coffee."

Tasha half-lifts her face, her hand still rests on my chest, and the other arm is wrapped behind me.

"Good morning," she says in a shy voice.

"Good morning," Marguerite says with a full smile. "We don't want to disturb you. We brought you chocolate croissants, apple turnovers, and some coffee from your sister's shop. We will leave you now to eat together. Come down later, only when you are ready. No rush. We understand it is your first morning as husband and wife."

Marguerite winks at Tasha. Tasha smiles. I feel the upward lift of her cheeks against my chest.

"Thank you," Tasha says, sitting up and separating herself from me. "This is so thoughtful."

"We are so glad you married Pierre," Colette says with such earnestness in her tone. "I hope you can tell how happy we are to have you as our new sister."

I cringe. Pulling off this farce felt relatively innocent. I am a man of morals. I don't lie to my friends and family. With the exception of hiding my pen name and career from them for a few years, I have always been very open with them. Hearing Colette call Tasha a sister douses my denial in a bucket of guilt. No lie is without its ripples. I only hope they are not too badly hurt when Tasha and I end things next year.

26

TASHA

Stop saying that marriage is "just a piece of paper."
... so is money, but you still get up every day
and work hard for it.
~ Unknown

"You what?!" Heather's mouth pops open, her eyes nearly as wide as the O her lips are forming.

We're in Catty Coffee after the morning rush, only a few regulars hanging out at the front of the shop. I've been picking up shifts here and there to help when needed. I'm cleaning the espresso machine the way Heather taught me, and she's wiping down counters and rearranging the baked goods in the display case, filling in gaps from what we already sold today.

"I pretended he was ... you know ... and I shouted out his name." Lowering my voice, I add, "I might have moaned."

It's been over a week since that mortifying morning, and I'm finally telling my sister the sordid details of what happened.

"Oh. My. Gosh. Have you lost your mind?"

"Maybe?"

"What did he say?"

"He joined in, groaning out my name and then saying the sexiest things you ever heard in French."

"That accent! What was he saying?"

"I know, right?! And who knows. It was French. But I heard some words I recognized. Oui ... Cher ... Je t'aime."

I don't tell Heather about the sleep talking recording I have. The one I possibly replay daily. I've translated it, and whew-eee. That's some sleep talking. If only he meant what he said in his dreams.

"I was mortified when his sisters came in winking like they had just caught us doing married things."

Heather giggles. "Well, you *are* married."

"Not like *that!*"

Heather shoots me a look and I lower my voice.

"But you'd like to be."

"I'd like to be something ... not married yet. But, yes. I do have feelings for Pierre. Big feelings."

"Awww. You should tell him."

"I can't. He needs me for this whole year. How am I supposed to spring this on him? Hey, Pierre. You know how we're faking that we love each other? Well, I actually might be falling for you. That would complicate everything. Blur the lines. Possibly ruin our friendship. Definitely make things awkward as all get out."

"Falling for him?" Heather turns and puts both hands on her hips. "Wow. Really?"

"Yeah," I say, not able to keep the tone of defeat out of my voice. "Really."

I have been falling. This past week since Pierre's family

left, we've been living under his roof—our roof, whatever—sharing meals, sitting comfortably together on the couch with our laptops open, each working separately, making coffee side-by-side in the mornings ... it's all been so domestic, and comfortable.

My feelings for Pierre had been dangerously strong before our wedding day. Then we exchanged vows and kissed at the altar. That was followed by our wedding night and the morning after, where nothing honeymoon-ish happened, but it feels like *something* did.

There have been a few times I caught Pierre glancing at me when I was puttering around arranging fall decor or cleaning up a mess. I always turn my head away quickly, but each time I know he was looking. I want to say he seems like a man interested in a woman, but I think it may just as likely be appreciation for my sacrifice or the deepening of our friendship—or maybe it's just him getting used to sharing a space he used to have all to himself.

I finish up at the coffee shop, hug Heather goodbye and stop by the butcher. I've never been to the butcher a day in my life. We always got meat on sale at Publix in the max pack and then froze a good portion of it to reheat and eat later. But Pierre is French, and I know they like their food fresh. I told him I want to cook dinner tonight. It's a surprise what I'm making. Let's hope it's not a disaster.

I've definitely taken on more than I can chew. The tenderloin steaks will be pan seared and then I need to make a complex sauce for those. The resulting dish is called tournedos à la bordelaise. Or tornadoes of embarrassment if I don't get it right.

I hope to make braised baby artichokes with tomato coulis to go on the side. I'll be preparing these baby artichokes Heather was able to get for me on special request from a guy she knows at the farmers market. I'll sauté up a bunch of carrot slices, garlic, onion and herbs, and then I'll add the prepared baby artichokes once they've soaked in lemon. Maybe I'll be burning the beef by the time I get the veggies going. It's a lot. I should have just made a quiche. That I can do.

Oh my gosh, why am I trying this? When I lived alone, a can of minestrone soup or a blue box of macaroni served me just fine for dinner. And Domino's. I could always count on Domino's.

No wonder these French women are so slim. By the time they cook everything, they've probably burned off five pounds in stress, and I'm sure they barely want to eat very often if it takes this much effort to prepare their intricate meals. But then there are the croissants. And the baguettes. And the tarts. God bless all those French carbs.

Forget it. The mystery of French slenderness will go down with the great mysteries of all time. What actually happened to Elvis? And what is Dolly Parton's real hair color? These are things we'll never know.

Speaking of French tarts, my old friend, Emmy Smart, has gone out of her way to bake us an apple frangipane tart with salted caramel sauce. It's sitting in the passenger seat next to me. I say we throw the steak on the barbecue despite the chill fall air outside. We can simply boil the artichokes, and then we'll eat this tart out of the pan with a fork.

But I can't do that. I started this gourmet French-fest, so I'm going to see it through.

"What have we here?" Pierre says, taking my grocery bags from me and peering into them when I come through the door.

"No peeking! It's a surprise."

"That's too thoughtful of you."

"Don't say that until the food is on your plate. You may want to order pizza just in case."

"Nonsense. I'm sure you will do fine."

Famous last words.

An hour later I'm shouting at the beef to "Wait a freaking minute!" while I de-fuzz the center of each baby artichoke. Twenty baby artichokes. I feel like the Old Mother Hubbard of Mediterranean vegetables. So many I don't know what to do.

Pierre sticks his head cautiously into the kitchen.

"May I help?"

"Gah!"

"I take that as a yes," he says, rolling up the sleeves of his oxford shirt to reveal his forearms.

I won't be that woman who's so cliché that she has a thing for a man's forearms. I'm a romance novel connoisseur. I've read about forearms for most of my adult life. I often thought, what's the big deal? Well, I'll tell you what the big deal is. I'm about to lose my balance at the sight of Pierre, his hair slightly rumpled from the way he runs his hand through it when he is working, his thick framed glasses perched perfectly on that French nose of his, the stubble dusting his jawline, and the way his arms stick out of his now-rolled-up sleeves.

Judge me all you want. I'm officially a forearm girl.

At least now I am, for Pierre. I'm every kind of girl for him. Only, he doesn't know it.

"Okay, Cher. What do you need? Put me to work."

"Rules," I say, half-joking, half-desperate to keep some semblance of structure between us so I don't turn and leap into Pierre's arms, finally letting loose all the emotions I've been tamping down for weeks.

"Ah, the rules," he wags his eyebrows. "They say rules are made to be broken, no?"

"Which ones?" I swallow.

"I would guess that would be up to us."

He leans nearer to me from behind, his breath tickling across my neck as he whispers into my ear. "Like if I wanted to tell you how beautiful you looked tonight while you are cooking me supper. We could decide if that is breaking the rules or simply me being appreciative."

"Uh."

I am rendered speechless, my knees wobble and I basically collapse backward after swerving a little, landing in Pierre's steadying embrace, the back of my body flush against the front of his.

"Of course, I don't want to cross lines," he adds, again with the breathiness on my neck.

Doesn't he know what that does to a woman? He could ask for my life savings. Not that it's much, but I'd give it over in a nanosecond if he keeps this up.

"You're ... you're guh ... good. You're good." There. I got that sentence out.

He's not backing away. His arms are wrapped gently from behind me, running softly up and down my arms.

"What are you cooking here?" he asks, the perfect picture of composure while I'm unraveling like a spool of thread under the influence of two kittens.

"Here?"

"Dinner?" he asks.

"Oh. Yeah. That. Dinner. Right."

He chuckles and I feel the vibration through my back.

Dinner? Who needs food?

"It's um. Beef." I clear my throat. "Tournedos à la bordelaise."

"Cher. You are making me a French dinner?"

"I'm pretty sure I'm making a mess of your French dinner."

I turn as I laugh, and man, oh man, was that a mistake. Pierre is here, right in front of me. The stove is behind me. And I'm looking up into his hazel eyes, a pair of tongs in my grip. His hands are still gently running up and down my arms in soothing strokes.

What are we doing?

Go with it! A voice in my head cheers on like someone in the colosseum, eager to see the bloodbath that follows their chant. My heart will be the victim of this battle.

Still, as I look at this man, the tender way he is studying my face, the soft smile on his full lips, the gentle way he is caressing my arms. This isn't friendly, am I right? We aren't trying to pull something off for a crowd or a publication. We're not attempting to convince Immigration. This is just Pierre and me, and a beef dinner that may be moving toward the realm of Cajun at this point if I don't turn down the burner.

"You are breaking rules four, five and seven." My words are breathy, a warning with an invitation tucked silently in the middle.

I'm not pulling away. As a matter of fact, my tongue darts out to wet my lips before I realize what I'm doing.

"Mmmm. Rules four, five and seven. No touching, no pet names, no compliments?"

"Yuh-yuh-yes," I stutter out in a breathy tone that I don't even recognize.

Kiss me! Kiss me!

"Well, now that we are such rule breakers, maybe we should consider rule number one?"

No kissing.

I barely recognize Pierre. He's still the thoughtful, careful, exceedingly handsome man who's always so put together and slightly unreachable. But this man in front of me is hungry. And not for baby artichokes. There's a longing in his eyes that I finally recognize because it is the mirror image of my own desires.

"Would you mind?" he asks, his eyes searching mine.

Pierre seems suddenly shy and apprehensive, as if his earlier teasing is now under question. I don't mind at all, and I know one of us needs to be the one to break through this barrier. We've agreed on lines for our own good. But now those lines are not what we want. At least if I'm reading him right, they aren't. So, I'll take one for the team. I don't mind being the one to start something. Not when it's so clear it's the very thing we both want.

I reach out slowly, bringing the palm of my hand to his cheek.

Pierre reaches behind me and clicks two burners off.

Efficient.

Also sexy.

Whatever. Everything he does is sexy.

I run my hand down his stubble and hum. I hum like it's my job. The feel of the scratch on the sensitive skin of my palm sends chills everywhere. It's sweet relief, touching him after bottling up all this overwhelming want and these monumental, unexpected feelings.

"Cher." He says it in a low, quiet voice, like he's savoring a truffle.

"Pierre."

I look in his eyes. We stand there, my hand on his cheek, his hands now gripping just above my hips.

The tongs clatter to the floor when I go on tiptoe and brush the lightest kiss across his lips. Pierre makes a soft rumbly noise of appreciation in the back of his throat. Like a bear if it were rolling over to get sunshine on its belly. Go with me. That's what he sounds like.

Pierre cradles the back of my head and tugs me closer. And then he's kissing me. No longer asking for permission or waiting for my signal. He got the green light and now he's in charge. His fingers weave into my hair. His other hand comes up to cup my cheek. One of my hands roams around to the back of his neck where I run my fingertips along the nape of his neck, playing with the short hairs there. My other hand splays across his chest. His heart hammers beneath his pecs. Beating for me.

We kiss for longer than we ever did before—because this kiss is ours. It doesn't belong to social media or Stuart or Immigration. We're not convincing anyone, except maybe ourselves.

Pierre moves his lips from mine, returning to softly peck them, then lingering at the corner of my mouth, kissing my nose, my forehead, and down my neck.

Beef, shcmeef. Who needs dinner when I've got Pierre kissing me like this?

He pulls back and the smile on his face tells me everything. His arms are still around me, holding me close, keeping me steady.

"Well," I say.

"Well," he echoes with a smirky look on that gorgeous face.

"We should maybe cook," I suggest.

"Hmmm. I think so. I've worked up quite an appetite."

He leans in and kisses me softly before letting his arms drop away from my sides. Neither of us tries to make sense of what just happened.

Pierre picks up one of the baby artichokes I haven't finished defuzzing and gets to work. I turn the burner on, trying to salvage the sauce for the meat. We work in companionable silence and then we devour the dinner that turns out to be not half bad.

After our meal, with a fire burning in the fireplace, Pierre feeds me bites of apple tart off his fork even though I have a slice of my own sitting right in front of me. I return the favor, slipping bites into his mouth and watching my fork slide back out between his lips.

We talk about his work in progress, the books I'm recording, and his upcoming trip—everything but that kiss we shared before dinner, the one that turned my entire world on its ear.

27

PIERRE

A writer only begins a book.
A reader finishes it.
~ Samuel Johnson

I've never had writer's block. It's not that I'm exceptional, or maybe I am. I've just never hit the wall with my writing. If I get stuck, I take a walk, read something, call Rene, or go to a cafe.

After that kiss Tasha and I shared in the kitchen last night, I am fully stuck.

You would think a kiss like that one—a kiss worthy of one of my books—would spur me into writing some of the most romantic scenes of my life. But all I can think about is how Tasha and I need to talk. And then I think of how dangerous a talk could be. I need her. If I chase her off, the tour will be forfeited.

Who am I kidding? It's no longer simply business for me. I need Tasha, and not because I have to contract with someone to be my fake wife. I need her in ways I don't think I've ever needed another soul.

My head spins.

What is she thinking?

What does she want?

Does she feel what I feel?

And what do we do if we are in a fake marriage, but we're developing real feelings?

My mind circles through those questions and then circles again, like I'm riding a child's merry-go-round at a park.

I stare out the windows at the leaves on the trees. The colors are vibrant, belying the fact that their lives are coming to a close. They look more alive now than they did when they were a mass of green.

What if our kiss is like this autumn foliage, blazing bright and giving me false hope?

But what if it isn't?

What if Tasha is open to a real relationship?

What if she's actually falling for me?

Am I falling for her?

I don't even have to ask myself that last question. I've already fallen.

Sometimes people sneak up on you when you aren't even looking for them. I didn't see Tasha coming. But when I look back over our relationship, back to that first encounter, there was already something unique—a connection, a feeling of familiarity I've never felt for anyone else except those people closest to me. I felt like I knew who she was even though we hadn't officially met yet.

I lived all these years, not knowing Tasha existed. But

maybe a part of me knew, because I felt restless and incomplete. Now that I've found her, I don't think I can ever live without her. I hope she feels the same.

The front door opens. Tasha walks in, finding me staring out the back windows, the screen on my laptop blank. She glances down at it from her spot behind me. I twist my head and meet her gaze.

"Writer's block?"

"Maybe. I've never had a block before."

"Never? I thought all writers had writer's block at some point or another. Doesn't it just come with the territory?"

"I usually can tell when I'm heading toward an impasse. I do something to shake my brain loose so it never gets this far."

"What about today?"

"I'm stuck. I can't figure out what direction to take my characters."

"Do you want a sounding board?"

"A sounding board?"

"You can tell me where you are in the story, and I will help you brainstorm where it might go. Or I'll listen while you bounce thoughts off me."

"That's not a bad idea."

I pause and look up at her again. She's still looking over my shoulder at the blank screen.

"Are you sure you're not just trying to finagle a sneak peek at my book before it's published?" I tease.

"Oh, I definitely want a sneak peek at whatever you're writing. But that's not my motive."

"Okay. Well, let me know when you are available, and I'll take you up on your offer."

"Now works."

Before I can say anything else, Tasha drops her purse on the floor and moves around to the front of the sofa. She sits next to me, not far away in the other corner, but close enough that her knee grazes my thigh when she folds her leg up under herself.

"Okay, so what's the gist of the story so far, and where are you stuck?"

It takes a moment to focus. I smell her vanilla and cinnamon scent, catch the light of the fire in the fireplace playing off her skin and hair. I remember our kiss. I'll never forget that kiss.

Talk to her about your kiss.

The day before I leave on tour? What if she gets upset, or brushes me off? What if she wants to leave? Stuart's irritated and impatient voice fills my ears. He would be beyond upset with me.

What have you done, Pierre?

"Pierre?"

"What? Oh. Yes. Well ..."

I gather my thoughts and fill Tasha in on the basic plotline of my book. I describe the characters and their arcs up to this point.

"So, it's time for them to kiss or continue to avoid one another?"

The question feels ironic when she says it. Her one eyebrow raises and she looks at me expectantly. Is she subtly implying we're at the same impasse?

"Yes. I need to decide if it's time for them to kiss. Or, should this burn and tension continue to simmer for a few more chapters."

"How does each course of action serve the story?"

"Yes!" I say with more passion than is needed. "Of course!"

Tasha giggles. "What?"

"That's what I lost sight of. How does their decision move the story?"

"So, do they need to kiss or wait?"

"They need to kiss."

We need to kiss. Or I need to kiss Tasha. My gaze drops to her lips. I remember what it felt like when she settled into me at the stove. Her hands in my hair, her palm cataloging my arm and chest muscles. The feel of her hair slipping through my fingers, the softness of the skin below her ear as my lips grazed her neck.

"Agreed," Tasha says, snapping me out of my reverie.

"Only ..."

I have so many unanswered questions.

Fear. It boils down to fear.

I'm afraid of losing her.

"Only?" she echoes.

"Nothing. Maybe you can help me write the scene."

"Help you write a kissing scene?"

Tasha's face is a puzzle—one I can't decipher. She blushes lightly. Her cheeks take on the momentary tell-tale pink, and then fade back to their normal porcelain color. Her eyebrows raise slightly in toward the middle of her forehead, but the rest of her face is neutral. Her beautiful brown eyes soften.

We shouldn't have kissed.

What am I saying? We definitely needed that kiss. Holding back the chemistry coursing between us would have been like putting a cap on a bubbling beaker in a laboratory.

Is chemistry all we have? Or is there more?

Now is not the time to find out. I'm leaving midday tomorrow for New York and Boston.

I glance at my blank computer screen.

"No. It's fine. I can write my own book. I'm sorry. You really helped me a lot already. I feel unstuck. Ready to kiss … to write a kiss. To write about their kiss." *Agh. What is wrong with me?* "How was your day at Catty Coffee?"

I try out the local slang, hoping it puts an air of casual comfort into our conversation while shifting the topic off us … and kissing … and romance.

"Catty? Look at you, using the town nickname. You're officially a Harvest Hollowan."

"Hollowan? I thought it was Halloween?"

"That's the holiday."

"We had that holiday for a few years in France. Mostly in the larger cities. It never really caught on. And, I am officially a Frenchman for life. One who happily landed in Harvest Hollow."

"I'm glad it's happily." Tasha sighs.

Her eyes search my face. Then she claps both palms onto her knees.

"Well, I'd better get dinner on. I'm making something far less complicated tonight. Chicken pot pie and a salad."

"Sounds delicious. And you don't have to cook for me every night."

"You cooked twice this week. I'm just taking my turn. When you're gone it will be soup or cereal every night unless I join Heather and Nate for a meal. I may as well treat us both to some home cooking while you're here."

"Thank you."

Our eyes lock. I want to read so much into the way she is looking at me. I wish my expression could speak for me.

When I get home. That is when I will talk to her. We have to talk. And we will.

28

TASHA

But she had dreamed of being his for too long.
He had quite ruined her for
a marriage of convenience.
She wanted everything from him:
his mind, his body, his name
and, most of all, his heart.
— Sarah MacLean

The house is quiet with Pierre gone. It's been three days since he left. I feel like Goldilocks, sneaking into someone's house. Nothing fits quite right— too hot, too cold, too big, too small, definitely too empty. It didn't feel that way when Pierre was here. He made me feel comfortable, nearly at home—just right.

I'm still in my pajamas, snuggled on the living room couch, a fire going in the fireplace to stave off the morning chill.

One recording is out of the way, another one scheduled, and I have two job inquiries I need to respond to.

There are a few author assistant tasks I could do, but my current read is too engaging. I love when that happens. Love, and hate. A few hours can pass before I realize I haven't done laundry, haven't exercised, and haven't answered emails. But my heart is full of the sweetness that comes from reading something captivating—from traveling into other lives and places through the written words of a gifted author.

The house phone rings. It rarely does since everyone uses cell phones these days. I let it go to voicemail since this is officially Pierre's home.

"Pierre? C'est ta soeur, Marguerite. Tu te souviens de moi, non?

I've been studying French more since the wedding. I can pick out a few words. It's. Your. Sister. Marguerite. Then something about him remembering something or someone? I'm not sure.

I stand from the couch, setting my Kindle on the cushion and walking to the kitchen to answer the phone. I stay there, appreciating this beautiful view of the woods turned into a burst of fall foliage while I answer. The wind gently ruffles the leaves, sending them into a synchronized sway while some flutter to the ground, adding to the already accumulating carpet on the forest floor.

"Hello? Marguerite?"

"Allo? Is this Tasha?"

"Oui. Yes."

"Oh! You are adorable. You are trying to speak French. This is good."

"Thanks. Trying is the key word. It's not the easiest language for us Americans to learn."

"Oui. If only you can catch a head cold, then your throat

and nose will make all the noises you need." She laughs at her own joke and I join her.

I really like Marguerite. Pierre told me we would hit it off. He was right. I feel like I've known her my whole life. There's an ease between us.

"So, please. Tell me why is my brother not answering my calls? Is he okay?"

"Oh. Yes. As far as I know. He's on tour. He's in New York, actually. He'll be in Boston a few days from now, and then back home."

"Ah. Home is Avignon. Do not forget. But his home for now, yes."

"Right."

"Well, I was worried. But now I am not. He is probably busy. Saving his calls to talk to you when he has time."

He hasn't. I don't know what I expected, but Pierre hasn't called once since he left. It's fine. Why would he call? It's not like I'm actually his wife. And he is busy, as Marguerite said.

"So, how are you, my sister?"

I blush. It's awful carrying off a lie with his family and mine. For some reason, I don't care if the rest of the world thinks we're married or not. But those people I care about, my booksta-besties on Instagram, my parents, his parents, his sisters, even some of my old classmates in town ... I feel awful for deceiving them.

It's for a good cause. You are doing him a favor.

A favor. I'm not doing myself any favors. Kissing him might have been the worst decision of my life. Or the best. I touch my lips, letting my fingertips drift to the spot under my ear, remembering his kisses, the way his breath skated across my skin.

"Allo?"

"Oh, sorry. I'm good. Fine."

"Ah. That is not good. If you are the same as we French women are, then fine is never fine."

I chuckle. "Yeah. Well, it's lonely here without Pierre. I miss him."

I can't believe I just admitted that out loud—to his *sister*!

"Awww. Ma belle. You miss my brother. No one has missed him besides my mother for as long as I have known him—which is my whole life, of course."

I'm suddenly overwhelmed with an insatiable need to know as much as I can about Pierre and his history.

"No one?"

"Definitely not that chat of a girlfriend he had."

"Chat?"

"Cat. She was like a kitten and then like a vicious tiger. Not good. She shredded his heart with her claws. Nasty woman. Ah. But she is gone. I won't discuss her now. He has you. And you are a treasure."

"Thank you."

"You need to do something distracting. Your beloved will be back in no time, and I am quite sure he misses you as much as you miss him."

"How do you know?"

I'm a glutton for punishment, apparently, so eager to catch a crumb of validation telling me what I feel for Pierre might be more than one-sided. If Marguerite only knew.

"I see him. A sister knows her brother. You know? We might be able to fool our parents. But we can never fool our siblings. We see through everything. And my brother is so in love with you. It does my heart good. You have brought him back to life."

I have? Can that be right?

"Well, frangine. I will let you go, as you say."

"Frangine?"

"It means sister, but in a casual way we call one another."

I smile, even though my heart feels like it will split in half. I would like nothing more than to have Marguerite as a sister.

"Au revoir," I say, using my French.

"Jusqu'à la prochaine fois. Kiss kiss."

I don't know what she said. I'll look it up later. The line goes dead. Instead of going back to my Kindle, I hop in the shower and get dressed. It's an hour before I'm supposed to get ready for a shift at Cataloochee, but I'd rather be among people than alone in this home with my thoughts.

The coffee shop is swarming with people today. Regulars. Tourists. People from Harvest Hollow who just want a coffee while they shop or meet up with friends. I put on a half-apron and the handmade name tag Heather made me and get ready to work.

Heather comes into the back. "We've got a problem."

"What's up?"

"Um. Peggy Grady was in earlier."

"That's always a little bit of a problem. What juicy bits of nonsense is she passing around today?"

"Well ..." Heather looks like her cat died. Only she doesn't have a cat. "Margie called Peggy this morning, so Peggy came running into the shop. She was actually walking, but she might as well have been running ... She was so eager to get her news out to the world."

Heather steps closer to me. Puts a hand on my arm. This can't be good.

"Peggy showed me some social media posts: One on the Harvest Hollow Happenings page, and another elsewhere."

"Okaaaayyy."

"About you."

"Why would there be a social media post about me?"

"It would be great if there were only one."

"What?!"

"It's sort of speculative," Heather hedges.

"What is?" My voice is higher now. Anxiety coursing through my bloodstream like ethanol-infused fuel in a racecar.

"Well ... you see ..."

"Spit it out! Um, please. Please, spit it out. I'm dying over here."

"Heather?" One of the other baristas, Shawn, pokes his head into the back.

"Um. Yeah. Give me a minute. Is it urgent?"

"No. Just ..."

"I'll be right out," Heather says with a smile toward her employee.

The door swings back and forth on its hinges as it settles back into a fully shut position.

"What is going on?" I ask.

"It's this."

Heather pulls her phone out of her pocket, swipes it open, taps a few times and hands it over to me. I read the post and my mouth falls open.

My head begins to shake back and forth slowly. "No." I look up at her. "No. No. No. This isn't happening."

"Calm down, Tash. It's just a post. It's speculation."

"Who could have figured this out?"

"No one figured anything out. It's speculation."

"Stop saying that word. Please."

"Okay."

Heather steps toward me and pulls me into a hug. I lean into her, hoping to gather strength from her as I always have. Someone posted a photo of my wedding day, but the caption is all about how Pierre is marrying me to maintain his legal capacity to stay in the states for his tour.

Basically, they nailed it. Exposed us. Our secret is out in the public eye.

Heather murmurs into my hair. "No one proved anything. This is today's gossip. You know what they say about gossip?"

"A lie is usually halfway around the globe before the truth even has its shoes tied?"

"No, silly. Gossip is like a house of cards. It's fragile and can fall apart at any moment."

"I've never heard that."

"Well, it's true. This will blow over like a house of cards. The next juicy tidbit will entice the people who live for details of others' lives instead of living their own."

"I can only hope."

I'm finally breathing a little more normally. My palms are still sweaty, but I'm coming back to myself.

"The irony is that it's not really a farce for me anymore." I look at Heather, my eyes nearly tearing up over the depth of what I feel for Pierre.

"The marriage."

"Well, it's not like I'd be married to Pierre this quickly. But my feelings for him are definitely not pretend anymore. Not even a little."

"I know. And I think it's time he knows that too."

29

PIERRE

Sometimes there is no next time,
no time-outs, no second chances.
Sometimes it's now or never.

~ Alan Bennett

"Excuse me, ladies!" Stuart announces to the long line of women, and a few men, standing at my table waiting for me to sign copies of my books. "I need to grab Pierre away for one moment and we'll be right back in a flash. Sorry for the inconvenience."

Stuart leans across my table and lowers his voice to speak to the next woman in line.

"Just a quick minute, I promise."

She smiles at Stuart with a flirty look of appreciation. I guess he is nice looking enough, if you don't factor in his domineering and somewhat high-strung personality. But maybe that's only how he is at work. No. I'm sure that's how he is everywhere.

We're day three into the book tour and I'm already wondering why I fought to stay in the states. Touring isn't horrible. My fans are amazing. It's just draining. I'm used to holing up in my home alone. Having Tasha there has been comfortable, except for the fact that I'm living with a chronic longing for more with her. But her presence feels so natural. She blended into my life seamlessly, like we were made for one another.

I miss her.

I shouldn't.

We haven't been together long enough for her to mean this much.

But love defies logic.

And my heart misses Tasha.

Stuart pulls me into a storage room at the back of the book store.

"Are you about to murder or drug me?" I tease.

His face is more serious than I've ever seen it.

"We're not here to joke around." Stuart shuts the door behind himself and looks around nervously. "Apparently some crazed fan of yours got wind that you and Tasha had a wedding. She started snooping around and she conjectured that you are in a marriage of convenience."

"What? How did you find all this out?"

"It's all over social media. She posted something and tagged your fan pages. There's even a hashtag."

"A hashtag?"

I stay off social media, preferring that Stuart and others he hires manage all that nonsense for me.

"It's a way of categorizing things. When someone uses a

hashtag, other people can start to use it. It becomes a way that posts go viral. Your hashtag is #PierresFictionalFall."

"Viral, meaning they spread? Like an illness?"

"Yes, Pierre. For Pete's sakes. Have you been living under a rock?"

"Next to one, mostly." I chuckle. Stuart does not.

I shake my head. So, a fan thinks Tasha and I are in a fake marriage.

"Did this fan go to the authorities?"

"As far as we know, no, she didn't. But she doesn't need to. This is causing a stir. The kind of stir you don't need."

"I thought you always told me all publicity is good publicity."

"Yeah. Scratch that. This isn't."

"Okay, so what do we do?"

I lean back on a storage rack. It wobbles, so I stand again.

"How are you so calm?"

Stuart has been frantically pacing, back and forth, back and forth, in this small room filled with boxes of books, shelf labels, cleaning supplies and end cap decor.

"I'm a logical man, Stuart. Getting emotional rarely solves problems. What do we need to do? Is my time in the states up? Am I going to jail? Will I pay a fine?"

"If Immigration doesn't get wind of this, you aren't in any legal trouble. And they would still have to investigate and find proof that you and Tasha are in a fake marriage. Us holding off on paying her until the year is out will help. There's no paper trail to prove anything except that you two chose to get married at an unconventional pace. Everything else looks legit. You had the ceremony. You live together. You have witnesses—even in your own families and friend groups—who will swear you are in love and in a committed marriage."

He sighs, still pacing, looking at me as he passes by, then looking at me again when he passes going the other direction.

"I don't know about the rest of what might happen. If only you were honestly married to an American—not merely pulling off a charade."

"I'm not."

"I know."

"No, I mean, I'm not pulling off a charade. I honestly care for Tasha."

"She's a great girl from what I've seen."

"She is," I sigh. "Stuart. I don't mean she's a great girl. I mean, I love her."

"You *love* her."

"I love her."

I love her. I do.

What does love involve?

Intimate knowledge of another soul, passionate and intense feelings of affection and attachment, a decision to commit to that person. I can check all those boxes without even blinking when it comes to Tasha. We have come to know one another quickly because of my circumstances. Not only could I easily list off her favorite things, I can discern her moods, anticipate her thoughts, and I live to hear her opinions and reactions. She delights me. I think of her when we're apart and I cherish the time we spend together. She makes me laugh, and smile, and see the world through a new set of eyes. And our kisses. Well, there's no shortage of chemistry between us.

Time isn't the only measure of love.

As a matter of fact, I imagine there are people on earth who have spent twenty or thirty years together who don't love one another the way I love Tasha.

"Yes," I repeat for emphasis. "I love her."

Stuart stops his pacing. He looks up at the ceiling and then back at me.

"I love her. Which means my marriage isn't a sham. Maybe it started that way, but I've fallen in love with Tasha. And I know it's early for marriage, but ... here we are."

"Well, this is great! This changes everything!" He pauses, seeming lost in thought. "Wait. Does she love you too?"

"I don't really know."

"Well, you better find out. Your future might be riding on that fact."

30

TASHA

Nothing haunts us like the things we don't say.

~ Mitch Albom

I tug my sweater closer around me. Even inside the airport, it's chilly this time of year. The weatherman said we may even get snow in the coming week. Snow! In October! It happens most years, especially in the higher elevations—just a dusting—enough to remind us Christmas is around the corner. But I'm still enjoying all things fall: pumpkins, colored leaves, hot cocoa, a fire in the hearth, warm bowls of soup, walks in the crisp air through the woods behind our house, all the apple treats ... I love it all. I'm in no hurry to kiss fall goodbye.

After Heather broke the news to me at Cataloochee, I hung my apron back up. Heather insisted I go take care of business. I rushed back to Pierre's home—our home—and packed a suitcase.

I need him.

We need to face this together. Either that, or I'm about to

find out there is no *we*. One way or the other, I have to get to Pierre. I called an old friend in town, Sue MacNamara. She went to school with Heather, and she runs a travel agency which handles local outdoor adventure bookings as well as national and international travel. She got me a pretty decent last-minute flight into LaGuardia.

I also contacted Bob since Stuart is on this leg of the tour with Pierre. Bob got me the details as to where Pierre is staying. I only noticed the itinerary and a Post-it note that said, *See you when I get back. - Pierre*, pinned to the cork board in the kitchen after I called Bob. So, Pierre didn't leave me as completely out of the loop as I thought he had.

I didn't call Pierre. He's immersed in this tour, meeting fans, signing books, giving talks, making special appearances. The last thing he needs is me interrupting a book signing or one of his other events just so I can trouble him about a social media post that's spreading gossip. Even if the rumors are true, calling him wouldn't solve anything. What we need to say to one another needs to be said in person.

I look up at the overhead screen hanging over the bench seats at my gate. It's got some midday talk show on. The commercials follow and when the show comes back, my jaw nearly drops. Pierre's beautiful face fills the screen.

What is going on?

A reporter is with him. They're both bundled in coats and scarves, standing outside a bookstore. He's on TV? I had no idea he was going to be on television.

The reporter leads with, "Today I'm honored to be with Pierre Toussaint, the author behind the internationally acclaimed, best-selling romance novels written under the pen name we all know as Amelie De Pierre. Welcome, Pierre."

"Thank you, Meredith. It's a pleasure."

His voice. I'm instantly soothed, and acutely aware of the distance separating us.

That's my *husband*.

"So, Pierre, it's come to our attention that a fan of yours started a rumor this week on social media. What do you think of that?"

They're talking about the social media posts? So, Pierre knows.

"I don't really use social media, Meredith. I know that's unusual, but I have people who work for me in a remote capacity. They all run my social media accounts. I just write the books."

"You just write the books." The reporter fans herself. "Oh, yes. Yes, you do."

Hey! That's *my* husband.

Pierre is his usual formal, aloof, kind, but not-available self. I settle back into my chair.

"So, back to this fan. What do you think of her rumor? She alleges that you and your new wife, Tasha, is it?"

Pierre nods. "Oui. Tasha."

Oui. Gah. I love when he says, oui.

"Yes, well this fan alleges that you and Tasha only got married on paper. She says you are in a marriage to help you remain in the United States. She's saying you don't have any other way to legally stay here. Basically, she's accusing you of a felony, and of deceiving your readers. Is there any truth to this rumor?"

Pierre is quiet. And for a moment I wonder if he's going to spill the beans and come clean on national television. I hold my breath and look at him, willing him to look into my eyes. I know, it's crazy. He can't see me.

Then he looks straight into the camera.

"I love my wife."

He smiles a gorgeous, private smile. It's as though he's smiling right at me. Of course, he isn't, but I feel that smile spread through me. That's my smile, the one that belongs to me, the smile he gave me on our wedding day while we said our vows. He may not know it, but that's my smile.

Pierre continues to talk into the microphone held by the reporter. "Tasha and I only recently met a few months ago, but she has been a fan of mine for years. When we met—at my book signing and meet-the-author event—we spent a number of days together. She is charming, captivating, easy to be with. Then, we found out we both live in North Carolina, so we connected when we returned to the east coast. And we have spent a lot of time together since our return. To some, our wedding may appear rushed. I understand that. Also," Pierre pauses, looking at Meredith and then back at the camera. "It is none of their business. The bottom line, as you say in America, is that I love my wife. I am not faking that. We are legally married and my heart is hers."

His heart is mine?

I clutch my chest, just to keep my heart from beating right out through my sweater.

Pierre loves me?

Is this real? Is he only saying words for the sake of quelling a lie?

I know he isn't. Deep, deep down, I know.

Pierre loves me!

I feel suddenly fidgety. I could fly to New York on my own nervous energy right now.

The reporter thanks Pierre and closes the interview with,

"Well, there you have it. Pierre Toussaint loves his wife. And to that fan, if you are really a fan, give the Toussaints a break. These two are newlyweds, obviously in love. Marriage is hard enough work without this kind of meddling interference making it harder. That's all I've got. I'm Meredith Jackson, here on the streets of New York. Back to you, Lucy."

Pierre stands in the background with a content expression on his face. It's a lot like the look he had when he was standing in the resort lobby the first day I saw him—the day I mistook him for a hot French professor. I was only wrong about one of those things. He's not a professor.

The screen goes back to the set where three hosts smile and discuss how sweet it is that Pierre and I are in love, and then they go on to welcome the cast of a current television series.

My flight is called and I can't get in line fast enough. In two hours, I'll be in New York. I'll find Pierre as soon as I land. I have half a mind to call him, but now, knowing what I do, I want to surprise him. I hope he likes surprises.

We've been a married couple who were not allowed to touch one another, kiss one another, say sweet words, or use nicknames with each other. All that ends tonight.

Pierre loves me!

31

PIERRE

Nothing haunts us like the things we don't say.
~ Mitch Albom

We just finished the second book signing of the day. Now Stuart and I are in an Uber heading back to our hotel through New York traffic. He's scrolling his phone. I close my eyes, letting my head drop onto the seat for the duration of the drive. I had two signings today and the spontaneous TV spot to clear up that mess of a rumor. I'm fatigued and ready for a quick bite to eat, and then my bed.

After Stuart cornered me in the storage closet, we returned to the table at the back of the bookstore to tend to my line of patient fans. My wheels were turning while I smiled and chatted with each reader as they approached the table, but Stuart moved more quickly than I could have imagined he was able. He called in a favor with an old friend who works at a TV station here in New York. As soon as we finished the signing, a reporter met us outside the bookshop.

Just tell them what you told me, Stuart had coached me before we walked through the double doors onto the sidewalk where the camera and reporter awaited us.

Which part? I had asked him.

This isn't a farce. Your relationship may have developed quickly, but you are a man in love. You are married to the woman you love.

That I could do. Finally, I am not lying to the press or to my readers. The only one who does not yet know the truth is Tasha—the most important person, the only person who truly matters.

As if my thoughts conjured her, my cell rings. When I pull it out of my pocket and see her face on the screen, a smile crests on my face.

"Allo, Tasha?"

"Pierre?"

"Oui. It is me. Are you okay?"

"Oui. I am now."

Oui. I love when she speaks French.

"Where are you?" she asks.

"Somewhere in New York City. We are on our way back to the hotel. Did you find my note? I left it on the cork board in the kitchen."

"I found it just this morning."

"Good. Well. Then you know I am staying at Hotel Beacon. It has a good view. We can see Central Park just beyond the San Remo towers from our room."

"Oooh. Classy."

Her teasing brings a smile to my face. I am no longer feeling quite as drowsy. Only four more days until I see her.

"Yes." She giggles. "You will be in Harvest Hollow in four days."

"I said that out loud?"

Now I feel like I am the one blushing for a change of pace. My cheeks feel heated.

"Ask me where I am," Tasha says. Her voice sounds different—light, airy, even flirtatious.

"Where are you, Cher?"

"Have I told you I love when you call me that?"

"You did. You mentioned it when I kissed you in the kitchen."

Suddenly Stuart's phone holds no interest for him. He is giving me a look. I give him one back—one that says mind your own business, please.

"Where am I? Hmmm. Where am I?" Tasha's voice is sing-song, teasing.

"Are you in my bedroom?"

I'm surprisingly emboldened by the way Tasha is purposely toying with me.

"Not exactly."

"Are you in the hallway leading to my bedroom?"

"Which bedroom?"

"I only have one bedroom."

"No. You have two. One in your home in Harvest Hollow. One in New York City for the next two nights."

"Yes. And one in Avignon, if we want to be specific."

"I am not in Avignon."

"That is good because the first time you go to my home-town, I will be the one to take you."

"Agreed."

Agreed? She is in a very playful mood, like a kitten who has had catnip. I like it very much.

"Where are you, then? Don't keep me in suspense."

"I am in ..." she pauses. "New York City."

"What? You are here. Cher. How? Why? Are you serious?"

"I am. I flew up this afternoon. We need to talk. I wanted to see you." Her voice grows quiet. "I missed you."

"I missed you too, Cher. So much."

"You did?"

"Oui. Tu m'as manqué comme mon propre bras me manquerait."

"Okay, I've been studying French, but that was too much. Translate please."

"I will translate when I see you in person."

"I'm right here waiting—in your hotel lobby."

"Ah, Cher. Mon ange. You came here for me."

"I did."

A few minutes after Tasha and I hang up, the Uber pulls to the curb in front of the awning stretching over the sidewalk from the tall brick and stone building where we are staying. I walk ahead of Stuart, rushing into the lobby. Amidst the dark wood, brass decor, sitting areas and large glass windows, I see her.

Tasha.

She sees me too, drops the handle of her bag, and runs toward me, throwing her arms around my neck.

We've never been this unabashed and vulnerable.

Tasha's clinging to me and my arms have wrapped around her of their own accord.

I whisper into the top of her head. "I'm so glad you are here, Cher."

She tilts her head up to me.

"I saw you on TV."

She saw me. She heard my profession. And she's here.

Her face looks expectant, soft—all mine.

"Let's go to my room."

I don't want to talk about this here with all these people milling around us. We've had enough public exposure over the past twenty-four hours. I need Tasha, alone, just the two of us.

"Okay," Tasha says, turning to walk to her bag.

I watch her walk away from me for a few moments. Then I follow her, grasping the handle of her bag and taking her hand with my free hand. I lead her to the bank of elevators. We ride up, fingers entwined, stealing glances at one another, but holding our words until we are truly alone and settled in our room.

I pull my key card and open the door, waving for Tasha to enter in front of me.

"Well, hello! The happy couple has made it!"

Stuart.

In the headiness of seeing Tasha, I had forgotten Stuart and I rented a suite—to share.

Tasha looks at me, her face scrunches up, lips tuck in, eyes widen, brows raise. It's such a transparent expression. Stuart chuckles.

"Didn't expect a third wheel?"

"Uh. No," Tasha says to Stuart. "I will be getting my own room anyway. Don't worry."

"No. No you won't," Stuart says. "How would that look? Here we're fending off a rumor that there's trouble in paradise. Sleeping in separate rooms will only fuel questions and suspicions. You'll stay here. After all, Pierre's side of this suite has two queen beds. Not that you have to use both of them, but that's not my call. I'll just be right over here."

Stuart points to the other side of the thin dividing wall between our two halves of the suite.

I give Stuart a friendly, silent glance. We study one another, man to man while the three of us remain standing in this tiny foyer of the suite.

Tasha seems to be taking in the pale green walls, tidy furniture and appointments around the room. Her eyes drift to the window and linger, a smile growing as she appreciates the view of the Upper West Side of New York City.

I continue to stare at Stuart, willing him to take a hint.

"You know what?" he finally says.

Tasha's gaze flits away from the window to Stuart.

"I think I'll see if they have a single. It's on you, Pierre. You'll put me up in my own room, won't you?"

"Gladly," I say with a smile.

"Right. Well, I'll get right on that. I'll just ..." he hooks a thumb toward his side of the room. "I'll just call down to the lobby."

"Great," I say. "Thank you, Stuart."

I place my palm on Tasha's lower back, urging her into my half of the suite, tugging her suitcase behind me.

"I thought we'd be alone," I say, apologetically.

"It's okay," Tasha assures me. "I can talk quietly."

She turns to me and surprises me by standing on tiptoe and placing a kiss on my cheek. Just like that, like she kisses me every day, like I'm her actual husband, or boyfriend.

I stand there like a statue, suddenly unsure of what to do with my hands, my eyes, my words.

She just smiles up at me, our fingers still interlaced. She gives my hand a little, conspiratorial, comforting squeeze. Then she turns and plops onto the edge of one of the beds.

"I call this one. I want to wake up to an unobstructed view of those two spires out there."

"It's yours," I tell her, wishing I could locate my usual sense of calm and confidence.

Tasha looks up at me. "Sit down, Pierre. You're making me nervous."

I'm making her nervous?

I follow her directions, walking to the side table by the wall with the window and taking a seat in one of the two chairs there.

Tasha lowers her voice, "I was going to tell you this before I saw you on TV. When I went into Catty Coffee to work today ... Wow. That was just today. It feels like a week ago! Anyway, Heather told me about the social media storm. I left the shop immediately, called Bob, got a ticket ... and, well, I came here. But on the way ..." Her face lifts, focusing on mine, our eyes saying everything to each other. "Well, I saw you. Can you believe it? I was at my gate and they happened to have an overhead screen and it just so happened to be tuned to the channel showing you being interviewed."

"It's practically a miracle."

"Pierre," Tasha stands, walking toward me. I spread my legs, allowing her to slip nearer to me. I wrap my arms around her waist and look up into her face. She runs her hand through my hair. I reflexively shut my eyes, reveling in the feel of her touch, the overwhelming emotions surging through me.

I can't let her bear the burden of bridging this gap. I stand. She steps back, making room for me.

"Well! I got another room!" Stuart's booming voice interrupts the moment.

If he hadn't been responsible for finagling that whole

televised interview today, I might clock him. He's so oblivious.

"I'll be out of your hair now." He chuckles. "Not that you two lovebirds will miss me. I imagine I could do a naked tap dance right through the room and you wouldn't even flinch."

That is an image I didn't ever need taking up space in my head. *Ever.*

Tasha's laughter fills the suite.

"Stuart!" she shouts out through her laughter. "Oh my gosh!"

He grins at Tasha. "I always knew I liked you."

I draw her closer. Not that Stuart's a threat. It's just, Tasha's mine. This bubbly, gorgeous, selfless woman is mine.

"Well, I'll be on the floor below this one. If you need me ... which, you obviously won't. Don't forget tomorrow's schedule."

He turns to walk to the door, his suitcase sitting in the entryway.

"Oh, and room service is on me! Or dinner out. Whatever you kids decide."

I smile at him. "Thank you, Stuart."

"You're my bread and butter, Pierre."

I know I'm more than that to him. He goes the extra mile, partly because that's who he is, and partly because I matter to him.

The door clicks behind Stuart and I turn to Tasha, running the back of my hand along her cheek from her ear to her chin.

Before she can get ahead of me again, I speak. "I love you, Tasha. I know it may feel fast, or crazy, or too much. But I love you. It's not infatuation. I'm not an impulsive man. I feel like

I've been waiting my whole life for you to drop your stack of books and allow me to help you gather them. You've been so good to me. But it's not only what you do that I love, the ease with which you care for others, the way you so seamlessly fit into my otherwise private life. I love you for who you are. For the way your eyes light up over the smallest things, the beauty you bring into each situation, your heart. And so many things I can't even find words for. I am an author, though. I will find the words if you give me enough years together to search for them."

She is crying. A tear tracks down her cheek and I swipe it gently.

"I love you, too. How did this happen? I wasn't looking for you. I just wanted my books signed by Amelie De Pierre." Tasha laughs through her tears. "And there you were, this sexy French professor."

I chuckle. "I'm not a professor."

"I know. But I thought you were. I saw you in that lobby, leaned up against the wall, looking so pulled together, so confident, so continental. And so very out of my league."

"Ah, Cher. You are wrong. You are out of my league, ma ange."

"I looked that up. My angel. I love it."

"I love you."

The words fall easily now. Words I've only said to my family and Camille. She didn't deserve them. They were perfunctory then, coming because they should. We had reached a certain length of time together and it felt like I ought to say the sentence, mark our relationship with a declaration. It never was because I couldn't help but say them. With Tasha, these words are like water bursting through a dam. They don't even hold the fullness of what I feel for her. Woefully inadequate, that's what they are. But they are what we have.

I reiterate my heartfelt feelings for her in my mother tongue. "Je t'aime."

"I love you, too."

Her eyes flick between mine, searching for something, inviting, playing with me again.

I lean in and run my hand along her neck until it rests at her hairline. I gently tug her toward me. Tasha meets me halfway, brushing her lips against mine, and then our kiss becomes more passionate. I hold her, running my hands through her hair, over her back, trailing down her arms, until our fingers entwine. Tasha lifts our enjoined hands and places them between us. I feel her heartbeat beneath my skin.

My body is humming. The only thing in the world is Tasha. Our kiss is sweet, promising, then frantic, then soft. She runs her fingers through my hair, lightly dragging her nails across my neck, leaving a trail of goosebumps in her wake.

I pull back, needing to see her face, to look into her beautiful brown eyes, to assure myself she's here, reciprocating this love I feel for her.

I cup her cheek and she lifts her hand, cupping mine in her palm. She runs her fingers along the stubble that's grown in throughout this overly-long day.

"I love your jawline," she says, smiling at me so openly that I feel leveled. "And these." Her fingers skim the edge of my glasses.

"You love my glasses?" I swallow a lump forming in my throat.

I need to get out of this room before I pull my wife onto

one of these beds and show her all the ways I love her. We may be married on paper, but we are in this strange uncharted land: in love, but still discovering one another. Legally wed, but never having dated. Having promised one another the deepest vows two people can express to one another, but all in the name of my business.

"Let's go out to eat!" I nearly shout the words.

"Um. Okay." Tasha giggles. "Take me out on the town, hubby of mine."

32

TASHA

And why not? If you love her, tell her so!
~ Edmond Rostand, Cyrano de Bergerac

"We're dating," Pierre says for the fourth time. I smile over at him from my spot on the couch. My stocking-clad feet are propped in his lap and he's lazily stroking across my fluffy socks with his fingertips.

"How can you be dating when you are already married?" Pierre's father's face is etched in confusion.

"Um. You want to field that one, Cher?" Pierre asks me.

I lean in so my face fills Pierre's phone screen a bit more. We're FaceTiming his family—my idea. He would have rather called than do a video chat.

Or not. Not. Definitely not.

He said, *This is my life. I'm an adult. Yes. They are my family and I adore them. But this—explaining the convoluted start and the resulting twists and turns of our relationship—I could do without.*

But I insisted. If Pierre and I remain together, which we definitely plan to do, these people are my in-laws. I need to straighten out my relationship with them while Pierre and I figure out how to date when we are already married.

"Bonjour, ma famille," I say, calling Pierre's family my family.

Pierre glances over at me with fondness. I know he loves it when I speak French.

With his head behind his phone so his family can't see him, he mouths, "Je t'adore."

He adores me.

"Moi aussi," I mouth back, completely forgetting the eyes of his family are all trained on me.

"You too?" Marguerite giggles. "Awww. Were you telling my brother you love him?"

I blush. "I was." I look into Pierre's eyes. "I do."

I clear my throat. "As you all now know, Pierre and I had an unconventional start to our relationship." His family nods, waiting for me to continue. "And now we have had time to talk and think. We decided, since our first months together were so unusual, we're going to go back to fill in what we missed. So, we will date."

"But you are still married?" Pierre's mom asks.

"Oui. We are married," I assure her.

"We are happy for you two," Colette says. "Take your time. You are wise. Date. And then, well, you are already married, so someday soon you will move upstairs, no?"

Pierre grabs the phone. I'm giggling.

"Mind your business, Colette. That is all you need to know. We are dating. We are still married. We are in love. Now, go live your own lives. Maybe find some men of your own to bother."

Spoken like a true baby brother.

I'm still giggling.

We explained to our parents and Pierre's sisters the whole truth after he returned home from Boston. We had to tell them since the news of the social media posts and his televised correction reached them. But at that time, we hadn't yet decided how to move forward. We knew we would stay married. He still needs our marriage in order to complete his tour. Besides, we are madly in love. It's ridiculous how in love we are. If I weren't in this relationship, I'd probably be tempted to gag over the sweetness of our connection and how often we demonstrate our feelings for one another through our constant little touches, impromptu kisses, and sweet, flirty texts.

Marguerite and Colette were relentless when we first confessed our farce, teasing me about the way I faked moaning out Pierre's name the morning after our wedding.

We were sure you were married. After all, what friends make those noises from a bedroom in the early morning hours?

I turned the deepest shade of red ever. I didn't need a mirror to confirm it. My face felt like it was on fire, despite the cooler fall temperatures in North Carolina.

After more conversation, and Pierre's family filling him in about things in France, we say our goodbyes, blowing kisses and promising to connect again soon.

A chorus of "Au revoir, Tasha!" and "Bonsoir, Pierre!" rings through the phone.

Pierre sets his phone down once he hangs up the call.

He turns to me. "Go to your room, please."

"What?"

"Humor me, okay?"

"Okaaayyy." I shoot him a quizzical look, reluctantly lifting my feet from their cozy spot in his lap.

I look so disheveled, in an, *I'm just home hanging out with my boyfriend-slash-husband* way. I'm wearing an old Harvest High sweatshirt, yoga pants and fluffy socks. My hair is up in a messy bun. I can't believe I looked like this on that Face-Time call. There's comfortable, and then there's way too comfortable. His family looked their usual polished and pressed selves. Maybe one day I'll be more like them—more French.

I walk to my room, shut the door and look around.

Why am I in here? What is Pierre up to?

My phone pings.

Pierre: *Hello, ma belle petite amie.*

His beautiful girlfriend.

Me: *Pierre, have you seen me today?*

Pierre: *Oui. Of course. You are all I see.*

Me: *You're way cheesier than I thought you'd be as a boyfriend ... husband.*

Pierre: *Cheesier? What does my love for you have to do with cheese?*

I chuckle to myself.

Me: *Cheesier. Corny? Um. It's like when someone is so*

over the top with their affection it's bordering on
ridiculous.

I still love being his personal concierge into the world of
American clichés and catch phrases.

Pierre: *Well, in this case, there is no cheese. I am serious*
as a heart attack.

Me: *Where did you hear that phrase?*

Pierre: *Nate said it.*

Me: *You need to stop copying Nate. He's literally the worst*
ambassador for the English language.

Pierre: *Whatever you say, Bae. You do you, Boo.*

I'm giggling now. And I still don't know why I've been
relegated to my bedroom while Pierre is obviously
occupied with texting me.

Me: *Why am I in my room? I miss your hands on my*
feet.

Pierre: *I miss my hands on your feet too.*

Pierre: *I wanted to ask you on a date.*

Me: *A date?*

Pierre: *We are dating now. I wanted to start soon. That way we can move along to being married.*

Me: *We are married.*

Pierre: *...*

I wait while those dots show up and disappear.

Pierre: *Will you go out on a date with me this Friday?*
I'm dying to know what he was going to say, but I won't press him.

Me: *I'd love to. Where are we going?*

Pierre: *It's a surprise. Much like when you surprised me in New York.*

Me: *One of the best days of my life.*

Pierre: *Mine too, Cher.*

Pierre: *I will pick you up at six on Friday.*

Me: *Pick me up?*

Pierre: *In your room.*

I laugh again. This man. He's really something else.

At first I didn't think we needed to go to the effort of dating. After all, we're already married. But the more we talked, I realized we both need this. We're allowing ourselves the gift of time to fill in the blanks we missed because of our choice to marry before we knew we were in love. I want to honor what Pierre so wisely called, "the rebuilding of our foundation."

Me: *May I come out now?*
Pierre: *Please. If you would. I miss you.*

He misses me.

I'm still blown away at how deeply I am loved—by Pierre Toussaint, of all people.

EPILOGUE

TASHA

I am so far beyond in love with you,
I can barely function.
I want to marry you. Like yesterday.
~ J.A. Huss

"A re you nearly ready?" Pierre's slightly impatient voice carries through from the living room.

"I am!" I shout back.

I fussed a little extra with my hair and makeup tonight. Pierre just got back from Wisconsin and I missed him, as I always do. I want to remind him of what he left behind, not that he needs reminding. He calls me every day he's away now. And when he returns, he dotes on me to make up for the time we've lost.

We've been dating for seven weeks. In the middle of which, Pierre toured South Carolina, Georgia, and then Kentucky and Tennessee. I went with Pierre on that second tour and visited my booksta-besties while he did some interviews and Meet-the-Author book signings. After attending one signing with him, we realized it was best if I did not show up to any others. Readers can become far too fixated on our personal romance story, making them lose sight of Pierre's books in the process.

A knock sounds at my bedroom door.

I open it, as I have been doing every date since we first started trying to reconstruct our beginning. Though, the further along we go, the less I feel it's necessary to rebuild anything. We're in love. How we got here is our story. I don't need to date my husband anymore. We've already promised to keep dating as long as we're together. What I really want ... well, what I really want is to start living my life as Mrs. Pierre Toussaint in every sense of the word.

But Pierre keeps asking me on dates. So, I'll keep saying yes until he feels we've reached some magical benchmark and we can actually live like we're married—and not merely in public.

"You look stunning," Pierre says, eyeing me from my feet to the top of my head and then settling his eyes on my face.

"Thank you."

Maybe this dating thing isn't so bad after all. Not when Pierre's looking at me like that.

"You look gorgeous. I love that tie." My voice cracks with unexpected nerves.

"I have a special night out planned for you, Cher. Here, allow me."

He walks to the hall closet, pulling out my dressier wool coat and holding it up while I slip my arms into the sleeves.

He turns me toward him once my coat is on, staring at me with something unspoken in his gaze. He seems pensive, his eyes roving across my face, his lips tucked in as if he's considering a serious thought.

Pierre bends toward me, and his mouth brushes lightly over mine, then he returns for a more full kiss. I lean into him, secure in his arms, lips buzzing from even this brief connection.

"You are so beautiful, Cher," he breathes the words into my hair, not even trying to hide the way he inhales after speaking. "And you smell delicious. I need to get you out of here before I cancel the plan and put a fire on."

"That sounds like a perfectly great idea," I say. "I could go for a night in with the fire blazing in the hearth, reclined in your arms, a warm drink for each of us on the coffee table ..."

"Mmm." Pierre hums, still holding me near.

"Do you want to stay home?" I offer.

"And kiss you for the rest of the night in front of our fireplace? Oui. But that will have to wait."

Our fireplace. He does that all the time, saying things like, *Let's go home, Cher*, or *I think we should put a wreath on our door and hang strings of lights on our porch for Christmas.* He never has treated me like a houseguest. The one remaining reminder that I have not fully been accepted as his wife comes at around ten o'clock every night when Pierre kisses me goodnight and then turns to walk up the stairs to his room—alone.

I've considered sneaking up there on several occasions. We're married. We're in love.

But something tells me Pierre isn't ready. Or maybe he knows what we need better than I do.

"Let's go," Pierre says, looping his arm around my shoulder and leading me out the door to his car. Bert

McStuffins stands proudly beside the front door in the same spot where we planted him on the day of our wedding. Only, now the trees around the house are nearly bare, and Bert looks a little more than well-loved after some rain storms had their way with him. I just can't bring myself to take him down, even though Thanksgiving came and went two days ago.

Pierre is quiet on the drive away from our home. We pass the lake, the dark evening sky making everything look more magical. Starlight and moon reflect off the water, the hills look like silhouettes surrounding a mirror of ebony glass.

We pull into town, and Pierre still hasn't given me any hints as to what he has planned for tonight. We've done karaoke at Upbeats, trivia night at Tequila Mockingbird, gone to a play at Harvest High School. Attended an end-of-season Appies hockey game at The Summit, and eaten out at most of the local restaurants, even DeLucca's, which is usually reserved for prom nights, anniversaries, and other special occasions. We even went kayaking and hiking.

And, on my favorite date of all, we went to Book Smart and browsed shelves together, buying a few books and then strolling over to Catty to get some coffee and pastries. When we got home from that date, Pierre read aloud to me while I reclined on the couch with my feet in his lap.

It should feel unbelievable, but it doesn't anymore. My boyfriend-slash-husband is still Amelie De Pierre, but somehow the novelty of his fame wore off before we even said, "I do." Now, he's just Pierre, that man who caught my eye in the hotel lobby and has been capturing my heart ever since.

We circle around a few blocks trying to find parking and finally find a space on the other side of the town square.

"Well, here we are," Pierre says.

"At the town square?"

"Yes. Do you remember?"

"Remember?"

Pierre hops out of the driver's side before he has a chance to clarify. When he arrives at my side of the car to hold my door open, he says, "Yes. Remember our first walk around the square, when you could barely look me in the eyes? You kept studying the fountain, trying to find words to say."

"After we met with Bob and Stuart? After they *proposed* to me?"

I emphasize the word *proposed*, still unable to reconcile how they thought it was okay to make such a huge request on Pierre's behalf when he didn't even know what they were up to.

Pierre chuckles, stepping up beside me and slipping his hand into mine. We begin walking around the square at a leisurely pace.

"That's the day, yes." He smiles warmly down at me. "Do you remember what you said to me?"

"Which part?"

"The part where you said, *Well, if it bothers you, Monsieur drenched rooster, do the honors.*"

"Oh. My. Gosh. You remember my exact words?"

"It was a big day," Pierre smiles so completely, his eyes crinkle around the edges. "The day you were asked to be my wife."

"I kind of like the time you asked me over strudel."

"I like that one too, only ..." He pauses, stopping us both in our tracks.

And then, right on the sidewalk, on the far side of the

town square, a block away from the hubbub of a Saturday night on Maple, Pierre drops to one knee.

He looks up into my eyes and continues what he was saying. "... only in my kitchen, while we ate your mother's strudel, I promised to be the best fake husband you ever had."

"Pierre." It's all I can say.

Why is he down on one knee? We are married. We said our vows. We've been dating to establish the things we missed out on by jumping into our marriage of convenience.

"Tasha. Allow me to do this." He's still on his one knee, looking up at me with deep sincerity. "Maybe this time around, when I propose to you, you will say yes because you want to be with me forever."

He looks so vulnerable, as if he doesn't know for certain that I'm his. Forever. He's the best thing that ever happened to me. Maybe we started this to bail him out of an immigration mess, but that motivation ended months ago for me. I barely allowed myself to hope what we had could be real until the day I flew into New York. Since then, I've had no question as to what I want with Pierre—what we're building together.

"Pierre, I will. I already am. I'll say yes to you every day if you want me to. You are my forever—if I'm yours."

Pierre shifts, and I think he's about to stand up, but he stays on the ground, looking up at me.

"Ma ange, if I thought I had loved you as much as I possibly could, you have proven me wrong every day since our first profession of love to one another in that New York hotel room. I love you more each day. Please, Tasha Pierson Toussaint, be my wife."

"Yes. I will. Yes."

I didn't know how much I needed this moment—Pierre officially asking me to be his wife.

But Pierre knew.

Tears of happiness stream down my cheeks. Pierre stands and cups my face in his hands. He bends in to kiss me. When we separate, he turns us so we're looking across the square toward downtown. The entire stretch of Maple street is coming to life with lights in the shop windows and on the lampposts. It's a tradition, the first Saturday after Thanksgiving, we light the town.

I look up at Pierre, my husband, and ask, "Do you want to stroll down Maple?"

"No."

His answer is firm.

"What? Why not?"

"Because, I have plans. And they involve taking my wife home and getting her settled into our room. Maybe we can recreate our wedding night … only this time you will not be calling out my name merely to impress my relatives."

"What?" I playfully swat at Pierre. "I was not trying to impress your sisters. Oh my gosh. You're insane!" I'm laughing and blushing at his words.

He chuckles. "Well, I want a do-over. Isn't that what you called it?"

"When we first met and I made a fool of myself dropping my books?"

"Yes. You asked for a do-over."

"I did."

"I want a wedding night do-over. This time, I will not pull out the couch and make it into a bed. I won't be sleeping across the room from you. And when you wake, you will be curled in my arms, where you belong."

I'm glad he's holding my hand as he leads me back to his car. I think my knees might go weak with the way he's talking to me, the gravelly tone his voice has taken, and the look in his eyes when he glances over at me.

"I thought you'd never ask," I tell him. "I thought you might date me forever."

"I wanted to give you what you deserve, Cher. You never hesitated to step in to help me. But in the process you lost the early stages of building a relationship with me. I wanted to restore those experiences—to date you, to build up to the day when you and I could truly live as husband and wife."

"And today is that day?"

"It is."

Pierre nearly runs to the car, pulling my door open and barely waiting for me to buckle before he's pulling out and driving what seems to be at least fifteen miles over the speed limit back to our home.

I start giggling.

Pierre looks over at me. "What is so funny?"

"You are. I hardly recognize this out-of-control version of you."

"I'm sorry, Cher. You are right. I will slow down."

He depresses the brake pedal, bringing the car to a pace that feels far too much like a leisurely Sunday drive.

"Don't you dare slow down. You aren't the only one who's been waiting for this do-over."

"Est-ce correct? Est-ce que tu me voulais autant que je te voulais?"

"Oui, mon mari," *My husband.* "I have wanted you as much as you want me."

Pierre's smile lights up. Even in the dark of night I can see his grin. He depresses the gas like an Indy 500 racer and

speeds us up the winding roads to our home. *Our home.*
Where we will finally live as husband and wife.

Nothing separates us now.

Not a pretense we're sharing.

Not the uncertainty about whether we're harboring
unspoken feelings for one another.

Not the need to make up for our mistakes.

We're barely in the door when Pierre turns to me. He
pulls me in and kisses my lips tenderly. This kiss feels new,
unrestrained in a way I've never experienced with him.
Pierre's hands are not staying put in safely demarcated
places. His breath is heavy, his kiss deep. The lines we had
drawn are erased. The rules? Out the window. Burnt to the
ground in the heat of the passion flaring between us.

Pierre pulls back from our kiss and momentarily
recovers himself, smiling widely like a kid on Christmas
morning, certain he got the present he asked for.

He shakes his head in disbelief and then cups my cheeks,
kissing me again, murmuring words in both French and
English between his kisses to my lips, my cheeks, the tip of
my nose, my neck, shoulders, the shell of my ear. His words
come out like drunken gibberish, everything he says making
me so eager for him. I shuck my coat while he continues to
kiss me, backing me toward the hallway, leaving a trail of our
clothing in his wake: his tie, my boots, his shoes, socks ...

"I thought you didn't like it when people leave things
lying around the house," I joke.

He gives me a look full of heat and longing, and then,
one minute my feet are on the ground, the next, Pierre is
scooping me up, laughing at my joke, and planting soft
kisses along my neck as he walks me upstairs, carrying me in
his arms as though I weigh nothing.

I'm squealing from the combination of surprise and adrenaline, with a healthy dose of pure bliss in the mix. But I don't squirm, instead I lean into his embrace, loving the feel of his arms holding me. He's possessive, yet gentle. Playful, yet determined. He knows what he wants and I'm fully aware of what's to come.

Pierre Toussaint, internationally renowned romance author has literally swept me off my feet and is carrying me to his bedroom. *Our* bedroom. What is my life?

"You can leave your clothes everywhere, Cher. I promise not to complain one bit."

I giggle as he kicks the bedroom door open and walks toward his bed, the bed I slept on the night we said our vows.

Only, tonight, and every night from here on out, my husband and I will be sharing this bed together.

Don't miss the rest of
the Sweater Weather series!
**Catch the rest of the fall vibes
in all the stories on Amazon.**

What's Next?

Thank you for reading *A Not So Fictional Fall.*

I hope you enjoyed Tasha and Pierre's story as much as I enjoyed writing it (which is a whole, whole lot).

Want more of Pierre + Tasha?
Read their Bonus Epilogue at
https://BookHip.com/KQPFPQQ

SHARE the book love ...
Something you can do really quickly:
If you loved *A Not So Fictional Fall*, you can help other readers find this story by leaving a review on. Amazon

IF YOU want to go back to Marbella Island ...
Riley and Cameron take off from Bordeaux Ohio with their two best friends, Ben and Madeline, to head to Marbella on historic Route 66. Fall in love on this road trip!
You can find *Are We There Yet?* on Amazon.

Read more Savannah Scott romcoms ... if you haven't read Savannah's well-loved *Getting Shipped* series, you can find all the laughs, small-town shenanigans, and love stories with all the feels on Amazon.

~

To hear about release dates, be the first to know about sales, and get sneak peeks behind the scenes at Savannah's writing life, sign up for Savannah's weekly email.

Sign up at
https://www.subscribepage.com/savannahscottromcom

All the Thanks

First of all ... I want to thank **Kiki Oliphant** (Emma St. Clair) and **Courtney Walsh** for dreaming up this series, and then for inviting me to be a part of the magic that is Harvest Hollow.

And the whole **Sweater Weather team of authors.** I feel so blessed to have been in the midst of this talented group of storytellers as we created this town and shared the creative process.

Gila Santos, thank you for coming through and helping affirm the direction of this story. You are so gifted and I'm so grateful that you share your gift with me.

Tricia Anson, thank you for being one of the best proofreaders and personal assistants out there, and for being a treasured friend. Thanks too, **Kari Cheney.** You two are the keepers of my sanity. Here's to the snort laughs we share, answered prayers, and all the goodness we share nearly daily. You two are a gift to me.

To my **Awesome Shippers** and the **AMAZING Bookstagram and Bookish Community** on Instagram and Facebook. You bless my socks off—as evidenced by my nearly-constant bare feet.

Jon, my not-book boyfriend, Thank you for believing in me and supporting me. There aren't words for the way you have made it possible for me to pursue my lifelong dream of becoming a full-time author. Special thanks for all the private stand-up comedy I get to have on the daily with you.

And to the readers who faithfully read Savannah Scott romcom books — that's **YOU**. Thank you for believing in me and loving the stories I weave. ***You are the best!***